FRONTIERLANDS

Frontierlands

Britain's Survival in the Making

HAZEL SHEFFIELD

torva

TRANSWORLD PUBLISHERS

UK | USA | Canada | Ireland | Australia
India | New Zealand | South Africa

Transworld is part of the Penguin Random House group of companies
whose addresses can be found at global.penguinrandomhouse.com.

Penguin Random House UK, One Embassy Gardens,
8 Viaduct Gardens, London sw11 7bw

penguin.co.uk

Penguin
Random House
UK

First published in Great Britain in 2026 by Torva
an imprint of Transworld Publishers

001

Typeset in 12/15.5pt Minion Pro by Six Red Marbles UK, Thetford, Norfolk
Printed and bound in Great Britain by Clays Ltd, Elcograf S.p.A.

The authorized representative in the EEA is Penguin Random House Ireland,
Morrison Chambers, 32 Nassau Street, Dublin D02 YH68.

A CIP catalogue record for this book is available from the British Library.

ISBN: 9781911709312

Penguin Random House is committed to a sustainable future
for our business, our readers and our planet. This book is made
from Forest Stewardship Council® certified paper.

For Ian, Stan and Larry

Contents

INTRODUCTION

Hastings

'Another world is not only possible, she is on her way. On a quiet day, I can hear her breathing.'

—Arundhati Roy

A LIGHT GOES ON IN a vacant building. A key turns in the stiff lock of a sealed door. A boot leaves a print in the dust of a forbidden landscape. Each of them a small but revolutionary act in abandoned places.

These places surround us. Gated fields, never crossed. Forests too dense to enter. Old factories on the edges of towns, left to ruin. Empty shops, vacant houses. Skyscrapers sitting uninhabited, built only to hoard wealth.

But far out on the periphery, people are crossing boundaries to build alternative futures in the ruins of the past. Futures based not on market dominance, scarcity and mob rule, but collective ownership, rooted in care. These people are rehearsing for a time when it will not seem normal that so much land and so many buildings are locked away, waiting to be sold or redeveloped for profit. They are practising for the end of the known world.

This is a book about those people and places on our frontiers. Left behind – or left alone – some of these places have become what Arundhati Roy once called portals, or gateways between one world and the next.[1] I found one of these portals once, on a damp June afternoon in 2019, on the south coast of England. By then, I had spent half a decade travelling the length and breadth of the UK writing about what I loosely called 'economic alternatives' to the for-profit companies I covered as a business journalist for national newspapers. Over time, my vision had sharpened. I was beginning to notice true challenges to the status quo when they appeared. This particular portal was in the least likely place: an alleyway in the seaside town of Hastings. The alley led behind a derelict printworks,[2] connecting it with some junk-stuffed caves carved into the cliff face, a public library and some ancient stables ironically named 'Rose Cottage'.[3] All these places had different owners of one sort or another. The council owned the library and landlords stacked up the other properties in their portfolios.

Each of the buildings was in disrepair. Craning my neck to look up at the old printworks, I saw how every one of its openings had been imperfectly sealed with a mish-mash of materials. One hundred and twenty windows: one hundred and seventy pieces of smashed glass.[4] Corrugated iron had come away in places. Wooden boards rotted and peeled. Plastic sheeting flapped. Pipes and ropes criss-crossed the surface, leading the eye down to graffiti-covered hoardings. Here was a piece of heritage that had become a mausoleum. Its workers turned to ghosts, its stories sealed inside: no way in and no way out.

In the shadow of the printworks, the alley showed signs of new life. Some local organizations had come together to form a community-based property developer.[5] In 2013, they had taken a 'meanwhile lease' for £200 a month on the basement of a nine-storey office block next to the printworks. Over the years, they transformed the alley: putting in drains, tarmacking the surface and stabilizing the cliff face. In 2019, they raised £15,000 to create a pocket park and began to build handmade planters and colourful benches hidden in the ancient caves where loitering teenagers could shelter. The interventions breathed life into that gloomy passage, leaving traces of the joy found in collective action, which shone out all the more in the dark days of lockdown.

The printworks had been through thirteen private owners since printing operations closed in 1984, most of whom did nothing but let the building rot before putting it up for sale again. But the alley had been saved from this fate by a strange quirk of history: it belonged to no one. In belonging to no one, it became a symbol of what could happen when it was cared for by everyone. Over many years, the buildings of a self-renovating neighbourhood assembled around it, like a constellation appearing in a cloudy night sky.

I'd never seen the old printworks in Hastings before that visit in 2019, but I knew of countless buildings like it. A creeping epidemic across every corner of the UK. It's impossible to grow up in Britain without being confronted by empty places where people no longer have the right to pass. It's there in our history, beginning with the Enclosure Acts that put common land and open fields into private hands, creating one of the most concentrated patterns of land ownership in the world.[6] Over the last decade, I have tried several ways to quantify the full scale of empty buildings across Britain. I've experimented with crowdsourcing, commercial datasets and the Land Registry. While the full picture remains elusive, the problem seems to be getting worse. Political decisions have contributed to the creep of neglect, like a disease that has infected our towns and cities, neighbourhoods and homes. We don't need to be told that one in seven high-street shops lie empty: we can just take a walk through the nearest town centre.[7] During a crisis of high rent, homelessness and unsuitable housing, one in sixteen residential properties sit vacant, a total of 1.5 million across England, according to the Office of National Statistics (ONS).[8] Since the Conservative government abandoned a dedicated programme to tackle empty homes in 2016, the number of disused properties has risen by 32 per cent.[9]

So much has been lost since the rhetoric of austerity took hold. In many cases, councils responded to budget cuts by putting land and buildings up for sale, desperate for cash. The cuts forced the closure of libraries, playing fields, museums, swimming pools and day centres for the elderly and disabled. Many of these public services were in beautiful municipal buildings. In 2019, I partnered with the Bureau Local for an investigation into the scale of the losses. We created a map that allowed people to search their local area and see what their council had sold. Our investigation #soldfromunderyou found more than twelve thousand public spaces disposed of by councils since 2014/15.[10] In that time, councils raised a total of £9.1 billion from selling property – some of which funded council redundancies. Some communities stepped in to save public buildings, stretching to operate them on a volunteer basis, without public resources. But many of the losses meant a shuttered door, the lights out in a library or a youth centre, a gate across a field where children once played.

Less well documented is the way these closures impact the mind. The journalists Polly Toynbee and David Walker conducted a qualitative study of this situation in their 2020 book, *The Lost Decade: 2010–2020*. They found that the cuts had created a culture of mistrust among neighbours and the decline of meeting places: 'a sense of common belonging diminished'.[11] This sense of abandonment – of doors slamming in people's faces – has been linked in studies to political polarization[12] and the vote to leave the EU.[13]

These losses have limited our capacity to respond effectively to climate change. The disaster preparedness expert Lucy Easthope describes community spaces as 'lifescapes' where people can go and be together to heal from disaster: pubs, shops, mosques, scout huts, museums.[14] Easthope says that in a pandemic or a heatwave or a flood, it is how well you know your neighbours, and how much you can help one another, that will make the difference between life and death.

We saw this acutely in the pandemic. A decade of cuts left the country fatally weak ahead of what was described, by the president of the Royal College of Psychiatrists, as Britain's 'biggest existential threat to mental health since the Second World War'.[15] Many people with depression and anxiety felt their symptoms worsen in the dark days of lockdown. Some, suffering from severe respiratory diseases, experienced trauma. People's sense of their own safety and wellbeing declined as they were deprived of social contact.

In the longer term, the combined effects of poor health and social isolation created a kind of downward spiral. We now know that social isolation is linked to deteriorating cognitive function and faster cognitive decline.[16] And it can impact people's political beliefs, with some studies linking isolation with the rise of extremist political views.[17] The neighbourhood policy vacuum created during austerity, followed ten years later by a pandemic, created the conditions for the complete fragmentation of society at street level.

It felt like a long reckoning, especially for people of my generation. I was born a year before Margaret Thatcher made her famous declaration that there is no such thing as society, 'only individuals'. Her words arrived during a fever dream of privatization – the dismantling of apparatus that had for centuries bound us to one another through industry, community and shared social needs. Four decades later, the statistics seem to bear out this absolute devastation of our sense of belonging to anything greater than ourselves. In its place we have seen increasing isolation promoted as personalization by social media and big tech companies seeking to quantify our complex humanity in data points to be bought and sold. The fever dream feels more like a nightmare as pandemics and extreme weather reveal the truth: that we cannot get through these disasters alone. Our survival depends on our recognition of our interdependence with one another and our environment.

What would it take to break out of our silos, peek behind the hoardings and the fences, and start seeing ourselves as intimately connected to the abandoned world – to see the impoverishment of our own souls in each shuttered window, each barred door? Most social change is chosen: we join WhatsApp groups to make collective decisions with neighbours, or cooperatives to find more equitable, sustainable ways of buying food or building housing, or we sign up to volunteer at local homeless shelters, or with the elderly and vulnerable.

But in a real disaster, the science shows that these actions – to help one another, to join with something greater than ourselves – become involuntary. This runs counter to common belief and what Western thought has preached ever since Cain killed his brother Abel in the Bible.[18] We have been schooled to see human beings as intrinsically selfish, prone to hoarding, putting the wellbeing of themselves and their kin above that of a stranger. That argument, history says, is untrue. During pandemics, flooding or heatwaves, most of us are compelled to act altruistically to feed or shelter one another. When the writer Rebecca Solnit documented the emergency response to five disasters, from epidemics to earthquakes, in her 2009 book *A Paradise Built in Hell*, she discovered that 'the image of the selfish, panicky, or regressively savage human being in times of disaster has little truth to it.'[19] She drew on decades of scientific research into the behaviour of people after the London bombings in the Second World War, to cyclones, storms and floods across the world, alongside her own reporting. 'When all the ordinary divides and patterns are shattered, people step up . . . to become their brother's keepers,' she writes. Not only do they step up, but by engaging in meaningful, collective endeavours, many also speak of joy.

Several of the stories in this book come from places on the fringes of a centralized economic system in which they experience a permanent state of disaster. In the past few decades, accelerated by recent political events, the world has returned to a kind of 'robber baron' capitalism. Tech moguls have captured power by emulating the worst excesses of nineteenth-century industrialists, with outright monopolies and worker exploitation. Governments have dismantled social safety nets, allowed profit-making to creep into education and healthcare, and vilified the most vulnerable for their dependence on others.

This state of permanent emergency has inspired multiple, messy, complex and forward-looking responses, many rooted in neighbourhoods where the symptoms of crisis are most acute. We can all learn from these places. They are rehearsing for the rest of us not just how to cope, but how to break out of the doom loop and imagine the world anew. Inside the word emergency, Solnit reminds us, is the word emerge.[20]

So often, the new things look like old things. The alley in Hastings is extraordinary because it has come full circle. In 1800, the surrounding neighbourhood was little more than a silted-up beach in a natural harbour behind a headland known as the White Rock. The beach appeared to be beyond the boundary of the town and had no obvious owner. In the first three decades of the nineteenth century, as Hastings grew, this patch of land became a kind of squat for the town's developers, attracting tradesmen and labourers who built up an ecosystem of houses side by side with a shipyard, laundries, carpenters and bakers, forges and piggeries.[21] One local myth goes that the residents of the triangle, cut off from the town by a small stream, declared independence and raised a flag of the Stars and Stripes – and some Hastings residents still refer to this area as the America Ground.[22] But its independence did not last. The residents, fighting it out for landlord-free land, often ended up in conflict with one another. It was the increasing nature of these clashes in 1825 that drew attention to this ungoverned land. In 1827, a Crown inquiry decided the valuable ground, being former beach, belonged to the government, and so in 1828, one thousand occupants were given seven years' notice to quit.

The alley, which had once been part of the cliff rather than the beach, avoided privatization. In the decades that followed, a wealthy Scottish businessman by the name of Patrick Robertson redesigned the area, building Robertson Street[23] and the whole of what is now known as the Trinity Triangle. Small businesses moved in, starting with a butcher that opened on the site of today's HSBC Bank. From the 1870s, a newspaper empire, F. J. Parsons, rapidly expanded its influence, building the seven-storey printworks and neighbouring office block. Behind the streets, the alley was the noisy, bustling centre of this publishing industry, bringing together skilled tradesmen as part of the Parsons empire of artists, printmakers and bookbinders.

Then in the mid-eighties, not long before Thatcher made her society speech, the fortunes of the district – known as White Rock after the old headland – came crashing down. The newspaper industry collapsed and F. J. Parsons sold out of the area, leaving the shuttered printworks rotting in the heart of the neighbourhood.[24] Green moss grew over the layers of brick and tarmac in the alley. Cigarette butts collected in the cracks. It became a wasteland. The freeholders of the connected buildings took their rights, dumped their rubbish and avoided responsibility.[25] Pigeons lived among the stench of weed and urine. Graffiti artists used it as a canvas. But no one owned it, so no one tried to rescue it.

The alley was all that remained of the landlord-free district that first formed in the silted-up harbour. It held the potential for community stewardship and renewal. But in the 1980s, at a moment of entrenched privatization, the freeholders of the adjacent properties had no interest in caring for it as a collective. That old English tradition of common land had been forgotten.

In English history, commons were communal areas – usually grassland, heathland, fens or moorland – where ordinary people who owned no land could subsist by grazing their animals and collecting firewood. In 1500, around half of England and Wales was common land.[26] These rights were gradually eroded in a process known as enclosure, which was enabled by Acts of Parliament, or 'parliamentary enclosure' in the eighteenth and nineteenth centuries. But the idea of the commons as an in-between place, stewarded by the many, is returning. In 1990, it was used by the economist Elinor Ostrom to suggest that there are more than two solutions to the problem of the management of common resources, such as forests, land, water or air.[27] In Western societies, natural resources are either owned and managed by the government, or they are sold to private owners, who operate largely without accountability to people or state. Ostrom won the Nobel Prize in 2009 for her work showing a third way. She demonstrated how communities themselves could define the rules for using or managing such resources, not outside the sphere of the regular economy but within it. She studied how communities did this in practice.[28] In Valencia, she documented farmers who, a millennium ago, dug canals to irrigate their farmland, established a set of rules about access to the water and established a water court of elected representatives that still meets to handle disputes to this day.[29] In Japan, she learned how millions of hectares of uncultivated forest and meadows were stewarded in common by collectives of households called *kumi*, with rules about when plants could be harvested and when villages were required to perform maintenance work like burning or cutting.[30]

Ostrom shows us that the idea of the commons is not a newfangled invention, but a returning to the wisdom of the past. Not just to England before enclosure, but to traditional knowledge and the customary laws of indigenous peoples all over the world. She demonstrated how collective stewardship gave people kinship with their environment, and kinship with one another.

In Hastings, Jess Steele absorbed these ideas into her emerging thinking about the alley as an urban commons: a place that could be stewarded by its people, who in turn would be transformed by the act of stewardship. It was just a humble alley. But as common land, it was the symbolic centre of a whole neighbourhood, equitably owned and collectively managed. Both the collection of buildings and the collection of organizations that develop and run them are known as Hastings Commons.

Hastings Commons was the result of a long-standing community campaign to reimagine the White Rock neighbourhood. A few passionate locals had come together to save the Hastings Pier in the middle of the neighbourhood from closure in 2006, inspiring a massive campaign. Later, they turned their attention to the wider neighbourhood, forming the community-based property developer that acquired the office block next to the printworks. Over several years, they acquired a cluster of buildings on the edges of the alley. These buildings – the office block, the print factory, the stables, even the junk-stuffed caves in the cliff face – became part of a hyperlocal real-estate portfolio of

9,000 square metres of difficult, derelict and eccentric properties, all within 150 metres.[31]

The buildings are partly held by the community in a trust called a community land trust, in a way that protects them from speculators. For the Hastings Commons, owning the buildings is the key to their survival as common-pool resources. Jess believes outpricing on the open market is 'the modern form of enclosure'. The long-term goal is for the shares in all the properties to be fully transferred to the community land trust, where they will be held for the good of the community in perpetuity. This process means the staff, track record, systems, processes and culture of the social enterprise property company remain, while the community gets 100 per cent ownership of and benefit from the buildings. That company, Hastings Commons, develops as a self-governing ecosystem of organizations engaged in a long experiment to support the White Rock neighbourhood to be self-renovating. It's a bold endeavour with a long time-horizon, and an antidote to the forces of gentrification that might price local people out of homes. For those involved, the renovation of the neighbourhood is not the purpose of the Hastings Commons, but a symbol of a greater flourishing of the human spirit that emerges as part of that process.

These kinds of transformational processes and projects depend on an unreliable patchwork of loans, community shares and philanthropic grants, locking organizations like the Hastings Commons in unsustainable cycles of funding applications, interest repayments and short-term programmes. It is complicated work, made more complicated by the fact that it goes against the established system of buy and sell and instead focuses on what happens in between, in the cracks in the market. On ideas not about linear growth and profit but stability, maintenance and care. But for all these reasons, the Hastings Commons captured my imagination. During the pandemic, I moved into a flat directly opposite, fascinated by the promise of that dark, unloved space at a moment when life felt totally upended. From 2010, the Conservative government's austerity project dismantled the public infrastructure that was our best defence against the social upheaval that comes with planetary crisis. Also at this time, new ideas emerged about how neighbourhoods might themselves respond. Many were quickly recognized by the mainstream. Ostrom won the Nobel Prize in Economic Sciences for her work on the commons in 2009. In 2010, a collective of architects came together under the name Assemble to host a cinema in an old central London petrol station, putting forward a slower way of constructing with, not for, communities while repurposing existing materials and structures. In 2015, Assemble won the Turner Prize for a project refurbishing homes in the neighbourhood of Toxteth in Liverpool that had been left to rot by the government's doomed Housing Market Renewal scheme. In 2011, another architect, Indy Johar, began to talk about a civic economy, where institutions are rooted in the activities of people in specific places.[32] In 2016 he founded Dark Matter Labs, a think tank that has worked with many local governments and the EU to redesign food, housing and land systems in a way that recognizes the entanglements between climate change, social inequality and global finance. These thinkers and practitioners all identified the need for new ideas about scale and process. They saw the importance of the neighbourhood as an ever-changing intersection between people, production and the environment. And they promoted the potential of neighbour-hood activity not to replace central governance, but to provide a counter-scale, restoring the balance away from unchecked market dominance and state power.

Fifteen years later, we are beginning to see the realization of some of these ideas in neighbourhoods, especially on the periphery. In Hastings, multiple shareholders, most of them local people, pay as little as a pound to join the Hastings Commons Community Land Trust. At regular meetings, members hear updates about tenants as each part of a building is opened up to new and often experimental uses, even while renovations continue. Jess calls this way of encouraging people to occupy buildings while they are thinking what to do with them 'phased organic development'. The process makes a virtue of the slow-moving work of renovating the buildings, proceeding in good faith according to the needs of those who step forward and the funding available. Through this approach, the buildings in the neighbourhood have been developed for multiple uses, from providing affordable accommodation for those on hous-ing benefit, hosting youth clubs and tool- and skill-sharing, to creating office space for digital businesses and mental health services. These kinds of activities make people feel they have a stake in the future – and that they are less alone.

What if, instead of being left to rot or be destroyed, other neglected land and buildings could be rehabilitated in this way? Empty homes might be renovated for those desperately in need of shelter. Empty shops could be reimagined in ways that conserve their embodied energy and celebrate heritage. Vacant or mistreated land might be brought under the stew-ardship of broad associations of people living nearby, with a vested interest in its proper care. It sounds far-fetched: why would private landlords give up the keys to empty assets, or landowners agree to turn over their fallow land to the hands of the many? The language of our time dictates that these are assets for hoarding. We swim in the soup of our market economies, unable to imagine a way in which collective stewardship might transform the places and the people that we love.[33] But human history is rich with alternatives: the commons, cooperatives, the abundance of gift economies, where giving does not always come with the expectation of receiving. Each has the potential to change the future. Our way of living is leading us to catastrophe. But it has never been the only way. On the edges, people are excavating the old ways. Nurtured by visionaries and artists, these old ways will become essential to our survival as certainties of the world – economic growth, stable environmental conditions, global supply chains – are revealed for their frailties.

Frontierlands is a book about these alternatives and how they work in parts of Britain where local people are already rewriting the future. According to Onion Collective in Watchet, there are at least two thousand groups across the UK working towards what they call 'alternative futures'.[34] In these more hopeful iterations of what lies ahead, the economy is no longer merely linear and for-profit but vast and diverse, valuing unpaid labour, mutual aid, gifting and other forms of sharing and exchange.

The work is complex and experimental. Many of the chapters in this book are about places that are trying out multiple ideas about alternative futures, while also intersecting, by necessity, with the present reality of a failing system. These are people trying to get more money circulating locally, while also redefining ideas about care work. They are neighbours growing food, while also experimenting with democratic ownership structures. They are communities working for racial justice, while also retrofitting a factory. In each of the chapters, we explore different economic models that draw on the idea of gift-giving and relationship-building, rather than pure exchange. They are cooperatives, community land trusts, tool libraries, community energy projects, urban farms, and artists who see art as a practice of imagining rather than as a profit-making commodity.

There are many different ways to explore these experimental futures. *Frontierlands* starts on the edges of our island, on the frontiers of Britain, and travels inwards through forests, mines, factories and viaducts, into the heart of the city, before landing in the home, the body and, finally, the mind. In Chapter 1, we go to the furthest reaches of the country, to a former harbour in the Bristol Channel. Harbours were once places where Britain's world expanded, tracing new trading networks all across the globe. Today hundreds lie shuttered, neglected or disused. But on one unlikely quayside in one of the most isolated towns in England, a group of women have built a £7 million arts centre to welcome this emerging network of people ushering in the next world on the peripheries of the old.

In Chapter 2, we consider how two competing ideas about the economy – one circular and one based on linear growth – play out in the abandoned amusements of a seaside town. Artists have been reclaiming these old palaces of pleasure and leisure, using creativity to explore the health-giving properties of the places where land meets sea. In Chapter 3, we break into the lunar landscape of an abandoned mine and encounter artists experimenting with clay and exploring our understanding of care work through our relationship with the earth's materials. In Chapter 4, we travel inland, cracking branches as we enter a forbidden forest, and consider how a different approach to education might transform our ability to adapt to catastrophic weather events. In Chapter 5, we visit just one of the hundreds – maybe thousands – of derelict factories that litter post-industrial Britain, to see how they can become centres for shelter and survival – even reinvention – in emergencies. In Chapter 6, we follow the story of some of the inventive ways skilled tradesmen, those who will build the next world in the ruins of the old, survive in the cracks of cities where market capitalism is at its most rapacious. In Chapter 7, we visit the shuttered shops, pubs and bars along a derelict high street and see how, thanks to two remarkable women, a sailors' thoroughfare is becoming a route to a regenerative future. In Chapter 8, we come to the neighbourhood and the home, the place where all these ideas converge in our daily lives and nightly dreams. We end our journey with the body. After a visit to Gateshead, we come full circle to Hastings. In both places, the rehabilitation of empty buildings is having a surprising impact on vulnerable people's physical and mental health.

I call these empty or derelict buildings and land our frontiers because they have for decades been shunned, or shut out of our ideas about progress. Untouched, they have become a new kind of wilderness, just as impenetrable as impassable thickets of undisturbed woodland or impenetrable mountain ranges, but much closer – indeed, all around. Yet it is precisely here that I have discovered new ideas about how to live in a time of crisis, ready to be carried into the mainstream. Wendell

Berry, the American novelist and poet, observed in the mid-seventies the great importance of understanding 'the marginal possibility, the marginal place, and the marginal humanity', which provides a 'counter-theme in our history, so far always subordinate to the theme of exploitation, but unbroken and still alive.'[35]

This is a book about Britain. But it is important to note that in American mythology, the frontier was the line between territory captured by invading Europeans and the homelands of indigenous peoples. The horrors that have faced indigenous peoples in the name of progress are an indication of how far we have strayed from their wisdom. Only now are we realizing how much we have to learn about how to live in balance with the world. What if we could see land, with all of its layers of history, exploitation and neglect, as kin, ancestor and teacher?[36]

The idea of land is at the heart of all the ideas in this book and in its title *Frontierlands*. Many interlocking systems have created what the historian Adam Tooze calls the polycrisis facing humanity.[37] But behind it all is land: whether we have the right to live on it and extract from it, whether we choose to exploit it and abandon it, or whether we return to it for nurture and repair. Can we heal our relationship to land, before the damage we have done to it destroys us? Tooze says that crisis fighting and technological fixes only lead us to coping strategies, ignoring the underlying trends of environmental breakdown. We need a total break with business as usual: an understanding that everything is about to change, but that this intertwining of our fate with the planet's can become a revolutionary force and a path to alternative futures. In Britain, as in many places around the world, we have seen the high waters of capitalism and colonialism retreat to leave a wilderness of abandoned places, left fallow by a system of exploitation. It is in some of these places that a counter-narrative now brews. So we start our travels at the ultimate frontier for an island: its craggy borders with the sea.

NOTE

'It matters what stories make worlds, what worlds make stories.'

—Donna J. Haraway, *Staying with the Trouble:*
Making Kin in the Chthulucene

TELLING THE STORIES OF COLLECTIVES is fraught with challenges. I have often grappled with limits of my storytelling tradition: a mash-up of the Fleet Street efficiency I was taught as an apprentice at trade magazines, and the flowery narrative style I learned studying in the US. Both centre stories on the individual. The hero narrative is so ingrained in the way we tell stories in the West that those without a main protagonist read as though something is amiss. I worry about losing readers by bringing in too many names, or if I need to provide some kind of key, like a character list at the start of every chapter.

There are other storytelling traditions. Outside the West, stories are more likely to reflect the collective identity of a community or the interconnectedness of people with nature and the cosmos. Mystical stories from religious traditions, like the Christian parables or the Sufi Tales, focus on spiritual enlightenment through simple scenarios or allegory. I don't experiment here, but I want to suggest that we need a different language for the new worlds I describe in these chapters. We need a way of telling stories about collectives that better reflects the reality of the work, which is often done by many hands and faces that change over time.

The stories in these pages demonstrate the limits of individualism and the power of togetherness. These are not tidy narratives. But it is their mutuality, their adaptability, that allows these projects to persist, despite conditions – free markets, corrupt governments, underfunded local authorities – that make the work nearly impossible. I have tried my best to give expression to this, despite working within a storytelling tradition that wants beginnings and endings, heroes and villains. I hope to show that other ways of being are possible, if not vital – especially on the periphery, where the accepted ways long ago failed.

1

HARBOUR

Watchet

'The corollary of a centre that lacks the incentive to imagine something different is a periphery that has no choice but to do so.'

—Onion Collective

1.1 ART ON THE EDGE

The number 28 bus that travels from Taunton to Watchet is a squat single-decker that sways down country lanes. I wait for it one Wednesday in February, pulling my raincoat around me against the cold. My rucksack is crammed with its familiar cargo: laptop, audio recorders, cameras and pens. It had been years since I quit my job at the newspaper and started travelling the country in search of stories of economic alternatives, but I still got an ache of anticipation in my guts every time I set out on one of these trips.

I heard something was happening in Watchet in West Somerset, a town almost entirely cut off from the rest of the county save for a single road. A collective of women had returned to this part of the country after years working in cities. They called themselves Onion Collective. Over a decade they raised £7 million to build an arts centre on an abandoned quayside in a place with a population of fewer than four thousand. I knew I had to go. The question was how to get there.

No trains go to Watchet. Two independent railway lines had closed long ago. Once, they had carried tens of thousands of tonnes of iron ore, mined on the mineral lines of Exmoor, to Watchet harbour. Here, great vessels took the lucrative cargo across the Bristol Channel to the belching, smelting steelworks of Newport in Wales. By 1862, more than a thousand ships were passing through each year.

But when the mines ran dry towards the end of the nineteenth century, the freight trains stopped running. A passenger service survived until the seventies. Today, Watchet station serves only a heritage steam train: a magnificent, slick black creature that chuffs noisily through neighbouring villages on a summer timetable. It was a nostalgia trip, but it didn't sound like a practical transport link for a world-class arts centre.

Regular passengers get stuck 20 miles inland at Taunton. I alight one Wednesday at 10am. The taxi rank is empty. I slip down a side road and wait, several minutes past the scheduled time, for a half-empty bus, which lurches out of the town and down roads that dwindle to country lanes, buffeted on either side by long grass verges.

The villages are so pretty, they could have been plucked from picture books: first Bishops Lydeard, a settlement named after a Belgian-born clergyman elected Bishop of Wells at the time of the Domesday Book in 1086. Then Crowcombe, named after the southern English word for a valley at the bottom of a hill. The 'combes' are deep wooded valleys, riven between open heathland, covered in gorse and heather. Even in February, when the trees are bare, the land retains a kind of lushness. Ivy is wound thick around wintry tree trunks. Snowdrops dare to raise their heads from muddy verges.

Suddenly, the coast appears on the horizon as the land drops away through Williton, a roadside town. I'm at the foot of the Quantocks, one of the most beautiful parts of the English countryside. The landscape inspired Samuel Taylor Coleridge and his friends Dorothy and William Wordsworth to begin work on *The Rime of the Ancient Mariner* one night in November 1797, when they crossed the scrub on the way into Watchet, perhaps taking the description of the Mariner as 'long, and lank, and brown; As is the ribbed sea-sand' from Watchet beach at low tide, the morning after their walk. It's low tide again by the time I arrive at the one bus stop in the town. The end of the line. The bus makes a slow circuit around a block of public toilets and heads straight back inland. I turn heel to see clouds hanging low over the coastline.

For centuries, Watchet harbour had been the heart of the town: its industrial centre and connection to the wider world. Then for ten years, it rotted while developers and the council argued about what to do with the land. For a moment, I close my eyes and remember my first visit to Watchet, exactly five years before. The East Quay was an unloved patch of land, blocked off by gates and covered in broken vessels. It sat next to a marina so desperate to be dredged that all the boats were marooned in mud.

But no more. I open my eyes and it appears: the East Quay arts centre. A mad Lego construction of colourful containers made of steel and concrete, piled high beside the sea. It is shaped like a big pink V: two fingers up to those who said it couldn't be done, two arms out to hug the town. A gallery with architectural credentials to rival any Turner, Tate or Bilbao, right here in one of the most isolated places in England.

I slip down the main road on to the quayside, into its arms. Here are repurposed shipping containers, flowerpots and a poster: 'No art on a dead planet'. The front door swings open and in a scrum of people around the doorway are the women who made this happen – Naomi Griffith, Jessica Prendergrast,

Sally Lowndes and Georgie Grant from Onion Collective. They are smiling and handing out coffees as they gently usher people through into the main gallery for the beginning of the day's activities: a symposium about artists on the edge.

In the main gallery, a hundred people gather to talk about what it means to make art this far away from 'the art world' – and how acts of creativity might help us navigate the possibilities that exist at the boundaries of the economy. 'Why edge?' Jessica says at the start. 'This theme of peripherality is something we talk about a lot.' Watchet, partly due to its isolated location, was given the dubious honour in 2016 of having the lowest social mobility in the whole of the UK. The Onions have spent the last decade frustrated by the idea that places like Watchet are left behind. 'It's a place that hasn't been left behind, it's been left alone and we have escaped some of the ravages of capitalism,' Jessica says. 'We have nature and beauty. We also have a bit more freedom than others. The accepted way of doing things is being challenged. In liminal spaces like this we find that we can begin to think and act in a new way.'

Behind Jessica, on the electric-blue wall of the gallery, hangs a private collection belonging to the writer Jeremy Cooper. Postcards, paintings, ceramic tiles – even a balloon made by the artist Gavin Turk for his son – have been selected not for their monetary value, but as talismans from friend-ships, symbols of love, memory and loss. The exhibition is typical of East Quay. It has hosted explorations of queerness, menopause, cults and class since it opened in 2021. Inside these walls, the women and the gallery curator, George Harwood Smith, celebrate artists and collectors who question the market as a mechanism for valuing creativity. Edge cultures finding a home in the strange gallery on the frontiers of the country. If life had gone differently for the Onions, this gallery might never have existed at all. The four women who founded the collective are all brilliant thinkers, schemers and friends. Each could have been spirited away from the West Country by the promise of better jobs and better schools for their children. But each had attachments to West Somerset that drew them back. Jessica has a theory about attachments. Social connections like the kind she made studying economics at Oxford and working for a think tank in London help people 'climb the ladder' or 'raise their aspirations' away from places like Watchet. This narrative – just like the idea of social mobility – implies that staying in Watchet is undesirable, that the people here, and the town itself, are to be escaped. But the nature of attachments binds us to these places and links us to their fortunes. Connections are about the success of each of us as individuals; attachments are about the wellbeing of everyone as interconnected beings. Connections imply escape, dereliction; attachments imply rootedness, responsibility. Connections could have got Jessica and the other Onions out of Watchet long ago. Attachments brought them home.

1.2 LIFE IN THE CRACKS

The story of how a radical £7 million art gallery came to be in one of the most isolated towns in England starts, like so much of what goes on in Watchet, in the pub. In her late twenties, Jessica married her university boyfriend and, when she became pregnant, convinced him to move to Watchet to raise their family.

Back home, Jessica banded together with her sisters, Naomi and Hannah, and her friends, Sally, Rachel Kelly and Georgie, for support. The women fed one another's babies when someone had to work. They passed long evenings taking it in turns to read bedtime stories at weekend sleepovers while splitting bottles of wine around kitchen tables, putting the world to rights. Through a combination of love and sheer isolation, they grew into kindred spirits, leaning on one another to stay sane.

On Thursday evenings, Jessica and her friends would escape. As the sun headed towards the horizon in the Bristol Channel, the women would softly close their front doors on whatever chaos was going on in the household – a toddler refusing bathtime, a four-year-old demanding another story – and weave their way through the streets of Watchet, across old railway tracks, past the abandoned boatyard and the community library, towards the effigy of Yankee Jack, the so-called father of sea shanties, whose bronze statue sits and looks down on the boats. One by one, the women arrived through the doors of a quirky bar called the Esplanade to find a spot on the red seating, beneath seafaring murals on the walls and the ceiling covered in electric guitars.

They drank pints. Lots of them. They talked, like everyone does at the pub, about the people they knew and the things going on around them. Because it was so cut off from the rest of the country, Watchet was tight-knit. As well as rolling hills and the beach, literary connections and maritime glory, the town had more than a hundred different groups run by volunteers: choirs, book clubs, wildlife clubs, girls' football, Christmas fairs.

When the social mobility commission put West Somerset at the bottom of its rankings in 2016 and again in 2017, it remarked that the area suffered from the triple threat: it was coastal, it was rural and all its industry was gone. Watchet's councils had disappeared inland, its paper factory and its working harbour had closed down. The town had the lowest wages and the lowest productivity among small- and medium-size enterprises in the whole of England. Young people commuted for hours on unreliable bus services to attend college. The hollowing out of public services and the retreat of industry inland had been the result of market liberalization and privatization policies that began in the eighties. But the long arm of that political shift could be seen in 2016, when 60 per cent of the electorate in West Somerset voted to leave the EU. The top five leave-voting areas during the referendum were all on the coast, from the leafy Lincolnshire port of Boston, to Thurrock on the muddy flats of the Thames Estuary. They had all been left out of traditional ideas of progress and condemned as deprived. People kicked back. The gap was widening between what the market would deliver, and what the state could provide.

But in that gap, between the edges of these traditional place-making forces, Watchet's independent spirit triumphed. It became a town where people learned to do it themselves. The kind of place where people left their doors unlocked and children roamed between their houses, the neighbours always keeping a watchful eye. If you needed your tap fixing or a pair of curtains shortening, someone in Watchet would sort you out. Or they knew someone who could.

Like Jessica, many of the women in Watchet had studied for university degrees and worked in well-paid city jobs. Back home, it was harder to maintain that trajectory. So they, too, fell into the gaps. They worked part-time, doing communications or marketing for local businesses and third-sector organiza-tions. And they took on the majority of the parenting while their husbands commuted to Bristol or Taunton for full-time jobs. The life-sustaining work of raising children – the care work of young parenthood – was rendered invisible.

Fifty years earlier, in New York, the artist Mierle Laderman Ukeles had come to a similar realization about her place as an artist and a mother within a capitalist system. In 1969, she wrote an exhibition proposal called 'Maintenance Art' in which she explored the experience of becoming a mother. 'Being a mother entails an enormous amount of repetitive tasks. I became a maintenance worker. I felt completely abandoned by my culture because it didn't have a way to incorporate sustain-ing work,' she told an interviewer.[1]

In one performance, she spent eleven months shaking hands with and personally thanking the 8,500 sanitation workers in New York City. For 'Maintenance Art', she proposed living inside a museum where every day a container of waste, 'polluted air' or 'ravaged land' would be delivered and dumped, after which she would process it in pseudoscientific ways in front of visitors. With each performance, she sought to unite her work as an artist and the 'maintenance work' of giving and growing life.

In 2006, two economists, Julie Graham and Katherine Gibson working under the pen name J. K. Gibson-Graham, found a way to make visible the invisible work that props up the world as we know it. They used the metaphor of an iceberg to repre-sent economic activity. Only a tiny amount is seen: paid work for publicly traded, privately owned companies. All 'alternative' forms of labour disappear under the waterline, including char-itable volunteering, gifting, mutual aid and the unpaid care of children. Without this work, which forms the majority of all labour, the iceberg would collapse. But to comprehend this we have to learn to 'see' what a prevailing system depends upon: the free labour it extracts from the many in order to sustain power. In Watchet, it was impossible for the women to unsee the maintenance work that went on in the underbelly of the iceberg. It was where so much of what was good about Watchet resided: in neighbourhood meet-ups, shared childcare, local support groups, mutual aid. Relationships – or attachments – were the things that made Watchet the place the Onions wanted to be, despite the challenges of living literally on the edge. In Watchet, these relationships didn't seem like fringe concerns; they felt like the whole world. The Onions wondered: what would the economy look like if care and community and creativity were at the centre?

Years later, long after the gallery opened, Onion Collective visualized this alternative economy as a flower. In their flower diagram, the new world emerges from the centre, while the dominant narrative of extraction and exploitation falls away like plucked petals from the edge. The new world is about stewardship over long time frames, about personal and communal connection to earth and the land. The new world was born in the grave of the old one, in the forgotten spaces. In Watchet, it found a home on the East Quay.

1.3 BRITAIN TURNS INWARDS

When did you last visit a harbour? When I was a child, each summer holiday would bring a 6am start and the long car journey to a different corner of the English coast. I remember the fish shack by the harbour at Lyme Regis, where we'd get crab sticks and eat them right away, prawn cocktail sauce dripping from our little fingers. The vastness of Poole harbour, watching yachts leave frothy trails in the water as they zoomed past. The sliver of beach at Tenby harbour in Wales, eating sandy sandwiches surrounded by tall houses in shades of blue and pink. Harbours were for seal spotting, crabbing, ice creams on an evening walk. They were safe, nostalgic places.

It wasn't always like that. Once, England's harbours were vast and dirty industrial centres: symbols of the danger and excitement of the high seas, and home to the horrors of the slave trade. Expanding global trade links from the 1700s turned seaports into hubs for employment and commerce, bringing wealth to surrounding settlements. Researchers at one university counted 391 acres of wet dock on the British coast by 1830, and at least fifty harbours.[2] Another study counted 479 ports on the coastline at different points between 1550 and 2000.[3] Harbours didn't appear by accident, but were created by decree. Acts of Parliament were used to create public trusts or private corporations with the powers to charge tolls and build or repair harbours, piers or docks. They became major economic centres and important instruments of the state, as some of the first formal taxes were applied to imported goods to fund overseas wars. Many were large employers until the sixties, when the introduction of container shipping required fewer workers to load and unload cargo. Container shipping favoured ports with deep water and strong road and rail networks. Trade dwindled at older ones, like the Port of London, while new ones like Felixstowe expanded.[4] As the country turned inwards, towards cities, places like Watchet became increasingly cut off from commerce and opportunity. A handful of harbours and marinas survive as tourist attractions like the ones I visited as a child. Hundreds of others have gone into decline. Just like it took Acts of Parliament to create them, it takes public investment to maintain a harbour against the weather. Failure is expensive. When the sea wall in Dawlish in Devon collapsed in February 2014, closing the main railway line from London to Cornwall for two months, it cost £50 million to reinstate the line, but wider disruption to economic activity cost the country £1.2 billion.[5] Yet so few coastal places have the protection they need, even with worsening predictions for rising sea levels and ferocious winter storms. In 2018, the UK government increased its projections for sea level rise compared with 2009.[6] Those projections are expected to keep rising throughout the twenty-first century, under all emissions scenarios, threatening the running of existing ports, and swallowing up seaside infrastructure including harbours and marinas entirely. As climate change increases the severity and the frequency of bad weather hitting ports and harbours, the pressure on commercial port users and public authorities to maintain and protect these environments will become more intense.

To the Onions, Watchet's harbour became a symbol of how the town had been taken from,[7] plundered for its natural resource and the labour of its people, then abandoned. The working harbour had closed in 1993 after a commercial shipping group with a subsidiary in Watchet went into liquidation, with the loss of many local jobs. It finally reopened as a marina for pleasure boats in 2001.[8] The council promised to develop a former boatyard, on the unloved east wharf of the harbour, within eighteen months, in return for half a million pounds in funding from a government development agency.[9] They got the money. But nothing happened on the land for seven years. Then, on the eve of the 2008 financial crisis, the council granted planning permission for a property developer to build a complex of shops and apartments including luxury flats.[10] Locals were outraged at the idea of luxury apartments in a place where plenty of people struggled to find suitable housing. But still nothing happened. When planning permission ran out in 2010, the district council mothballed the site and it mooted plans for a temporary pay and display car park. Meanwhile the East Quay sat, gated off, in the centre of the town.

The first time I visited in 2020, Watchet's harbour was beginning to show signs of strain after many years of neglect. A storm had blown in overnight, smashing a hole right through the sea wall and threatening to flood the marina. Excavators crawled over the quayside, chasing boulders back into the sea defences. It was shocking to witness the fragility of the neglected infrastructure. But for the people of Watchet, the state of the old harbour was no surprise. The women that would go on to form Onion Collective regularly got on to the subject on Thursdays during their evening drinks. In the summers, sitting outside on the esplanade opposite, the women dreamed of what they might do if they had the right to steward the East Quay. Workshops to celebrate Watchet's seafaring history, with boat making or maritime craft. A meeting place for the lonely and work experience and training for the young.[11] Each time someone shared a new idea, Jessica and Naomi took note, until they could not unsee the possibilities.

One Thursday night in the autumn of 2012, the two sisters asked their friends Rachel and Georgie to stay behind. They were finally through with waiting for something to happen. 'We're going to start a company,' Jessica told them, draining her pint.

'We'd like to see if something amazing could happen on East Quay,' Naomi said.

Then Jessica jumped back in: 'And we want you to do it with us.'

Rachel and Georgie looked at each other. They, too, had ended up in Watchet after years in the city. Rachel had managed multi-million-pound production projects for the BBC and Channel 4, and Georgie had a decade's experience in communications, including a stint at the British Film Institute.

Georgie knew that if anyone could make something happen on the harbour, it would be Jessica and Naomi. In their twenties, the sisters had joined a campaign in nearby Minehead to stop the council moving a library that had ended with them winning £3.2 million from the National Lottery to set up a youth centre and world-class skate park. Because the skate park was independent from the council, it was still going, even though similar youth services across the country had closed down. Even so, it would be a huge risk to do something in Watchet. They would have to beat a private company to take on land in the heart of their town – land that had already been fought over for a decade. They knew that nothing about it would be easy. But they couldn't know quite how many hoops they would be made to jump through; how they would have to pay over the odds, justify themselves endlessly, and hawk back rage as they were belittled and bullied by people who saw them as 'just mothers' on the edge of the country, in the gaps of the economy, without the right to make demands.[12] Georgie felt nervous. Rachel felt excited. Together, they agreed.

1.4 BIRTH OF ONION COLLECTIVE

In 2012, Onion Collective was born. The women registered the business as a not-for-profit community interest company, a kind of social business that is designed to work for local good. Though they didn't know exactly what they were going to do on the East Quay, they did know how they would start: with months of research into what the people of Watchet wanted.

At first, people laughed at the strange name. The women had chosen it because it sounded organic, layered and distinctive. Someone made a joke about them making grown men cry, which wasn't exactly true. But plenty of people underestimated the women in Onion Collective.

During their early research, the Onions met with the head of a local business consortium. When they asked for his ideas about what industries might suit the town, he looked them up and down and then suggested they try 'something with cakes'.

The people of Watchet had better ideas. When they asked people in the pubs and clubs what Watchet needed for a stronger future, they gave one hundred different answers, from tourist attractions, to stuff for teenagers, to concerts, swimming pools and meeting places. The Onions crunched the information to figure out how it might all fit together. They wanted to build on the brilliant things Watchet already had to offer, like its seafaring history, its many creative people and its beautiful surroundings.[13] Using these ideas, the Onions came up with a plan for the renovation of the local boat museum and the addition of a visitors centre as a place to celebrate Watchet's maritime heritage. By this point the East Quay had been locked off for more than a decade. The Onions felt the need to act quickly. The sisters won funding for three years of art studios and workshops in shipping containers under the project name Contains Art. Faced with the reality of inhabiting freezing metal boxes on the seafront and little to no money for renovation, they recruited fifty local volunteers. Together, the volunteers – many of them artists and women – learned on the job how to clad interiors and construct floors, cut windows and wire up the electrics.[14]

In the years that followed, many of those volunteers rented the studios and visited the exhibitions. They brought their children to workshops to make postcards, or pictures of rocks and fossils, flowers and bees. Slowly, the temporary occupation evolved into conversations for a more permanent building on the site: something magnificent and distinctive, steeped in Watchet's history, where a new generation of townspeople could reimagine their future.

Then, in 2015, something happened that would change Watchet for ever. On Christmas Eve, 176 Watchet men and women lost their jobs at the paper mill, Watchet's last major industrial employer. For 250 years, skilled workers made brown paper for cardboard boxes and paper bags, wallpapers and wrappings. There were still orders on the books when the London-based owners DS Smith suddenly announced the mill would close.

People in Watchet felt gutted at the inevitability of the factory closure. These were loyal tradesmen, many of whom had worked at the plant for many years. The company blamed the decision to close on the loss of a big order and the investment needed for modernization. That year, DS Smith celebrated growth in total shareholder returns of 350 per cent over five years, three and a half times greater than the benchmark index, the FTSE250.[15] Meanwhile, in a town on the outskirts of England, more than one hundred people woke up on Christmas morning without a job.

It had always been important to the Onions to reflect Watchet's history of papermaking in their plans. But now that task took on a new urgency. They commissioned a Bath architecture firm to draw up designs for a building that could bring together the many elements described by people in Watchet: two galleries to bring world-class art and artists to town, a classroom for learning and sharing, permanent workshops for Watchet's many talented makers, a cafe and accommodation pods looking out to sea. In the centre of the building, they included studios for a paper manufacturing business called Two Rivers Paper, which produces watercolour paper so fine it is in demand all over the world.

Even more than jobs and art, Jessica and the Onions wanted East Quay to be a palace to what was possible in a town where people were told over and over again that to do anything good they had to leave. In 2018, they won planning permission, and in 2019, underwritten by the local authority and supported by a foundation called Esmée Fairbairn, they raised £2 million in order to qualify for a game-changing sum from the government's Coastal Communities Fund of £5 million.

Even with these pieces in place, the challenges continued. After getting planning permission in 2018 and starting the build in 2019, the cost of materials spiralled because of the pandemic, on top of existing price increases affecting cladding after the Grenfell tragedy and imported materials after Brexit.[16] Onion Collective were constantly praised by funders and onlookers for their resilience in the face of so many setbacks. But the Onions began to loathe the idea of resilience: the idea that their achievement would be in beating the endless obstacles that came with going against the system. They realized that they didn't want permission from the old guard so much as a different system entirely. One that saw the point in preserving heritage, in celebrating people's skills and knowledge and in foregrounding those whose contributions had for so long been overlooked. Onion Collective hadn't set out to be post-capitalist. But as the challenges mounted, they realized they were fighting for a different kind of economy. And they were not alone.[17]

1.5 IN AN EMERGENCY, THE NEW WORLD EMERGES

Just before lunchtime on the day after Boris Johnson announced lockdown in March 2020, Sally logged on to Zoom. On the screen appeared people from the four corners of the country, coming together to share ideas about how to respond to the crisis where they lived.

It was one call of many. Up and down the country, one thousand mutual aid groups were set up in that first week of lockdown. In the following weeks, two million joined local support networks on Facebook, while a hyperlocal social network called Nextdoor saw its daily users rise by 90 per cent.[18]

In the Zoom call, people talked about their most pressing

issues, including reaching people with no access to tech and the internet, and the supply of food. 'Buy food, make meals, freeze them,' said Iain Chambers, the manager of a community pub in Brighton called the Bevy, who turned the pub kitchen over to making freezer meals that they distributed in the community. He was worried about carrots and onions – whether they would arrive from Spain. It was too early in the year for UK supply. His worries proved correct when supermarket shelves started to empty of vital supplies of toilet paper and fresh food.

The pandemic was the first time many people in the UK experienced food shortages. Supply chains designed to fill shelves just in time fell apart under increasing demand. Between May and July 2020, about 10 per cent of people were using food banks, according to a survey by the Food Standards Agency.[19] When the UK went into recession in August, those on low incomes felt their incomes fall even further due to rising unemployment and fewer working hours. Researchers found that four times as many people were suffering from food insecurity in 2020 compared to 2018. People reported going full days without eating meals.

On the Zoom calls, Sally learned how community groups in Anfield, hundreds of miles up the coast from Watchet, were helping one another to get food to those in need. A food bank that normally distributed donated cans and tins started assembling boxes of fresh food from local businesses. A community-led bakery switched from match-day pies for the nearby Anfield stadium to making seventy loaves a day for the food banks and a local community centre, and lunches for staff at the local Asda. A neighbouring butcher donated meat, and some of the local pubs started making frozen meals to send out to those in need.

The whole system had changed, the people on the Zoom call explained. The economy was working the other way round. Local businesses pivoted to make sure they were responding and supporting one another in a mutual way. In Leicester, one health centre called B Inspired started delivering food bank parcels. In Bristol, another health centre called BS3 set up a Covid response team to deliver people's shopping and prescriptions. Pubs all over the country started delivering meals. A cooking school in Hackney raised more than £40,000 in a crowdfunder to make and deliver food to people in need.[20]

Sally had her own stories to share. Because of its many community organizations and associations, Watchet was able to form a mutual aid effort with a huge number of volunteers at lightning speed, mostly focused on getting food to those in need. It was about trust, the groups on the call agreed. But few of them realized the true value and strength of the trust they had built up in their communities, through years of working closely with their neighbours. It was so strong in places that it was able to replace even money. In Watchet, volunteers set up an emergency phone line for shopping orders. They got the local Co-op and other independent shops to agree to delayed payment. They used card machines to take contactless payments for shopping on the doorstep or over the phone, allowing relatives and friends to pay on behalf of vulnerable people. Then volunteers were sent to the Co-op to collect and deliver the shopping. On the Zoom calls, Sally learned about communities that had set up a small float to be used as a last resort, to pay for shopping and prescriptions when people were unable to use cheques for relatives and friends. In a crisis, it seemed, trust could go a long way.

Even as she feared for her children and the future, Jessica began to see the community response to the pandemic as a revolution. As supermarket shelves emptied and the delivery slots disappeared, the system of getting food to the consumer just in time collapsed. In its place, a web of smaller producers and socially minded enterprises emerged, delivering locally grown vegetables, bread and medicines by hand to people too vulnerable to leave their homes.

By talking to one another, the groups doing this work identified their shared ideals. They banded together for the first time, finding common ground even though they were so far apart. Sally and the Onions talked excitedly about a societal shift. They had the sense that Watchet would never feel so isolated again.

After the pandemic, many of the wildest hopes about revolution faded from view. People had said normality would never return, but somehow it did. The regular group calls dwindled and the people on them returned to the ongoing work where they lived.

But there was one small difference. People knew what would happen in the next crisis. Cities would fall silent, supermarket shelves would empty, trains would stop – and neighbourhood networks would come alive. The Onions and many other groups like them began to think of the pandemic as a kind of rehearsal for the catastrophes that were coming down the line with climate change. What they needed was some way to document this emerging network. Some kind of map that could guide them into the uncertain future.

1.6 THE NETWORK

What would you do in a crisis? In Sweden, every household gets a little red booklet. The Swedish government wants its citizens to plan for the day the heating stops working, or the shops run out of food, or bank machines stop giving out cash. Or if the petrol pumps run dry, or the mobile networks go down. 'In just a short time, your everyday life can become problematic,' the booklet says.[21] 'Think about how you and people around you will be able to cope with a situation in which society's normal services are not working as they usually do.' In Sweden, it's your responsibility to prepare for the first seventy-two hours of a disaster. The booklet goes on to list all the essentials that people should stockpile, from cooking oil, to candles, to cash.

Even in the US and Australia, there is a culture of disaster preparedness. There are more than 20 million Americans who engage in prepping, while the Federal Emergency Management Agency determined in a 2023 survey of Americans that 51 per cent are 'prepared for a disaster'.[22] In Australia, the Red Cross has its own disaster preparedness app.

Most of us in the UK are not preppers, nor do we have a booklet like the Swedish or an app like the Australians. But we might have something more important. Because when communities are asked to take shelter, the thing that truly makes a difference to survival is not a bag of tricks or a plan of escape. It's a place to congregate. The disaster preparedness expert Lucy Easthope has advised the government on everything from the Grenfell fire, to the 7/7 bombings, to the coronavirus pandemic. She calls these places 'lifescapes': communal spaces where people can gather and heal, like pubs, shops, mosques, scout huts and art galleries.[23] Easthope says that in a pandemic or a heatwave or a flood, it is how well you know your neighbours, and how much you can help one another, that will make the difference between life and death.

Take Chicago. In July 1995, a deadly heatwave rocked the city. As temperatures climbed towards 40 degrees Celsius, roads buckled and the train rails warped. Cars piled up. Children stuck on buses got so sick and dehydrated they had to be hauled out and hosed down by the fire department. As every ancient air conditioning unit was plugged into the mains, energy use hit record levels and the power grids failed, leaving almost fifty thousand households in the dark.

On 13 July, the temperature reached 41 degrees Celsius. After about forty-eight hours of constant exposure to these kinds of temperatures, the body begins to shut down. Thousands of people went to the hospitals, forcing accident and emergency units to close their doors. Ambulance crews drove around the city for miles looking for available beds. Hundreds never made it through the hospital doors. Soon, the dead were piled high outside the morgues. Police officers waited hours with corpses. Morgue workers searched for refrigerated trucks to hold the overflowing bodies.

It was an unprecedented disaster. But later, studies showed that some people were more vulnerable to the extreme heat. The people who did worse were isolated: they lived alone, rarely left the house, and they had no friends and family to check on them. Men, not women, were more likely to die – because elderly women kept their friendships going, the researchers found, whereas men became more isolated as they aged. While Latino people make up 25 per cent of the Chicago population and are disproportionately counted among the poor and sick, just 2 per cent of the dead were Latino.

In his book *Heat Wave*, the American sociologist Eric Klinenberg explained that it was not necessarily better family ties that made some communities more resilient to heat than others, but the fact that some districts were safer and more vibrant for residents, so they could more easily find shelter in air-conditioned stores or local churches. When another heatwave came, just a few years later in 1999, the city of Chicago made a plan to facilitate more places where people could go for help. Along with a strong public warning, the city opened cooling centres and provided free buses to them, phoned the elderly and sent the police and city workers to check up on old people living alone. The death toll was 110 residents – much fewer than in 1995. To truly prepare for another disaster, Klinenberg argued, communities must become better connected.[24] 'The only way to prevent another heat disaster is to address the isolation, poverty and fear that are prevalent in so many American cities today,' he wrote. He could just as easily have been writing about the UK, or any other country. Because what matters in a time of crisis is not how much money you have, but whether you have places to go and people to look out for you.

After the pandemic, Onion Collective got a name for themselves as people who made things happen in unlikely places. Foundations and other community groups wanted to know how to transform that sense of being left behind into one of opportunity. Onion Collective came back with a list of ideas. One of these was making explicit the ways that communities are linked. In a heatwave like the one in Chicago in 1995 or a pandemic like the one in 2020, these links saved lives. What if we could see those relationships, even before disaster struck? Onion Collective knew, partly because of the pandemic, that the country was covered in groups working against the idea that every man was for himself. They had also been developing a digital mapping tool to allow communities to reveal their hidden connections. But they had no way of measuring just how many groups existed. Then, in 2024, they were asked to do just that. A charity called the Joseph Rowntree Foundation asked them to research whether funding was reaching groups who were in some way working towards what they called an 'alternative future'. First they had to decide what that meant. Then they had to figure out how to measure the scale of activity across the country.

What does it mean to work towards an 'alternative future'? Alongside Gibson-Graham's iceberg, three models became the inspiration for the Onions' own petal-shaped model. First, a 'three horizons' model by Bill Sharpe, which shows how regimes fade away before eventually being replaced by alternatives.[25] Then a 'Two Loops Model', by the Berkana Institute in Colorado, which also shows the old system dying and the new system rising to replace it – but with emphasis on the role of 'pioneers' of these alternative futures, and how they join together to form networks as they become more dominant. But their favourite, and the one they most related to, was developed initially by the Dutch academics Arie Rip and René Kemp. It is called 'Multi-level perspective'. On this timeline, alternative futures are practised as niches in a dominant system and come to the fore when external factors, like weather events or pandemics, open up opportunities. The Onions felt this model described the way so much of the work of imagining a new world happens on the frontiers of the old one. When they came to design their own model of the transition to the next economy, they wanted to signal that, far from being extreme, people practising alternative futures occupy a more moderate position, one that embodies the circularity of the natural world. It was late-stage capitalism, they felt, that relied on an extreme form of exploitation and extraction, despite its dominance. That's how those groups practising alternatives ended up at the centre of their flower-shaped model, alongside their values: rootedness, trust, attachment, sharing, stewardship. On the edges of the flower, represented by dying petals, the views of the dominant system fell away: colonization, corporatization, commoditization, linear growth, extractivism and exploitation.[26]

Tracking down the people doing this work proved to be a hard task. Many did not advertise themselves as post-capitalist in a system in which they were intertwined and, for the time being, dependent. So the Onions embraced a snowball approach, asking organizations they knew embodied alternative futures to nominate other like-minded groups. These groups answered surveys to help the Onions understand their work and how it was funded. Eventually, they gathered the names of one thousand groups who said they were, in some way, working towards creating an alternative future. When they extrapolated from this research, they were able to estimate that the true number of groups doing this work was more like two thousand. Thousands of organizations, all over the country, working to bring into being a world that does not yet exist.[27]

But more than that, beyond the rejection of capital as the central mobilizing force, the Onions were able to show, for the first time, what these alternative futures might look like. The results showed a constellation of activity in every sector, touching every aspect of life.

1.7 CENTRING THE EDGE

When things get really tough, Jessica goes to the sea. The sound of the waves, the rolling stones, the horizon: something about being at the edge of the land makes her see things differently. Looking out at the water reminds her of the safety of Watchet, her corner of the West of England, where she feels rooted and secure, even though she can hear the rush of the waves and the pull of the earth, the reminder that everything changes and just keeps going. She feels caught between this world and the next world in a liminal space where everything is uncertain. But the movement makes her feel calm.

If it's after May – any earlier and she finds the water too cold – Jessica leaves the safety of the shore and swims out towards the horizon, into the waters of the Bristol Channel. On clear days she swims out into the flat muddy estuary, away from the land, and turns around to look back on her little piece of home, to see it from a different angle. It reminds her of the size of the world, and how small her place is in it, and the long arc of time, which draws the heat out of the daily minutiae of building and running a building while keeping her children fed and happy.

But her favourite days to swim aren't the still ones. She likes it when the sea is choppy and the wind is up, and the waves tip her sideways, the horizon coming in and out of view. She likes the feeling she gets right at the threshold of safety, when she knows she should probably turn back, but instead she goes a little further out, just to push at the edge. She thinks of the anthropologist Victor Turner and his description of edgemen as people who are 'betwixt and between' the structures of society. He wrote about how such people could act for social change and challenge accepted power structures. She recognized in this description something of the way she worked, pushing at the edges of what is possible and acceptable, and in the work of her friends around the country. For all of them, the space at the edge – that liminal place – is where the hope is. It's a stunning place that she can't help but swim towards – somewhere where things are different and she feels free.

Jessica describes this ritual in her opening speech at the symposium for artists on the edge in the East Quay Gallery in February 2025. As she talks, there are murmurs of recognition from the crowd. There's Kate Adams, all the way from Hastings, who has for decades been supporting neurodivergent people to make art. Kate has a collection of over five thousand physical works, displayed in galleries all over the world. Her collection shows how much bigger the world could be if only we could see all the people – the divergent, the different, the diverse – hidden from view. There's Lyn Barlow, now in her sixties, who runs a crafting group in the neighbouring village of Williton. Not long after the East Quay opened, the Onions supported Lyn to create three sewn panels describing her life in care, in Brixton squats and as part of the anti-nuclear protests at Greenham Women's Common. It was Lyn's first exhibition, sewn together with help from her crafting group in her living room and local churches. Onion Collective exhibited it alongside two touring tapestries by Grayson Perry. The exhibition showed not only that Watchet could host the art world, but that, more importantly, it was home to people making worlds with their art.

On the sidelines, still in his splattered apron, is Jim Patterson, who has for six decades been making some of the finest watercolour paper available anywhere in the world as Two Rivers Paper. His small manufacturing business, once hidden away in an old mill, is now in a studio at the heart of the East Quay arts centre, where the door is always open to passers-by. His company shows the reality of manufacturing the materials we need to create worlds: raw fibres and water and sweat and labour, pushed to the frontiers of the country, to the edge of the art world, but still existing in the cracks. In between these faces I see one hundred more: artists and makers and collectors whose work exists on the margins, embodying vital values of care, community and circularity.

What happens in the next world? All around the country, people from different neighbourhoods, different backgrounds and different disciplines agree on certain things. The world they are working towards is built on trust, compassion, hope and humility. It is regenerative rather than extractive, collective rather than individualistic and healing rather than harmful. When Onion Collective did their survey, all the people they spoke to were comfortable as defining the future they are working towards as 'post-capitalist'.

But from there, the many groups splinter into their own specialisms. Not all of the organizations the Onions encountered were working in one place: some were regional, national or online. Among them is Centric Lab, a research lab that uses neuroscience and ecology research to understand how the places we live impact our health. And Dark Matter Labs, the think tank working towards creating institutions and instruments for a more equitable and caring future. Onion Collective learned about more than one thousand organizations from their survey. But they wanted to know: how are these groups connected? How will they be able to help one another in the next crisis? So they made a digital map. Each of the organizations appeared as a little dot, with lines to show their connections to funders and to other groups. The funders appear in the middle of the network diagrams, like dandelion clocks with masses of circling white seeds. But the little seed heads disperse when the diagram is altered to remove these central figures. Without them, the other groups float off to the edges, untethered to any other. This map seemed to bear out the Onions' understanding of the work of building the next world happening in the margins, or, in the words of the writer Gal Beckerman: 'in the small, secluded corners where a vanguard can whisper among themselves, imagine alternate realities, and deliberate over how to get there'.[28] The work continues to survive and evolve, almost in secret, in the everyday. But it is in moments of emergency that the centre will expand. When that time comes, the pioneers will once again become a movement, one with the power to challenge the accepted ways.

2

HOARDINGS

Morecambe

'New ideas require old buildings.'

—Jane Jacobs, *The Death and Life of Great American Cities*

2.1 BOB TAKES ACTION

A milky dawn on Morecambe Bay is an invitation to consider the prehistoric. This is one of nature's frontiers: tucked into the coast of North West England, where four rivers – the Leven, Kent, Lune and Wyre – come together with smaller tributaries to make one enormous estuary the size of Malta. Each day, the sea rushes up to 12 kilometres towards the shoreline, turning sand into water in one of the largest tidal ranges in the world. The year is marked by a calendar of migratory visitors. From March, as the colder weather subsides, the distinctive ringed plover, the oystercatcher, the little tern and arctic tern lay their eggs on the Bay's quieter beaches, foraging for honeycomb worm, mussels and cockles in the reefs to feed their young.[1] [2] On sunny days in spring, the green flash of a tiger beetle can sometimes be seen speeding across the dunes to catch unsuspecting spiders and ants.[3] After sunset, the great crested newt emerges to perform his elaborate courtship dance, flashing his silver-striped tail by the light of the moon.[4] In summer, leatherback turtles visit from the Caribbean, teardrop-shaped and soft-shelled, searching for jellyfish to eat.[5] In late August, pink-footed geese arrive honking from Greenland and Iceland, travelling in large V-shaped flocks, marking the turn of the seasons as summer cools.[6] On extreme low tides, the bottom of the whole bay is revealed: a transitory land mass, alive with invertebrates that appear like a service station for circling seabirds.[7] Then the tide turns and the sea rushes back in again until it laps the edges of the surrounding towns.

For centuries, humans have found a home here, their fortunes ebbing and flowing like the tides in the Bay. These are the sandgrown'uns, people born on the shore.[8] At first their settlements were small, filled with fishermen trawling for shrimp and flatfish.[9] The railways arrived in the middle of the nineteenth century, bringing with them thousands of Victorians from the choking industrial cities of the North. They came seeking clean air and water. They believed the fresh air could heal their spotty lungs and that the saltwater could soothe their aching limbs. The trend earned Morecambe a new crest and motto, 'beauty surrounds, health abounds'. This – not the factories – became Morecambe's industrial revolution, turning it from fishing village to seaside resort, studded with all the grandeur of the era. Humans created new chapters in the history of the Bay, catalysing fresh transformations of the coastline in a landscape where the only constant ever has been change.[10]

The Victorians built pleasure palaces with their new-found wealth: a magnificent Winter Gardens with intricate mosaic floors and marble staircases with eccentric carvings of angels. On the seafront, daredevil showmen tumbled, five at a time, into an open air swimming pool, leaving spectators gasping in the stands. At the theme park over the road, passengers squealed as they hurtled around a train track in a figure of eight. Today the swimming baths are gone and for decades the doors of the Winter Gardens have been shuttered, leaving the plaster of the frescoes peeling in the dark. The theme park staggered through the decades, passed from owner to owner. In 1987, it became Wild West-themed, with a log flume and a viewing tower sponsored by Polo mints. They called it Frontierland. It felt like a suitable attraction in a place that was becoming another kind of frontier, not just between land and sea but between Britain's industrial history and its post-industrial future.

When the industrial centres of the North went into decline, the tourists were replaced with the poor as councils sent those in need of housing out to the coast. The fancy Victorian town houses of the West End were split into multiple units and sold off to private landlords. One pier caught fire, another washed away. The train station was closed down and the platform retreated inland. It wasn't long before Frontierland too was in trouble.

The tourists petered out, drawn overseas by cheap package holidays and the promise of good weather. The welcome gates at Frontierland were replaced with unsightly blue hoardings, taller than a man, leaving the viewing tower and the lifeless log flume to rot. There the hoardings stayed for twenty years, a two-hundred-metre-long barrier running parallel with the coast. Imagine a time-lapse video of those twenty years: the grass growing long between the sleepers of the rides. Paint peeling. Trespassers breaking and entering and leaving scattered cans and plastic bags.

For two decades, most locals never set foot on the ground behind the hoardings. They squeezed past one another between the road and the barrier as they travelled from the town centre to the houses and shops in the West End. Eventually rain and wind pulled the hoardings loose at their edges and some clattered, rusted and worn, on to the pavement, where people stepped over them gingerly as they went about their day. But many people carried with them the history of that site. Perhaps, when the hoardings blew down, they peered in to see what was left of the old Frontierland, to remember their summers speeding up the Polo tower for views of the surrounding coastline, or clinging to the boats around the twists and turns of the log flume. Imagine the time-lapse video ends one day when, zooming in, you see an old man pulling up in his car, stepping out and looking back and forth along the road to see if he is in the clear.

Bob Pickersgill had spent a lifetime painting lettering and murals as a signwriter, a job that had taken him from Liverpool to East Anglia and back again. But usually he got paid for his work. By 2021, Bob was in his mid-seventies, with black-framed spectacles like Eric Morecambe, the town's most famous comedian. He lived in a caravan with a small attached shed, measuring just ten by seven feet, and it was here, amid his tools and scraps of wood and boards, that Bob liked to hatch his plans.

Like many people, Bob was sick of the hoardings, especially once they blew down and people started walking all over them. Long nails stuck up on the panels, just waiting to puncture the underside of some unsuspecting sole. So, in the first days of January 2021, as soon as the shops were open, he went to a kitchen fitter to buy a piece of plywood big enough to cover a single panel. Back in the shed, he set the plywood on a rack, opened his oil paints and began a portrait of Dame Thora Hird, a famous actor born in Morecambe, whose father had managed a theatre where the shopping centre now stood. He painted her peering through a pair of distinctive round spectacles, a cup of tea raised towards a knowing smile. When it was finished, he stood back and wiped his hands on a rag. Not bad, he thought. Then he waited for a dry day to go and put it up.

Bob had put up plenty of signs before. But this one was different. He untied the plywood from the roof of his car, took out his electric screwdriver and, before the wind could get behind the panel and blow him into the road, he secured the first corner. A police car appeared in the distance, and Bob waited for it to slow down, prepared to defend himself against charges of defacing private property. But one police car flew past. Then another. None stopped. So Bob carefully secured the other screws, worrying all the time that they might not be strong enough, that the painting might blow away and crash down on someone's head. He didn't want to be on the hook for that. But before he had time to get worked up, the job was done.[11] He stepped back and for one moment took in Thora Hird and the twinkle in her eye. She seemed to say, 'I've got this, Bob.' Then he sped home, heart pounding, and put the kettle on to warm up. There was nothing more to do but wait.

2.2 LOOK AT WHAT WE HAVE

In humans, the act of hoarding is considered an illness. It was recognized as a pathological condition by the NHS in 2013, just after a financial crash that took everything from some people – even their homes – leaving them clinging to whatever they had left. As much as 5 per cent of the British population is said to suffer from it: some three million people agonizing over throwing away the slightest thing, at risk of death from falling objects, or disease from rot and decay.[12] The hoarder is a figure of ridicule, fetishized in reality TV shows with names like *My Hoarder Mum and Me* and *The Hoarder Next Door*. In these shows, producers perch mentally ill people on stools, surrounded by piles of upturned furniture, boxed toys and old newspapers and magazines, and prod them to reflect on their unstable upbringings while their families weep. Our fascination stems from a feeling that any of us could become hoarders. Our collective sense of scarcity and surplus has become dysregulated in the age of the internet, where we are told that everything we could ever desire is one click away. Hoarding is a condition of surplus – too much of everything – but it is most often linked to a condition of scarcity we call poverty. Poor people are four times as likely to hoard as wealthier people, according to a 2008 study.[13] Poverty brings with it all kinds of instability and need, problems that a hoarder seeks to address by hanging on to objects beyond their useful lifespan. Advertisers have for decades told us we can achieve happiness simply by earning enough to accumulate objects. The hoarder's response is to acquire objects anyway, even ones with no significance or value, in pursuit of some imagined relief.

Inside, we live surrounded by never-ending stuff, while outside the streets are full of hoardings. Next time you're in a built-up place, take a moment to look for these supposedly temporary structures. Notice the barriers around derelict plots, empty holes or building sites awaiting construction vehicles. Hoardings have two functions: to shield workers on a site and to stop intruders. When the economy is growing, speculators parcel up cities with plywood hoardings. Each surface is plastered with promises and marketing slogans dreamed up by developers, eager to sell their vision of the future. The word hoarding comes from the Old English *hord*,[14] meaning an accumulation of valuable objects cached for preservation or future use. Ancient languages had their own, similar words: in Icelandic, *hodd* meant treasure, while the German *Hort* was a refuge. Hoardings have always been liminal spaces, connecting a site of former use to its future one.

But in a recession, or in a place where capital is not readily available, hoardings can go from frontier to fortress. These barriers shore up the financial interests of speculators against the dreams of people who live nearby. Some scholars trace the root of 'hoard' to the Proto-Indo-European *kewd*, which means to conceal or hide – thus meaning simply 'something hidden'. Today we usually think of hoarding as the act of hiding and storing something away not always for future use, but to accumulate value. 'Though' we are fascinated by the tendency in its human form, hoardings in the landscape are so common as to be almost boring. Only sometimes does a community, sick of being barred, try to tear the hoardings down.

The problem of hoarding land and property is most striking on Britain's frontiers, in coastal towns like Morecambe. There is no end of evidence showing coastal towns are places of extreme deprivation. Around 10 million people live by the sea in England, or 18.5 per cent of the population (in Scotland it's even more – 40 per cent).[15] Data shows these places are more likely to be disadvantaged, with poorer housing, and a transient or elderly population as young people leave in search of a better life. Each coastal town has its own dubious accolade: Boston in Lincolnshire had the highest leave vote in the Brexit referendum; Jaywick on the coast in Essex is statistically the UK's most disadvantaged.[16] Hastings, where I live, has the highest number of young people who say they are in bad health.[17] Morecambe fares worse than most.[18] For a while, so many people were jobless in Morecambe that it was splashed across the tabloids as Costa Del Dole.

These statistics tell a story of rising inequality, threatening our ability as a species to come together in response to the planetary emergency. As the rich get richer and those in power more powerful, these individuals hold increasing sway over politics, just as we saw with the appointment of Elon Musk from Tesla and SpaceX to an advisory position at the start of Donald Trump's second term, at a moment when Musk was the wealthiest person in the world. Mainstream politics is shown to operate in favour of, even at the hands of, the wealthiest, creating a collapse of trust in politics among ordinary people. In this collapse, support for extremist views grows. Multiple studies have shown that support for far-right leaders increases as income inequality gets worse.[19]

Once in power, populist politicians – from Trump in the US, to Recep Tayyip Erdogan in Turkey, to Narendra Modi in India, to Giorgia Meloni in Italy – govern in the interests of the wealthy, dismantling social safety nets and deregulating the economy, increasing the exposure of working-class supporters to economic shocks and the misdeeds of corporations who seek to avoid social and environmental responsibility.

These problems don't just exist overseas. The UK has become one of the most unequal countries in the world, second only to the US.[20] The racist riots that erupted across the North of England in July 2024 came as little surprise in a political system that had for decades targeted minorities and migrants as scapegoats for politically manufactured inequality. You have less not because of us, politicians said, but because of them. During the 2024 riots in Southport in the UK, far-right leader Tommy Robinson used social media to call for people to join the disorder, telling people they needed to 'get there and show support'.[21] Months later, channels on Telegram with Russian links were found to be encouraging people in the UK to attack mosques and Muslims in return for cryptocurrency. Meanwhile, charities reported 2024 to be the most dangerous time to be a Muslim in the UK. One collected data showing Islamophobic assaults surged by 73 per cent.[22]

In places where inequality is at its most acute – those, like Morecambe, listed as the most deprived in national statistics – hoardings are the physical manifestation of a system that is based around the accumulation of wealth at the expense of the many.

Bob wanted to send a message with his mural: think of what we have, not what we lack. Think of Dame Thora Hird, Morecambe's 'most famous daughter', his mural read. Think of our families and our attachments, our history and our future. And to his surprise, many of his neighbours agreed with that message. Little did he know but Bob Pickersgill, veteran, signwriter and proud Morecambe resident, had just started a protest against the capitalist forces that had long been at work in his home town.

2.3 BEKI TAKES NOTE

Beki Melrose first saw Bob's mural on her way to work at the Exchange. Beki is a sandgrown'un, raised in neighbouring Heysham, who found her way back to the shore after training as a fine artist in Winchester. She loved the bubble of art school, putting on DIY shows in the day and partying at night. But when she left college she fell into a deep depression, unsure of what to do with her training in the real world.

With her mum's encouragement, she came back to Lancaster, Morecambe's neighbouring city, where she met her partner, Jo Bambrough. Jo liked mountain biking and hiking and helping people. For every creative idea Beki came up with, Jo had a practical solution. Together, they felt like they could do anything.

It was Beki who spotted the house in Morecambe, tucked away on an unmarked road in the north of the town. She convinced Jo to take a look. It was in a terrible state, with junk everywhere and metre-high drifts of mystery animal hair. But Beki felt a weight lifted being back by the sea. Jo was handy. If there was ever something she didn't know how to fix, she just set to and figured it out. And Beki was trained in the art of imagination.

Beki covered her mouth with her jumper to block out the foul smell and said to the estate agent, 'This is the one.' The estate agent couldn't believe her luck. She immediately promised to deliver her a vanload of bleach.

As well as renovating their own house, Jo was interested in creating a place where other people might gather at a time when many public services had disappeared. She had spent seven years as a youth worker for Lancashire County Council, until austerity stripped so much from the budget that she found herself recruiting teenagers for a project she knew the council had waning commitment to deliver. But she hadn't lost her desire to work with people. She imagined a place where people could show up for different reasons, with no restrictions on what they should or could be doing there. So she posted a message on Facebook inviting people to a meeting to discuss the idea. The response blew her mind.

At the first meeting, fifty people turned up. Beki and Jo couldn't make the tea fast enough. They wanted a place to show and sell their art, people said, since so many of them had moved to Morecambe in search of somewhere they could live cheaply and be creative, but there were few places to show or sell anything they were able to produce. By the third meeting, Beki and Jo, in partnership with their friend Melody Treasure, had rented a little terraced shop in Morecambe's West End, once its richest quarter and now its poorest. At the meeting, they drew a business plan on the windows using dry markers. Inside, they installed a counter to serve tea and take payments, and hung art for sale all over the walls. They called it 'the Exchange'.

Very quickly, Beki and Jo realized that they were offering more than a shop. Before long they were opening the doors to the Exchange every day for workshops, gigs or supper clubs. People thought they wanted a place where they could sell art, but really they wanted a place where they could be together in their creative endeavours. And the results of this collective action were brilliant and surprising. People made art rooted in Morecambe's history as a place of pleasure and leisure. But they also dreamed about events and exhibitions that looked to the future. One summer, regulars at the Exchange made a crazy golf course, spilling out on to the seafront, with each hole created by a different artist. One winter, the Exchange supported a local software engineer who came up with an idea to teach people to make their own miniature illuminations, filling the prom with thousands of tiny lights.

Some people came to the Exchange for the food and the company, like at Chinese New Year, when there was a paper-lantern-making workshop, sparklers and a hot meal of spring rolls and sweet-and-sour curry. Others used it as a springboard to new ventures. The software engineer started a prototyping business. The artists started putting on their own exhibitions and experimenting with more ambitious installations and events. Beki and Jo helped one regular, Jules Abraham, to put on a winter spectacle – an ambitious, immersive piece of performance art in a church.

Jules is a gentle giant of a man with big curly hair and a booming chuckle. He had returned to the North West after studying in America, and found work as a teacher and in a museum. But when his parents passed away he began to search for a new creative outlet to help him heal.

One day, he took himself to a drop-in group offering support with grief through creative projects. It was there that he met Beki, a support worker with an impish grin and cropped hair. Jo and Beki had just started the Exchange, and Beki invited Jules to come along to the little terraced shop, to see if he could find something there that would help him return to himself.

After Jules first visited the Exchange, he came almost every day. Over the summer, each time Beki and Jo needed help for one of their events, he was there. Within a couple of years, Jules found himself curating an exhibition of tiny artworks: more than a hundred tiny paintings and sculptures, displayed on miniature easels. He started to realize he'd been waiting for this kind of place his whole life.

As more people came to the Exchange, it expanded into a neighbouring shop. In search of more space, Beki and Jo secured a verbal agreement with the owner to temporarily occupy a Methodist church over the road.[23] The church was damp and cold, but the artists saw the potential for large-scale works in its cavernous rooms. In February 2018 they helped Jules to put on his spectacular. Jules wrote a story about a snowflake that wanders off and goes on a great adventure, before finding its perfect home in a frozen cave. He held a meeting for other artists to join the production, and together they filled the downstairs rooms of the church with lights, fabric and mirrors to tell the story of the snowflake's journey. In February, as people waited outside to be guided round the rooms, Jules realized that he was like that snowflake. He'd been drifting. But coming to the Exchange had given him direction. He'd found a place of possibility and vitality at a moment when his life had grown cold and still.

Beki and Jo approached the owners of the church to see if they could secure a longer-term agreement that would allow them to properly invest in its transformation. But in the summer of 2018, just when they thought they'd come to an arrangement, they received notice to leave.[24] The owners had decided to put the church up for auction. In response, Beki and Jo mobilized their community for a massive crowdfunding campaign to see if they could raise the money to buy it. They also started a petition to have the church registered as an asset of community value, a way of pausing the sale to give them longer to raise funds.

Though they raised their initial funding target and succeeded in registering the church as an asset of community value for future sales, the church slipped from their grasp.[25] The community simply couldn't find the £100,000 required to buy the asset at private auction at such short notice, and nor could the sale be paused.

It was a blow. But Beki and Jo had no time to wallow in disappointment. Morecambe is full of beautiful, derelict buildings. Even the ugly ones had potential. Increasingly, the artists that came through the doors of the Exchange wanted more permanent places to work together. Within a few weeks, Beki and Jo had secured a short lease on a unit of the Arndale shopping centre near the train station. The unit had been an Argos, before the branch closed, leaving another empty storefront in an arcade pockmarked with frosted windows. It had a warren of windowless storage spaces out the back. Even though the Exchange could only secure a thirty-day lease on the store, people leapt at the chance to turn the warren into workspaces. Soon each corner was full of desks and easels, half-finished paintings and screen-printed posters, and colourful objects. In the shopfront, the Exchange hosted exhibitions and workshops, and encouraged the artists to take part.[26]

After the church campaign failed, Beki and Jo stepped back from big buildings for a while. But another one began niggling at them. It was a former Co-operative department store, the jewel in the heart of the high street that ran through the West End. Once, the windows had been filled with Victorian finery: clothes and household wares to tempt money from the pockets of residents and tourists. But in a story that now sounds familiar, it had been empty for the past twenty years. This time, Beki and Jo seemed to be on to something. Lancaster City Council, impressed at their work on the church campaign, asked Beki and Jo to work on a plan for the Co-op, offering them rent below the market rate. So Beki and Jo started making plans for the building, involving more art, more creativity, more good things, renaming their organization Good Things Collective. In the summer of 2022, they brought together local high school students and heritage groups to research the history and values of the co-operative movement and how they might play out in Morecambe in the present.[27] It would take hundreds of thousands of pounds in investment to make the Co-op safe to occupy again. But with the city council on their side, Beki and Jo dared to believe that finally, they might be able to transform one of Morecambe's empty buildings for good.

2.4 ART OF THE NEW FRONTIER

Bob's painting on the hoardings tapped into something. Beki knew from a mile off that the mural was by him, even before she got close enough to see his signature. The hoardings were hundreds of metres long, with more than enough space for other artists to contribute murals of their own. So Beki invited Bob to give a signwriting workshop at the Exchange.

During the workshop, while his students were learning the painstaking art of getting all the letters the right size, Bob told the story of the Devonshire School of Lettering that once stood in the West End of the town. Just like many signwriters all over the country, Bob used to buy his brushes from there. Little did the participants of the workshop know that signwriting was part of Morecambe's rich heritage, another reason their town deserved a place on the map.

Beki loved the idea of transforming the hoardings on the seafront from an eyesore into an art gallery – and saw the potential of collective action to put political pressure on those in power to get the barriers taken down for good. The idea definitely fell into the category of a good thing.

But she really was swamped. The members of Good Things Collective were in the midst of trying to raise hundreds of thousands of pounds to start the restoration of the Co-op department store. At the same time, their work in the community was crossing over more than ever from art to social change. Though art had been the starting point, the discussions that went on in their workshops had grown into new areas: food, housing, jobs.[28] The collective had many members. But Beki and Jo were still organizing and coordinating the whole effort without any other staff. A lot had happened since they began selling local people's art in 2015.

If Bob and other local artists were going to create more murals for the hoardings, Beki knew they needed to have their own identity. This had to be a proper protest. So Beki and some of the first artists involved decided to form a different collective demanding change. They called it Art of the New Frontier. 'We want to celebrate the creative community that lives here!' they announced online. 'But ultimately, we hope our actions bring awareness to the fact that this is not OK for the site to have been left in this state for over twenty years.'[29]

It was a risky business. They didn't have permission to put paintings on the hoardings. If anything went wrong, and the art fell down or blew away and injured someone, no one was insured. But the project was popular with locals. The kitchen fitter agreed to give them cost-price plywood. Soon, people all over Morecambe could be seen slipping through doorways with their massive canvases. Bob's phone was alive with messages from people who had finished their mural. He collected each canvas, took it back to his shed and edged it with white plastic, ready to hang. By March 2021, he had fixed another three along the two-hundred-metre-long monstrosity. A reporter from the local paper turned up, and Bob stood for pictures next to the row of murals wearing dark glasses and a raincoat, hands clenched into fists, a stepladder at his feet. 'We care about the town,' Beki told the reporter.[30] 'And we think this can be a catalyst for change.'

The plywood kept coming. By the summer, Bob was putting up two or three pictures a week. There were paintings of deckchairs and Punch and Judy shows, reproductions of old train line posters, seahorses, mermaids and silhouetted birds. 'I really miss the Polo tower,' read the text on one. Eventually, almost the whole strip was covered in one hundred pieces of art.

It looked amazing, like Morecambe's answer to the East Side Gallery, the artworks that adorn what's left of the Berlin Wall. The pictures symbolized people's hopes and dreams, their memories and their desires. But it was also a sign of resistance. As well as working on the art, Bob sent a letter to Morrisons, who now owned the site, asking them to repair broken panels, and they agreed. Some of the artists coordinating the campaign gave out empty maps of the land and asked people to imagine what could go there. 'Swimming pool,' someone scrawled across the middle of the white space. Someone suggested a recycling mall to stop the fly-tipping in the West End, a major problem in the alleyways as people couldn't afford to call out the council to pick up old mattresses and fridges. Someone dreamed up a snowboarding dry slope, another a sensory garden, someone else a half-pipe and a cat cafe. One map was filled with nothing but drawings of trees. Another read simply: 'Please, no super-markets, car parks or housing estates.'

Beki and a local councillor called Jim Pilling met with Morrisons executives to put forward the community's ideas. They decided to start small and that meant no demands for swimming pools or dry slopes. They just wanted two things: for the hoardings to go, and for the community to be allowed to use the land, even temporarily, for dog walking, sunbath-ing, picnics, or simply to cross from one end of the town to the other. Not for ever, just while the supermarket decided what to do with the land in the long term. It seemed like a reasonable request. The executives said they would think about it.

The community had spoken. Beki and Bob waited to see what Morrisons would do next. While the church project had failed, good things were happening. The council had agreed to a community asset transfer of the Co-op building. Morrisons seemed to be taking their proposals about the old Frontierland site seriously. There seemed to be a groundswell of support for change. They didn't know that hundreds of miles away, behind closed doors, investors were making plans for Morecambe on the back of an envelope that would change the rules of the game. Millions of pounds were suddenly in the balance. A juggernaut was about to come to town.

2.5 DREAMS OF EDEN

One day in October 2015, Dave Harland was sitting in his office, hundreds of miles south of Morecambe at the Eden Project in Cornwall, when the phone rang.[31] Dave grew up in the former china clay mining town of St Austell, just down the road. His mum remembered a bustling market town, grown rich from the deep deposits of kaolin, a white substance used in everything from porcelain to magazine paper to toothpaste. But after the pits had closed, many families were left without the means to make a living. By the time Dave was born, St Austell had gone into decline. As he grew up, like most people of his generation, he had one eye on getting out. He ended up working as financial director in Woking, preparing the books of a care home services group for acquisition, when he got headhunted for a job back in St Austell. To his surprise, the offer was too good to refuse.

The Eden Project is a tourist attraction built with lottery money at the turn of the millennium. The co-founders, including a brilliant businessman called Tim Smit, proposed filling an old china clay pit with giant domed greenhouses: futuristic looking conservatories made of clear plastic sheets stretched over steel hexagons. The structures trapped heat, making them a good place to grow plants and wildlife from the rainforest and the Mediterranean. Visitors came to see the plants and stayed for food and drink, activities in a visitors' centre, and to browse Cornish goods in the shop.

At this time, Eden was looking for someone to get it on a stable financial footing before embarking on expansion overseas. To Dave, an opportunity like this so close to his home town felt like fate. He joined in 2012, and, over a decade, rose through the ranks to become the CEO of an increasingly international brand, overseeing deals for new Eden Projects in China, Africa, South America, Australia and Dubai. The last thing he expected was a call inviting him to Morecambe Bay.

The voice on the end of the line belonged to the deputy vice chancellor of Lancaster University. He had a proposal for Dave. 'You ought to do an Eden Project here in Lancashire,' he said. 'Right on the coast in Morecambe Bay.'

Dave found Morecambe Bay on the map. It was at the other end of the country. But it was not far from many major towns and cities in the North West – Lancaster, Preston and Blackpool – and at the foot of the Lake District, a popular tourist destination in itself. He decided to go up and find out more.

On his first trip he found a top university willing to support the project as an educational initiative, including starting a new curriculum based on the ecosystems of Morecambe Bay. When he visited the Bay itself, he could see that its glory days were in the past. He felt that it needed 'a leg-up'.[32] But a tourist attraction requires tourists, so for Eden, the key question was: where would the tourists come from?

They did the maths. Around 1.6 million people live within two hours of the Eden Project Cornwall. Eden executives discovered that 10.6 million people lived within two hours of Morecambe Bay, and many more passed through the region on their way to holidays in the Lake District. That's ten times more people than in Cornwall. They couldn't believe what they were seeing. 'Let's just think about that for a moment,' an Eden executive called Si Bellamy excitedly told business leaders at a Lancashire expo in 2019.[33] 'The scale of reach with Eden Project North in Morecambe is on a different level to anything we've done before.'

So Eden commissioned some designers to make an initial drawing, which was released to the press in 2018.[34] They chose a spot on the promenade that used to belong to the Super Swimming Stadium, the heated open-air pool where spectators would watch, amazed, as five interlocked men jumped from vertiginous diving platforms and women competed in bathing beauty contests. The site was now simple green space, overlooking the Bay, metres from the site of the blue hoardings. In the green space, the architects drew a series of silvery, teardrop buildings inspired by the shape of mussels, with walkways guiding people down into the Bay. It looked futuristic. But it was impossible to say what was inside the domes, or what you were meant to do there. Dave went back to Lancaster University to show them the drawings. To elaborate further, he said, they would need £1 million.[35]

How do you pay for a project the scale of Eden? The park in Cornwall was conceived in very different times, when the government was actually looking for big regional flagship projects to spend National Lottery money on as part of its Millennium Commission. Although the commission took some convincing – initially turning down Eden's proposal – it eventually contributed £56 million. Another £50 million in public funding came from the Southwest Regional Development

Agency and EU funds – the latter no longer available since Britain left the EU. It took at least £20 million more in loans to get the project off the ground.

These days, that kind of money is trickier to come by. Lancaster University went to local councils and business leaders to suggest they split the £1 million four ways. The City Council did a back-of-the-envelope risk assessment of giving Eden the money, splitting the decision into 'for' and 'against' columns.[36] If they didn't do it, they wrote, the risk was that 'the area remains stagnated'. No alternative proposals were considered. Eden got the cash.

Then came the proper calculations. Eden went away and came back with a build figure of £125 million. It campaigned for the UK government to contribute £75 million, first from the Northern Powerhouse agenda, then from the Levelling Up budget. Achieving that kind of investment would rely on being able to prove significant wider benefits to the scheme, including regenerating Morecambe by bringing in hundreds of thousands of tourists a year, who might spend their money in the wider town. As for the site, as long as Eden could get the planning permission and raise the funds, Lancaster City Council said it would transfer the land for free.[37] All Eden had to do was agree to put a small percentage of each ticket sale into a trust to benefit the local community.

The drawings of Eden North, drip-fed to the press, got more fantastical. Lancaster City Council and Eden Project hired consultants to make their case to government for funding. They released fresh rounds of images showing those distinctive domes filled with the native plants and flowers of the Bay – the same flora and fauna that grows in abundance and can be enjoyed for free right outside. The pictures show giant sunflowers and shrubs leading up to viewing platforms. Performers dressed as giant native birds. Orange pods, suspended from trees. Within a year of Eden completing its feasibility study, Dave Harland told people that tourism in Morecambe was already up 135 per cent. He boasted that people were already making investment decisions based on the promise of Eden. He meant it to sound exciting, to entice the government to fund £50 million, and investors to come in with another £50 million. But to many people in Morecambe, it sounded more like a threat.

2.6 EVERYTHING CHANGES

I visit the Exchange in 2020, two years after the first images for Eden North are released to the press. It's a year after my investigation into property and land sold off by councils during austerity and I want to follow it up with an investigation into empty buildings, with the idea that if communities knew more about vacant buildings, they might be able to open them up or bid on them. But I find local people already in crisis mode. Eden North has become a vacuum, sucking up all the air in the town. Young people say house prices have increased so much they might never be able to move out of their home. A three-bedroom house, worth around £85,000 in 2017, has just gone on the market for £129,000. This is a dire development in the West End, where just 40 per cent own their own home, compared to a regional average of 65 per cent.[38] Almost everyone I speak to is renting, some making do with damp, blocked drains or leaky roofs, all the while living in fear that the owner might be tempted to sell up and kick them out, given the rising prices. An artist called Carmen Scott has already received a notice of eviction from her landlord.[39] She feels Eden has a moral obligation to help local people at risk of being evicted because of gentrification.

Property developers have started circling. People receive flyers and business cards through the letter box from London firms asking if they are considering selling their home. Others see people coming round the West End with clipboards.

Business owners start new enterprises or rename old ones to contain the word Eden. Everyone wants in. Now there is an Eden taxi company, a podiatrist and a cleaning company. A local hairdresser registers a company called Eden North Luxury Apartments and dissolves it again. Property owners begin to hang on to spaces in the hope of selling them on later for greater profit. The hoarding mentality intensifies: we have nothing, so we're going to save everything. And it is just as true of Lancaster City Council.

After Covid, when high street shops all over the UK closed down, researchers found that communities could only take on empty shops and buildings with local council support.[40] Councils had several options. They could use a mechanism for transferring buildings they owned into trusts for the benefit of the community. Or they could act as a broker, standing between community groups and private companies or landlords. But in Morecambe, after Eden Project receives planning permission, Lancaster City Council does neither. Instead it buys the Frontierland site behind the hoardings from Morrisons, spending £3 million of public money, and asks developers – rather than the people themselves – to send in their ideas.[41] In tender documents, Lancaster City Council asks bidders to think about accommodation for tourists. 'The site is a great location for a new purpose-built hotel,' it says.[42]

Back in his caravan, Bob is dismayed. He thinks the council buying the land is the worst outcome. That the space will once again be left to rot. Local councillors, it seems, have a short memory. Some twenty years earlier, in 1994, Lancaster City Council voted fifty-nine to one to award £300,000 to the television show host Noel Edmonds and his production company to turn a local adventure playground called Happy Mount Park into a Mr Blobby theme park.[43] But it ended in complete disaster. Just thirteen weeks after opening, The World of Crinkley Bottom – known to everyone locally as Blobbyland – closed down. Lancaster City Council spent more than £2 million of the public's money taking Noel Edmonds to court over the scheme, in what Edmonds called the biggest local government scandal of modern times.[44]

In 2004, the corporate director of regeneration at Lancaster City Council told a journalist that Blobbygate, as it became known, had taught the council that it could not run a theme park.[45] And yet, just a decade later, the authorities are once again handing over six-figure sums to travelling businessmen promising dreams to tourists, even as half the town is full of empty theatres, churches and shops.

Then comes the final blow: Lancaster City Council decides to replace the fencing with smaller metal hoardings, too small for the artworks to fit, expressing health and safety concerns at the state of the old boards.[46] It's 2023, not long since the one-hundredth artwork has been hung. Bob fears they will all end up in a skip. He asks the council, if it is going to own the land, why don't they just open it up for local people to use? But his suggestions are rebuffed. The hoardings have been up for twenty-five years. Now, Bob fears, they'd be there for another twenty-five.

2.7 SMALL THINGS

The visitors to Morecambe Bay are changing again. The eternal dialogue evolves between the non-humans and the humans of the Bay. People have warmed the earth, creating shifting weather patterns that affect the ability of some migrating birds to reach these milder shores in winter.[47] The silver-grey tern, with its majestic black cap, had all but disappeared by 2008 because of lost habitat and lack of food.[48] The UK government plans wind farms in the Irish Sea, sketching out the routes of miles of underground tunnels, tearing up the beaches.[49] The blades of wind turbines are deadly to migrating seabirds like the pink-footed goose and whooper swan who keep to their straight lines and fly in low light.[50] A holiday park, drawn up next to one of the Bay's nature reserves, threatens to bring thousands of visitors to trample on the fragile estuary home of the great crested newt and the natterjack toad.[51]

The developers are characters in a narrative that describes the natural world as a separate entity, there to be plundered. But as we enter an era of extinction and ecosystem collapse, it's becoming more and more difficult to see ourselves as 'above' changes to the environment; as immune from the effects of climate change. Every year of declining species in Morecambe Bay brings us closer to an unfolding environmental crisis that will inevitably envelop us all.

Eden Project offers a tired but familiar proposal: build something even bigger, even shinier. Commodify the Bay under domes and charge people for access. Harness its nature as something to sell. Value its precious species as exhibits for human consumption. The idea of pleasure palaces attracting tourists to the coast feels comfortable to the government and to investors, who have seen this model a thousand times before. A new government in 2024 promises the £50 million in public investment to Lancaster City Council, which plans to turn the entire sum over to Eden.[52] The council hands over the land, worth another £900,000, for nothing at all.

In January 2024, a government think tank assesses the council's plans to give a combined £50.9 million subsidy to Eden. It finds little evidence of how Eden North would improve the lives and wellbeing of local people, particularly how it might address lower life expectancy, poorer health and higher obesity rates, lower educational attainment, lower employment rates and higher rates of crime. The council says twenty years of failed initiatives to improve the fortunes of Morecambe prove that only a project of Eden's size and expense can have an impact. The think tank says these historic examples are irrelevant. It wants to know, what could be done instead?[53]

Once, I asked Tim Smit, the founder of Eden, that question. What might happen if he asked the people of Morecambe what to build? His reply was unequivocal: 'That would be the way to build the biggest piece of rubbish you can imagine.'[54]

But what if building something is about more than shiny new buildings? The case for new buildings at this moment in human history is vanishing. Buildings, measured for the carbon consumed during their construction and during their day-to-day operations, account for 40 per cent of global carbon emissions – larger than global emissions from coal-fired power plants.[55] In order to stay within 1.5°C of global warming, emissions from buildings need to be halved by 2030 and reach net zero by 2050.

As raw materials face scarcity and the carbon budget ticks down, radical architects like Dark Matter Labs are advocating for ways to retrofit and reuse existing buildings, and to design new ones for disassembly and reconfiguration. Like the nests of migrating birds, buildings need to be adaptable and reusable, recycling what is already there and breaking down when no longer in use.[56] And there is no shortage of beautiful, neglected land and buildings in Morecambe. Beki and Jo alone have demonstrated that building goes beyond bricks and mortar, by inhabiting existing places – the terraced shop that became the Exchange, the abandoned church opposite, the empty Argos in the Arndale Centre and the Co-op department store on Regent Road. And of course, the Frontierland site, stuck behind the hoardings. These places appeared like mushrooms: just when Beki and Jo thought they'd found the next challenge, another would sprout. They have shown that building can be just as much about creating connections between people, the capacity to imagine new possibilities and joy.

Beki and Jo aren't the only ones in Morecambe trying to rehabilitate its existing buildings. Since 2006, local people have been working to save the Winter Gardens, a Grade II listed

concert hall with a vaulted moulded ceiling. A volunteer restoration group meet at weekends to learn how to repair tiles
and cracked walls.[57] A businessman tries to revive the Alhambra Theatre, another Victorian theatre that was once one of the
great Northern Soul dance clubs, opening it up for festivals and
for drinkers at weekends. On Victoria Street, a local entrepre-
neur sets about restoring a traditional covered market, hoping
to turn it into a food hall.

How could Eden's £50.9 million in public subsidies, split
between these community-led initiatives, change lives in
Morecambe? Money going directly into the pockets of local
people, acting with the confidence of the authorities to take
on the beautiful existing buildings of their town. In emergencies, these civic spaces become our lifescapes. When extreme
flooding hit Morecambe in 1983, Morecambe Town Hall was
turned into an emergency advice centre to help people most
affected by the disaster.[58] In 2018, a local businessman opened
the doors to Morecambe's seafront theatre, the Alhambra, for
emergency public meetings. The meetings were held by local
people in response to news broadcasts of poverty so severe that
parents were relying on primary schools to charge their mobile
phones and wash their children's clothes. When the pandemic
struck, the town hall was once again opened up and turned into
a coronavirus testing centre. The local cricket club and football
stadium became temporary vaccination centres. By contrast,
during a crisis, most tourist attractions shut down. During the
coronavirus lockdown, the Eden Project in Cornwall closed to
visitors and let go 40 per cent of its staff.[59]

But there is no £50 million in Morecambe for local people's
plans. Beki and Jo's story is one of persistence in the face

of repeated displacement. They were evicted from the Methodist church in 2018. In 2020, with no immediate need for meeting space during lockdown, and so many other projects in planning stages, they gave notice on the little shop in the West End they had transformed into the Exchange. In 2022, NewRiver Retail, a London-based retail property investor, announced the long-awaited sale of Morecambe's Arndale Centre. Beki and Jo got thirty days' notice to vacate the old Argos. They spent an exhausting week packing up art supplies, moving the community Risograph printer and taking down the paintings and prints that covered the walls – each one a reminder of a community project or a person that had passed through the doors. And although they initially secured an agreement with Lancaster City Council to transfer the Co-op building into community ownership, by 2023 the council had changed direction.[60] It started working with Place Capital, an out-of-town developer, on a scheme for offices and housing.[61]

When I visit in August 2023, Good Things Collective find themselves, for the first time in a long time, without any bricks and mortar in which to host events.[62] All the buildings they have inhabited sit empty in the neighbouring streets, shuttered and still, despite countless community campaigns, thousands raised, false starts and broken promises from landlords and the authorities. To Beki and Jo, each one was a stepping stone on their way.

I meet Beki, Jules and two other local artists at a community garden on a once discarded plot in one corner in the West End. It's a glorious day. The raised beds are abundant with the fruits of earlier labour: tomatoes, courgettes, elderflower berries almost ready to harvest. On picnic tables, the artists lay out different kinds of seaweed – a recent passion of Beki's. For lunch, there are rolls of seaweed sushi, sweating slightly in the heat. Beki has brought jars and jars of home-made pickles. Foraged vegetables press up against the insides of the glass, swimming in salty brine. There are Tupperware containers of seaweed salad, showing a tangle of vibrant green. There is even a seaweed zine, printed on the Risograph.

The meet-up is part of a long season of summer events the Good Things Collective have planned in this micro-garden, in the hope that more people in Morecambe might take on some of the abandoned plots and use them to grow. Pushed out of the buildings, they occupy the streets. At each event, there is free food and friendly faces and a workshop of some kind, usually on the natural world. A mother has brought her two boys down and they chat excitedly while Beki hands them paper and pens. 'Can you draw this seaweed?' she challenges them and they fall silent and begin to study the plant.

All of a sudden, three young boys fly past on bicycles. The leader of the pack has his T-shirt tied around his scrawny waist. His skin is tanned a deep chestnut after a long summer bouncing around in the sun. 'Hello!' they yell cheerily, giving no sign of slowing down. But a few moments later, they appear again, loitering outside the garden on the corner of the street. 'Water?' Beki offers them. 'Lemonade?'

'Lemonade!' says the eldest, delighted, slurping it down in a paper cup and wiping his wet mouth with the back of his hand. 'Pens?' Beki offers them next.

'I'm no good at drawing,' the shirtless one says, little slits of eyes in a sweet, boyish face. But they sit down anyway, accepting the pens and making jagged black lines across the page.

'Good holiday?' Beki asks.

'It's OK. At least it's a break from school,' the boy says. He's going into year eight, he says, but he's on his last warning. One more incident and he'll be permanently excluded. It's hard to imagine when he's like this, hunched over his drawing, chatting about seaweed and how it can be eaten. Beki opens the plastic box to show the boys the sushi. The younger ones won't try it until the older one does. They all agree: that's not going to happen. Instead, the older boy takes a tendril of seaweed salad and dangles it in his mouth: a green sliver silhouetted against the blue sky. For a moment, he looks like he's going to eat it. Then he spits it into the vegetable beds and they grab their bikes, speeding off again, declaring that the youngest has a birthday party to go to.

I wonder if these boys will ever walk through the gates of Eden North. If they will see the 'immersive theatrical experiences' or the 'environment filled with plants'. A ticket for a child costs £16 in Cornwall. And the food is certainly not free. Shut out from the land and increasingly from the buildings, the energy of the community moves like hot lava through Morecambe's back streets. It flows into overgrown corners, connecting the townspeople to the surrounding nature. It challenges people to ask themselves how they relate to Morecambe's grand history, to imagine a future that has not yet arrived for their town.

There's no cure for hoarding in humans. But doctors recommend cognitive behavioural therapy, a way of gently reprogramming the brain. It would take a similar kind of reprogramming of the economy to rid the system of its obsession with scarcity and top-down development. The good things, the very things outsiders want to capture – nature, wonder, diversity, renewal – already exist in abundance in the Bay.

3

MINE

St Austell

'An earlier and more pertinent genealogy of landscape in Germanic Europe is that place in which political moots could be gathered to discuss *things*, that is, issues of importance. A landscape is a gathering in the making . . . My landscapes are moots in which many living beings – and non-vital things as well, such as rocks and water – take part. They come together to negotiate collaborative survival . . .'

—Anna Tsing, 'The buck, the bull, and the dream
of the stag: some unexpected weeds of the Anthropocene',
Suomen Antropologi, 2017[1]

3.1 BLACKPOOL PIT

The water of Blackpool Pit in Cornwall is luminous turquoise. From a distance it looks like alien glue has been poured into craters, the surface hardened like wax, surrounded on all sides by giant terraced banks. It's a school kid's diorama of life on some far-off watery moon. But up close, the lake isn't really that blue. Just like its name, which some say comes from the Cornish *poul an du*, meaning 'pool of black', the water at the lakeside glints darkly.

One morning in June 2021, before the day has properly warmed up, I approach the water and peer down at the foamy edge. It looks cool and inviting. I glance behind me to see if anyone is watching, knowing I am trespassing. Then I slip my clothes over my head, pile them on some rocks and step as lightly as possible over the jagged white shards and into the water. My feet are first to feel the chill.

Compared to my usual swimming spot in the sea off the south coast, the fresh water feels heavy. My body sinks. I watch my icy toes feeling their way across the craggy bottom towards the edge of a ledge. From there, the pit descends into absolute blackness: a drop of 200 feet.

Blackpool Pit is private property, owned by the French mining conglomerate Imerys. I am in the mining country near

St Austell on the South Cornish coast, where the rise and fall of the china clay industry has shaped the landscape and its people over the last quarter of a century: a story of enclosure and privatization in which the people of Cornwall have become estranged from their land.

The pit was once one of the biggest and most productive of the china clay pits in Cornwall, the centre of clay mining in the UK. People in the surrounding villages – known as 'the Clays' – live in the shadow of the giant flat-topped mountains made of quartz. After Aberfan, that fatal landslide in Wales, many of the mountains were levelled. One of the most famous, Watch Hill, still stands more than three hundred metres tall.

It is, technically, a heap of waste material. But it is covered in white china clay deposits, making it look snow-capped from afar. Creepers have grown over the old buildings, covering clay-firing kilns and rusting mining equipment. Water has filled the old pits, creating these startling blue mineral pools that are surrounded by a quicksand-like slurry made of mica, a mineral that was discarded as waste.

Seen from space, the pools split the moors like open wounds. These are the scars of systemic extraction: a monument not just to human desire for nature's minerals, but to a way of life. From the ground, they are mostly hidden from view.

Aside from a handful of nature trails, human activity here is banned by Imerys, which bought the British mining company English China Clays in 1999. In 2007, Imerys closed the Blackpool Pit, ending 170 years of mining history. That day, five hundred workers went home jobless.

Heavy gates were shut with chains. Imerys installed security guards and no trespassing signs. Local newspapers ran warnings from Imerys about the risk of drowning in the lakes – 'deep cold water poses a significant threat to life'.

Mostly, people heed them. So much so that when people were seen waterskiing on Blackpool Pit, it made local headlines. I see evidence of these pleasure-seekers. A big yellow digger sits on a ragged green carpet on the dirt track down to the lake, all that's left of the effort to make this into a runway for speedboats.

For many years, it was nearly impossible for ordinary people to explore this landscape within the bounds of the law. Until a decade after the closure of Blackpool Pit, when some local ceramicists approached Imerys with a radical idea. They wanted to open the gates and bring people back to reimagine the pits – to reacquaint them with its cold clay. The idea is an exercise in reconnecting with the earth. And an invitation to make something new out of the waste materials of industry.

The act of returning to this land is political. It's about how Cornish people were dispossessed, first of the moors and the stories they held, then of the mining country that made them proud and wealthy working families. And it's partly philosophical. The project gets to the heart of how to live on the planet without destroying it. By reconnecting with material – with a whole moorland – locked up and discarded as waste, the ceramicists are questioning the very nature of care.

But for one of the artists, this project is personal. After many years of working in London, Rosanna Martin is exhausted and looking for a way back to the feelings that first sparked her love of clay. Her family is from this part of Cornwall, and she digs not just for clay but for the markers of her heritage: her connection to the earth at a moment when she feels untethered.

The philosopher Jane Bennett asks, 'How would patterns of consumption change if we faced not litter, rubbish, trash, or the "recycling" but an accumulating pile of lively and potentially dangerous matter?'[2] In Bennett's suggestion, this discarded landscape is treacherous and vital. The world is no longer a passive thing from which we are at liberty to endlessly extract, but an active collection of components that transforms over time: like our bodies, like the stars.

From the water, I look up to the scrubby peaks towards Watch Hill, that famous waste mountain. Rosanna and her colleagues have invited people to join them on a walking tour – a field trip – through this forbidden frontierland over four or five hours.[3] The peak promises spectacular views out west towards St Agnes and Goonhilly and the south-westernmost point of England – the long thin peninsula known as the Lizard. A good spot from which to consider the changing landscape and our place within it.

Then something brushes my leg and I shudder. As the sun tracks higher over the man-made peaks of clay country, I retreat hastily to the shore, taking one last moment to savour the cold against my goose-pimply arms and legs, before scrambling back out to my clothes. Perhaps this lake – this landscape – isn't so lifeless after all.

3.2 BRICKMAKING AS RITUAL

After my swim, I head downslope to find Rosanna. A small plume of smoke is the first sign of human activity. A scrubby border demarcates an unofficial road, which opens into a flat area of the filled gravel pit. The hills around are streaked with falling rocks. Rosanna greets me with a dust-flecked, tired smile. She is quite pregnant, but you can barely tell under her giant vest and shorts. She wears leather boots covered in gravel and mud.

This is the patch of land that Imerys granted her, she explains. She called it Brickfield – a sister site to her studio Brickworks, an open-access ceramics studio in Penryn. As well as the land, Imerys donated several giant bags of ball clay and china clay that the artists have been using to make bricks. Later, more clay was found, undisturbed, at an abandoned brickworks called Wheal Remfry, by the last man to fire the last working beehive kiln before it closed in 1971: John Osborne.

John came to one of Brickfield's early workshops at Indian Queens Preaching Pit in summer 2019. The workshop was intended for people from the villages surrounding the mining sites. In fact, John was the only person to come. John couldn't help himself. He was in his seventies and hadn't made a brick for fifty years. But he remembered every bit of it: the names of the bricks, the designs of the kilns, the timings and the mix of the materials. 'Because of the love of it,' he said. He saw how Rosanna was making and firing bricks. Then gently, without ever criticizing, he explained how it was originally done.

Soon Rosanna and John were visiting the site of the old brickworks at Wheal Remfry together, entering the private land to scratch around in the grass and the gorse. When Wheal Remfry closed, piles of bricks were abandoned in the stacking yard. Rubble had covered over the old kilns. Ash, ivy and elder had grown over the rubble. A road was built after the millennium that cut the site in two.

With heavy gloves and scratching sticks, the unlikely pair excavated usable bricks and carried them off to use in their kilns. Soon they were bringing others from Brickfield with them: volunteers and artists repurposing abandoned materials for something new.

The Brickfield site tells the story of Rosanna and John's growing friendship and the evolution of the project. Two shipping containers provide basic protection and storage: the older one for tea and coffee, the newer one as a kind of open-air classroom with an awning offering a little cover in case of rain.

On the other side of the site, a row of pallets are stacked with drying bricks and covered in tarpaulin. In the middle sit two kilns made of found and reclaimed bricks from the old Wheal Remfry site.

The first kiln is a mash-up of a beehive kiln and a brick clamp kiln, the simplest way of firing bricks. Then Rosanna met John, and learned some of the old techniques. The second kiln has just been built in a traditional beehive shape under John's watchful eye. It's a majestic creation: perfectly round, squat and sturdy, with a tall metal chimney that reaches up to the blue spring sky. Around it, the site has become a workshop. Artists wearing protective gloves are bashing the nails out of planks of wood with a mallet. A jigsaw screeches as someone dismantles a pallet. All of this will soon be firewood: fodder for the kiln.

Firing the kiln is the main event at Rosanna's workshops. It's part science, part pure passion, involving days of chopping logs, hand-filling the kiln with hundreds of unfired bricks and sealing over the top with clay. Then follows a twenty-four-hour marathon, sleeping in shifts to feed the fire to its maximum temperature. It has to be hot enough to turn soft clay solid, hot enough to push scorched air around the bricks, so hot the stench of burning wood and firing clay stays in your clothes for days.

It's a ritual that connects Rosanna to John and Brickfield to the centuries-old tradition of brickmaking in Cornwall. It gives new life to waste clay and discarded bricks. It's a process of death and renewal that echoes the origins of brickmaking in Cornwall – and Rosanna's own path to clay.

In the UK, mining is most readily associated with coal. The British Isles is riven with scars from mining, an industry that has shaped British politics and culture – and continues to this day. There are around two thousand mines[4] and quarries in the UK. Some are still active. In Devon, a London-based company[5] is planning to excavate untapped seams of tungsten, used in missiles, television tubes and drill bits. In the Scottish Highlands, a private company is pioneering 'clean' gravity and flotation techniques to extract fresh discoveries of gold ore reserve, which are still extracted using poisonous mercury and cyanide in some parts of the world.[6] And mining may soon return to Cornwall. The 'clean' energy transition will actually increase demand for critical minerals including lithium, nickel, cobalt, manganese and graphite, which are essential for batteries; the rare earth elements used in permanent magnets in wind turbines and electric motors; and the copper and aluminium used in electricity networks.[7] By 2030, demand for lithium could reach as much as forty-five times the 2020 demand.[8]

Far more numerous than active mines, however, are abandoned mines and quarries and their legacy of derelict land, dangerous buildings and contaminated water. Nature has crossed these industrial frontiers. Colonizing plants, shrubs and small animals have reclaimed some sites. At others, as in

South Wales, authorities have brought in commercial companies to remove mine waste, flatten peaks of slurry and redirect or treat water.[9] But humans – dog walkers, nearby residents, would-be hikers – are often banned.

In 2008, the Environment Agency judged abandoned mines to be one of the most significant pollution threats in Britain.[10] Some disused mines discharge heavy metals and other pollutants into streams and rivers when it rains. Others are silently filling up with groundwater over time, liable to start polluting in the future. Discharges of metals such as cadmium, iron, copper and zinc are expected to make one in ten English rivers unsafe from an ecological and chemical perspective.[11] In some mined areas, important drinking water supply aquifers are polluted or threatened by plumes of sulphate and chloride.

Legally, no one can be held responsible for pollution from the majority of mines. It is only since 1999 that mine operators have any obligation to deal with the consequences of abandoning a site. So it falls to the Environment Agency, which has built a handful of mine water treatment plants around coal mines.

Even the agency admits this is insufficient, and that metal mines in the ore fields of Wales, the South West and northern England continue to pollute the surrounding landscape, as no single body or national strategy exists to tackle them.[12] Industry has taken what it can and discarded the land. Cornwall is pockmarked with tin and clay mines like Blackpool Pit: whole landscapes transfigured by extraction and waste. Clay is one of the most wasteful types of mining. For every tonne of clay quarried, the miners created nine tonnes of waste rock and mica.[13]

Originally, brickmaking was one useful response to all the waste from the clay mines. In the first clay pits in the seventeenth century, bricks were made from waste clay on site and used to build local housing for the miners and their families. By the eighteenth century, brickmaking had moved offsite, using newly formed deposits of waste clay that had washed downstream. The clay was mixed with sand and straw and other readily available local materials and fired in huge beehive kilns. So, the brickworks have a kind of symbiotic relationship with the extractive process of mining. One that might hold clues about how to rehabilitate abandoned industrial sites.

Rosanna was born in Cornwall and spent her childhood playing in the slurry water of Tuckingmill Creek, on her grandparents' farm on the Roseland Peninsula, upland from the River Fal.

Upstream, miners in the Western Pits were still at work excavating kaolin, otherwise known as china clay, from partly decomposed granite. Downriver, old sediment had caught in the bend outside Rosanna's grandparents' house, silting up the creek.

Historically, extraction pits were so polluting that the St Austell river, the River Vinnick, was christened 'the white river' because of its permanent discoloration with clay particles.

Every weekend, when the tide went out, Rosanna and her brothers would play in the slurry of Tuckingmill Creek, swimming, skating and sliding through the bright-white mud, flecked with iridescent mica. It was Rosanna's first contact with the material that would become her life's work.

Three decades later, Rosanna was working three jobs in London and struggling to find time to make art in her studio. She spent most of her time facilitating workshops for adults with learning difficulties and working as a technician at a drawing school. The cost of living in the city was strangling her creativity. A period of burnout hit. She returned to Cornwall, to recuperate with her parents. But the dearth of employment in the county can make it a hard place to come back to.

Rosanna knew she would have to make her own way and took a studio space in Penryn. She thought this was the dream: a place where she could do all the things she was doing in London as part of one project. She called it Brickworks, after the Trelonk brickworks on the site of her grandparents' farm, even though at the time she had never made any bricks.

But within a few years, she realized that managing a workshop was just the same as having three jobs: it left no time for her own practice. When the pandemic closed the doors on the ceramics studio, she felt a sense of relief. She began to wonder how she could bring her own practice together with her workshops and teaching, out in the open air.

The landscape around her grandparents' house at Trelonk was known to her through the family nicknames once used by her mother to navigate the fields: Parc n Ponds, Kennigey, the Mayhay. But it was locked off to her now: the pits closed by a private, overseas corporation, her grandparents' house long sold. She couldn't reach her grandparents' place by land without trespassing. So one day, she decided to go by water, and set out on a kayak to reach the bend. When she arrived, she leant over the side of the kayak and ran her fingers through the soft sediment, remembering the feeling from her childhood. Gently, she scooped some up with her hands and into the boat, feeling the boat sit lower in the water with the weight of her spoils. Ragworms,[14] common underwater millipedes, greeted her momentarily before burrowing back down into the mud in search of organic matter to eat.

In her many years of study and specialization, Rosanna had been drawn to the details of minerals. She had taken up an artist residency at the Eden Project in Cornwall in 2018, while running her studio, and spent time photographing particles of found materials across clay country.

The particles, just one millimetre in size, were unidentifiable, even at a microscopic level. For many years she collected these curious specimens and experimented with fusing them together with clay from Trelonk in the heat of the kiln to make intricate, geological sculptures. Rosanna saw in these new man-made materials a beauty and a complexity that revealed the long and strange process that brought them into being. In every unidentifiable speck, there was a whole system of extraction and its impact on a universe of geological transformation taking place concurrently over the course of millennia.

Rosanna had not been back in Cornwall very long when the founder of a local arts studio asked her to run a field trip of some kind. She began to wonder how an expedition might offer her a way back to the family land and its language. The name of her studio became a kind of premonition. She would take people to what was left of an old Cornish clay mine. There, they would make bricks.

3.3 EARTH STORIES

I find a group of people waiting in a makeshift car park on one of the plateaus of a former gravel pit. People chatter excitedly, checking their backpacks for home-made sandwiches, sweets and water. Two little dogs pull at leads towards the trail.

Here are teachers, council workers, pensioners and art students: people from the local area who saw the walk advertised as part of a local ceramics festival, and decided to take the opportunity to cross the boundaries that have for decades cut them off from clay country.

Zenna Tagney, our guide, stands among them. She has shiny black hair piled up on her head above big smiling dimples. She wears hiking boots like she lives in them, a neck scarf tied over a long-sleeved green T-shirt. Zenna knows the stories of old Cornwall. Back then, this land was very much alive.

While we wait for stragglers, Zenna gives a short introduction to the area. Clay country is unique, she explains. It is the only place in the UK where there has been large-scale extraction of china clay. This is because of its unusual geology.

Around 300 million years ago, during a period of mountain building called the Variscan orogeny, two continents collided to create mountain ranges across Europe, including the Ardennes and the Massif Central in France.

As the mountains moved, rocks melted into magma deep beneath the earth, forming crystalline granite. Over time, ice, wind and water wore away the surface of the mountains, exposing granite to air. As the granite weathered, some of the aluminium rich feldspars within the rock were chemically altered to create china clay.

Mining didn't start here until 1745. Before that, the landscape was green. Back then, the Cornish moors were dotted with villages and small coastal settlements, as well as landmarks that Zenna learned about in her parents' folk songs:

burial grounds, standing stones and other remnants from human rituals that told of ancient interactions with the land.

Zenna was born inland from Plymouth at Gunnislake, and grew up in Tywardreath, a little village on top of a hill near St Austell, to musician parents who navigated the landscape by folk stories and songs. The tales drew the relief of the land in vibrant colours. Each pool might be home to a sad mermaid, each hedgerow providing cover for a mischievous monster hiding in wait for a traveller to scare. In mine country, an encounter with a mythical dark-dwelling spirit called a knocker was said to bring good luck.

Zenna found new ways to tell these stories. Clay became her instrument. Using porcelain foraged from riverbanks, she fashioned pellars, or wise women, who created remedies from elements of the local nature. She experimented with piskies, naughty creatures who could lead you astray on the moors.

The stories are reminders of a time when ordinary people, or commoners, had the right to communal land – known as the commons – to make their livelihoods. This precious pasture became a place to graze sheep, light fires and raise children. From 1235, the Statute of Merton, decreed by Henry III, allowed manor lords to enclose common land, asserting their rights over woodland and pasture. The poorest people were pushed off the land. Those who remained were forced to work for a wage.

The enclosures not only transformed the land, but they changed the relationship between men and women. Men took on the duties of production: farming, mining, fishing. Women who had worked on the common land were now confined to the household and reproductive duties. Old women, meanwhile, once dependent on the common land for firewood, food and shelter, were forced to go begging from door to door.[15] The historian Silvia Federici has shown how these enclosures arrived in tandem with the witch-hunts. Women – especially old women – no longer shared in a communal resource and had to beg for subsistence. These elderly female beggars were often blamed for misfortune – a sick child, a lost harvest – and accused of laying a curse or a hex on the family.

It was considered blasphemous – somehow threatening – for humans to behave as kin with nature. Instead nature was to be quelled, to be dominated – it became a commodity. Within a few centuries, explorers arrived to sell the precious stones of the earth, forever changing the face of the moors. In the eighteenth century came William Cookworthy, a chemist and the son of a Quaker weaver from Kingsbridge, Devon. Cookworthy's brother, a sailor, had presented to him a fine, elegant white ceramic clay discovered on his overseas travels. This was porcelain, as yet undiscovered on UK soil. The mineral fascinated Cookworthy: as fine as talcum powder with a mesmerizing white sheen. He became obsessed with the search for porcelain at home. In 1746, he travelled to Tregonning Hill in Cornwall, where, in a bell foundry, local people were using what they called 'growan' to make moulds.[16] Cookworthy touched the soft sediment and felt its fine texture – soft to the touch – and he knew. This was kaolin, that rare type of decomposed granite his brother had found overseas.

Cookworthy took samples and began to test ways to use water to wash off impurities. He spent twenty years developing a new recipe for making porcelain, eventually applying to patent his process in 1768.[17] In Plymouth, in neighbouring Devon, he set up a porcelain factory to begin manufacturing fine china for export.

By the early nineteenth century, the St Austell deposits had emerged as the largest known resource of kaolin in the world. The material became widespread in other industries. Paper-makers used it to make magazines glossy, pharmacists put it in toothpaste as a whitener and in exfoliators to buff the skin, and manufacturers made toilet bowls from porcelain to give them a hygienic white sheen.

As demand soared, men were called to work in the filthy conditions of the pit. This was opencast mining, using high pressure jets of water to spray peat, soil and rocks from the sur-face of the earth. The explosions created a slurry of mud and minerals which gathered at the base of the pit, where it could be filtered and classified.

Granite, mica, mud and any other materials were taken by conveyor belt to be discarded, growing into mountains of waste products known as tips. Only precious kaolin was allowed to remain, pumped into tanks where the water used for its extrac-tion could be sucked away.

Men were needed for every part of the process: spraying the walls with pressure hoses to remove the clay, then processing and transporting the material ready to be exported all over the globe. The surrounding villages, some built with waste clay, swelled with new families who sent their men to work in the mines. The villages gained their distinctive name: the Clays.

By 1910, Cornwall was producing one million tonnes of china clay every year, accounting for half the world's supply. Three-quarters of the extracted material was exported overseas. In 1919, the three main producers merged, calling themselves English China Clays, which continued to dominate the market until it was bought by Imerys in 1999 for £756 million.

One of my walking group asks Zenna about Imerys.

'It's a French company,' she explains, adding that not everyone feels good about Imerys locally, because of what happened after it bought English China Clays. In that single deal, Imerys became the largest employer in Cornwall.[18]

In less than a decade, the company had halved the number of employees, a loss of eight hundred jobs. In 2006, Imerys closed down all mining in Devon and one of the seven pits of Cornwall's clay country, alongside one refinery and two drying units. It planned to move operations to Brazil, spokespeople said, because of the high cost of 'coating', an energy-intensive process where clay is mined, refined and dried for use as white pigment in high-quality paper, mostly exported to paper factories in Scandinavia.[19]

When we think of industry in Cornwall, we think of fishing, tin and copper mining and farming, Zenna explains. But china clay from Cornwall accounts for 88 per cent of total UK exports of this material, none more so than from the pits around St Austell.[20] Imerys still employs a thousand people in Cornwall and extracts a million tonnes of china clay each year from around twenty active quarry and industrial facilities.[21]

The mine closures were the second time Cornish people had been dispossessed of their land. The enclosures preceded the triumph of the rational over our mystical connections with the earth. Then, private companies and corporations claimed their right to this land for extraction and profit.

Zenna's tour takes us past signs forbidding trespassing and

warning of falling rocks. Up a rough path, two men in orange vests are inspecting a pile of rubble near a building. A van parked up opposite is emblazoned with the word 'demolition'. They look up to see us approaching.

They want to know what we are doing – whether we have the right. We have crept on to this land and now we are privy to the slow crumbling of an era of Cornish history. Eventually, after a slow climb, we reach a viewing platform built for visitors to the mines. The platform tells a story of the nation's pride in mining. A place from which the royals – those ultimate landowners – could gaze down upon man's domination of the landscape.

Queen Elizabeth and Prince Charles once stood here. Even more improbably, so too did Emperor Naruhito of Japan.[22] Up here I get a sense of the pit's scale. How tiny I was, inching into the edge of the water for a morning swim. Though the mines took a wrecking ball to the moors, it's impossible not to admire the majesty of the pits. Another kind of history, layered over the Cornish folklore that came before.

With Zenna as our guide, we can reach back in time, before industry took hold. Along a path of scrub and rocks she shows us the site of scores of barrows – human-made heaps of earth or stone often found on hilltops. Locals once recorded other markers here: the signs of a double burial and other mysterious rituals like stone circles and standing circles. 'So much of that has gone,' Zenna says. 'Unmarked.' As she talks, Zenna scuffs the path with the toe of her hiking boot in search of pieces of clay to squirrel away for later.

The stories have changed. According to Zenna, each ancient burial ground, each pre-industrial settlement that was destroyed to make way for clay mining was judged less valuable than the growth of the industry. She believes that, in that displacement, the many magical tales of the Cornish moorland – its populations of mischievous piskies and cove-dwelling mermaids – are replaced with one new story: the story of china clay.[23]

3.4 PRECIOUS STONES

We stop for a rest behind three boulders in a crater that is a little sheltered from the wind. There we sit in the scrub like little birds in a dust bowl, eating snacks from our laps. Zenna points out the matrix, a crumbly granite that disintegrates on contact. It looks like dust, but it contains the precious substance Cookworthy was after: kaolin. To take it from this land would be considered stealing from Imerys. Instead we crumble it through our fingers, feeling the softness turn to nothing. The stones here are another kind of signpost. A way to see into the past and to reimagine the future.

A mineral collector has come on the field trip alone. While the rest of the group listen with awe to Zenna's stories about mythical spirits and burial grounds, he looks studiously at the ground, bending to inspect the earth, searching for rare rocks and stones. Any flash of colour, or the glint of a hard surface, could signal a discovery.

The mineral collector works for the local council, but his weekends and holidays are dedicated to his hobby. He is part of the Russell Society – the national body for professional and amateur mineralogists.[24] He knows that clay country, because of the unique interaction between the earth's forces and human industry, yields many kinds of precious stones. A keen eye might spot the green flash of torbernite, a glint of blue apatite, or sparkling lilac fluorite crystals. Even, he says in hushed tones, yellow opal. 'You do get opal up here,' he says as if to reassure himself. 'If I find one you'll hear a squeak!'

According to the rules of the Russell Society, discoveries can be recorded, but the stones must remain in place. Since this land is private, removing them can be considered theft. Sometimes, however, a rare stone or two finds its way into the pockets of a collector. At home, catalogued and recorded on message boards online, the stones – and their location – tell their own history of the way the landscape has changed, from moor, to mine, to dwellings. Some of his most precious pieces are from places buried under housing estates, he says. No one will have access to those sources again.

Nearby, a former clay mine is being covered over with housing by Eco-Bos, a housing developer formed between Imerys and a Swiss urban development corporation. Though clay mining has gone into decline, Imerys still has other business interests in clay country. History is about to repeat itself. Another explorer, three hundred years after Cookworthy, has come to Cornwall in search of precious stones.

Andrew Smith first came to Cornwall in 2017 in search of lithium, one of the world's lightest materials, which is in huge demand to make batteries for bikes, phones and electric cars. He had already set up the Cinovec lithium plant in the Czech Republic – the largest lithium resource in Europe and one of the largest in the world. He had a hunch Cornwall, with its history of clay mining, might yield more of the precious mineral, since lithium is found in mica, which alongside kaolin is one of the components of granite.

In clay country he found his prize. He tells the story like this:

one day he was driving through the mines when he saw a sparkle at the side of the road. He stopped the car and got out to inspect the ground. He turned the rock in his hand – granite, and inside, the glint of mica. He had struck gold.

Smith took the rock home and sent it off for tests. Half a decade later, he signed a joint venture agreement with Imerys, giving them an 80 per cent stake in Imerys British Lithium. Before long, the company was promising to excavate enough lithium from clay country to power 500,000 electric cars by 2028, just as long as they could fund a processing plant at a cost of up to £1 billion. The newspaper headlines sang of a modern-day gold rush.

Halfway up Watch Hill, someone in the group cries out. We stop to see what they have found. Not yellow opal, the amateur mineralogist shrugs. Instead, in the palm of their hand, is a hard crystal of common quartz. Quartz, which comes from granite, is a waste product of the china clay industry. When granite is split into quartz, mica and feldspar, only feldspar has the potential to become kaolin.

The pink quartz in the palm of the walker's hand is nothing special to the mineralogist, nor to the miners. It is neither rare nor useful, and easily discarded by those concerned only with scarcity and function. And yet, just like feldspar and lithium, multiple forces brought it into being, from thousands of years of geological processes involving pressure and heat, plus the human processes using gravity, magnets and water to split the granite into its component parts. This stone is a connection to those earth systems and to geological time: an invitation to consider the world as not simply inert, but as an evolving system in which people still play a part.

As we ascend, the walkers compete to find the best specimen of quartz. Others look up from the path and begin to doubt they can complete the climb. It's not an easy hike, and slowly we split into two groups – those who want to continue to the summit and those who would rather make their way back down towards the car park.

Those of us who make it to the top are rewarded with the promised view of both of the Cornish coastlines, visible on the horizon: from Newquay all the way to St Austell Bay. The land is covered in the man-made mountains of clay country. Two villages, Foxhole and Carpalla, sit nestled in the valley between two sets of peaks.

The pits around them have long since been abandoned. Nature is returning, covering the rocks with grass and gorse and little pink flowers called stonecrop. The mineralogist, so concerned with rocks formed millions of years ago, considers the future for the pits that remain. 'They won't be here long,' he says. As we look to the future of the moors, he chronicles the past, one precious stone at a time.

Perhaps lithium mines will transform the landscape, doing to clay country what the clay mines did to the moors. Or housing estates will creep on to the quarries. Just a few miles away, the Eden Project sank an entire rainforest biome into one former clay pit: a tourist attraction that would have been unimaginable to the miners who once worked the earth.

In each of these dreams of progress, the landscape – from mineral to moorland – is inert, a passive body of rock waiting for humans and machines to do their work. But what if each mineral, each mountain, had its own evolutionary process or even its own purpose? What if these rocks are, in their own way, alive? Perhaps that sounds like the stuff of folklore – and indeed it is. But it is also, most recently, a discovery of science. One that threatens to change the rules of physics and unlock clues to the history of our planet – and its future.

3.5 HISTORY REPEATS ITSELF

In December 2006, Robert Hazen, a self-proclaimed 'hard core' mineral physicist, bumped into his old colleague Harold Morowitz, a theoretical biologist, at a Christmas party in America.[25] Morowitz approached Hazen with a question – not the usual 'where are you spending the holidays' kind of question, but one that would change the course of science. He wanted to know whether clay minerals existed during the Hadean period, when the earth was just forming, between 4.6 and 4 billion years ago.

Hazen was bowled over. No mineralogist in history had ever been asked a question like that, a question that dealt not with the chemical or physical properties, but with a mineral's place in time. He was immediately struck with the fact that the earth's mineralogy must have changed over 4.5 billion years in ways that had never thoughtfully been explored. After several sleepless nights, he embarked on a project to do just that, assembling a team of cross-disciplinary scientists including geobiologists, meteorite experts and petrologists, who study rocks.

Hazen and his team knew that the planets in the solar system were formed by just a few dozen minerals. Over time, the number of minerals increased to several thousand. Through his research, Hazen was able to determine when and how each of more than 6,000 known minerals were formed, with the surprising result that more than half of all minerals evolved through biological processes.[26] Minerals helped trigger life, then life triggered the creation of more minerals.

They realized that they were describing a form of co-evolution, an evolution in step with the emergence of other living beings. They called it 'mineral evolution': a brand new kind of science that considered minerals not as static, but as a dynamic system that increased in diversity and complexity – processes that in some ways echoed the evolution of life.[27] This was a groundbreaking discovery. Since the Ancient Greeks, metal and minerals had been depicted as cold and inert – as the opposite of pulsing, vibrant life. Hazen was able to identify three ways that mineral evolution was like other kinds of scientific processes that change over time. First, they had interacting components: atoms and molecules. These were not so different to the interactive components of cells and genes in the body, or musical notes of a scale or the ones and zeros of computer code – all of which could be combined in a vast number of ways. Second, there had to be a way to create those different configurations, from the earth mixing up atoms and molecules, to life in the womb creating new generations of genes, to composers coming up with notes to make music.

Finally, he proposed, there had to be some method of selection. Darwin explained biological evolution as the survival of the fittest, a process of passing healthy genes on to the next generation. In minerals, it was about being stable: not melting, or dissolving or weathering away. In music, or coding, the selection process was about achieving critical or commercial approval, or writing programs to serve certain functions.

The scientists even went so far as to say that their discovery constituted a new law of physics, akin to Newton's laws of motion, called the second arrow of time. The first arrow of time is described by thermodynamics, and says that in an isolated system, entropy, or the degree of randomness and uncertainty, tends to increase with time. This is the trend in the universe towards disorder and decay, the one-way arrow towards death. Hazen and his colleague proposed a second arrow of time that went in the opposite direction. Rather than a diminishment, it described an evolution – or increase – in the diversity and patterning of systems through time. It demonstrated a process of selecting for function, or the increase in functional information over time. That was a difficult idea for scientists. Scientists worked in absolutes. The word 'functional' required context. It required purpose. If true, Hazen's law suggests that there is something in the universe that is increasing order, increasing complexity – not in a random way, but in a way that selects according to purpose.[28]

If the question that had started this enquiry at the party was confusing, the questions that followed were totally mind-blowing. Hazen began to ask himself, do minerals have a purpose? Do atmospheres have a purpose? Does life have a purpose?[29]

These were huge unanswerable questions. But they opened up new avenues for understanding how humans interact with these systems.[30] The climate catastrophe was one example in which humans are trying to change their relationships to the earth, its fossil fuels and its minerals, in order to prevent the destruction of the human race. How might humans change their relationship to the earth if they knew that the earth had its own life cycle, its own purpose, that began billions of years ago?

Science may only just be catching up with the idea of the earth as a living, evolving entity. But many cultures outside of the West teach of a Mother Earth with whom humans must find balance and interdependence.[31] Indigenous peoples have for decades driven forward the climate movement. In 2008, Ecuador enshrined the rights of nature in its constitution, acknowledging that nature is its own legal entity with the right to exist, persist and regenerate its life cycles – not just the property of mankind to plunder.[32] In New Zealand, the Whanganui River was granted legal personhood in 2017.[33] A 2021 study by the Indigenous Environmental Network and Oil Change International found that indigenous-led campaigns and resistance stopped or delayed at least a quarter of greenhouse gas emissions in North America in a decade.[34]

In 2023, leaders of indigenous peoples from around the world warned the UN that the West's plans for a green transition, including mineral mining, amounted to a new kind of 'green colonialism'.[35] They told of onshore wind farms built on the reindeer herding grounds of the Sami people of Norway, nature reserves displacing Maasai people from their ancestral lands in Tanzania, and the fast-tracking of lithium mining on Native American reservations in Nevada.[36] History is repeating itself. The transition to 'greener' sources amounts to a doubling down of the legacy of colonialism, relying on further extraction and greater violence towards historically persecuted people. This violence is being perpetrated by countries who have already consumed way over their share of global carbon, when historical emissions during colonialism are accounted for.[37] What's worse, most materials and minerals essential to the transition are found in nations where colonialism has already created corruption and instability. Cobalt, a key component in the lithium-ion batteries that power electric vehicles and renewable energy storage systems, is found in abundance in the Democratic Republic of Congo, while lithium is mined in Zimbabwe and Namibia.[38]

Mineral extraction is leading us into a new age of imperialism. But climate change cannot be outsourced to these countries. Weaker food and energy supply chains, the appearance of rare and contagious diseases and the displacement of millions of people through climate migration: these are global phenomena – and can be manipulated by politicians to divide us using fear. But there is an alternative. In order to stabilize the climate and ecological systems that support all life, we need a new appreciation of our interconnections with other peoples and with the earth. We need new ideas and practices to change the way we relate to land, materials and each other, drawn from the ancient wisdom of people who have always better understood our connection to the earth.[39]

By firing bricks made of waste clay, Rosanna and the artists at Brickfield remind us of circular practices that were lost even from our own rational, industrial heritage. But they also create new connections with the minerals and materials of the planet as it exists today, reminding us that the earth too is a living, evolving entity deserving of care.

3.6 IF BRICKS CAN KISS

It is the night of the kiln firing at Brickfield. On site, John Osborne, the last man to fire the last working beehive kiln before it closed in 1971, is fretting. Rosanna wants to squeeze in all five hundred bricks from the workshops. But if there isn't enough air circulating between them, John says, it will be impossible to get the kiln hot enough. The hotter the kiln, he explains, the harder the bricks. Meanwhile Rosanna is concerned with a different kind of burnout – the previous year, they fired the kiln overnight after four scheduled workshops and then, fearing the temperature had dipped too much the following day, fired it for longer. Everyone was knackered by the end of it. Rosanna led the last of the workshops in a total daze. Later that night, she couldn't remember anything she'd said to anyone.

This year there is a community of brickmakers to share the work. Assistants Zenna and Bobi McFadzean make up a mix of clay and mica ready for John to make bricks with the following day. Three volunteers chop wood ready to feed into the kiln. I am asked to sieve the rocks out of a large heap of the 33 tonnes of clay donated by Imerys at the behest of John.

It travelled up here on a digger and was unceremoniously dumped against a bank of rock. Sieving sounds like a gentle job, but actually, it involves flinging spades of clay at a mesh grid the size of a door. The small enough particles pass through and land on a wheelbarrow covered over with a smaller grid mesh, which filters smaller particles so only the soft clay is collected in the wheelbarrow. It's dirty, physical work, but necessary since the deposit John found at Wheal Remfry is full of stones that must be removed before it can be used for bricks.

We continue like this in the muddy light of the late afternoon, the rhythmic sounds of rocks flung against mesh, the thwack of axes splitting wood, the stomp of muddy boots on hard ground. By the evening we are all filthy and starving, but happy in a way that can only follow hard physical work. Rosanna and I disappear to make our encampment. She will sleep in the back of her van on a mattress while I pitch up in a tent behind.

We are sheltered from the site by a bank of rocks and gorse, with a beautiful view out to the south coast of Cornwall. When we get back to the site, someone has been heating up dinner over the open fire: a feast of two curries, rice, naan and bhajis. The kiln has steamed now – all the moisture has evaporated. The firing has started. Zenna and Bobi's mothers, plus an aunt and a cousin, have pitched up in boiler suits and visors to push wood into the furnace to keep the temperature inside rising.

We break to eat; bread hot from the fire, curry cooling as it hits our tin plates. Over dinner, Rosanna draws up a rota of people to watch the kiln overnight. She puts us down for the 2am shift. 'It's a good one!' she says, almost convincingly. 'You can sleep either side.' I slope off to bed early to get some rest.

At some point, in the pitch darkness, I hear the door of Rosanna's van open behind me. My alarm hasn't gone off, my eyes aren't even open, but I know what the sound means and wriggle from my sleeping bag. Rosanna calls my name softly through the canvas to see if I'm awake. We agree to meet at the kiln.

It's 2am. Outside the tent, the full moon is high in the sky, visible beneath a thick layer of cloud. I can see the white lights of Cornish villages down in the valley. Some of the kiln's previous attendants have parked a second van a few metres away and sleep in reclined car seats. Zenna and her partner Jack Tagney are pitched up a little further along, but their tent is empty. I find them with Rosanna, next to the kiln, swapping notes about the amount of wood used and the temperature reached.

They wish us goodnight and head back to the tent. Rosanna tends to the fire, inspecting each grate with a prod from a stick that has been designated for this purpose. Then she heads to an old shipping container to make us cups of tea. She returns with steaming mugs and apples. I open a packet of digestive biscuits. For the next half an hour we take turns to stoke the fire, pulling on a visor and one stiff fireproof glove – comically large – before tossing wood into the molten abyss. The quiet night is filled with the crackle and pop of burning logs, each split by hand. The dirt and grime of the day's work bake into our skin in the heat. We talk about the new techniques and terminology Rosanna learned from John, words that suggest the love and the care that goes into brickmaking. One stays with her. If the brickmakers stack their bricks too closely together in the kiln, preventing the heat from hitting all the sides evenly, it leaves a mark in contrast to the shiny, metallic surface where the flames lick the stones. This mark is called a kiss.

Rosanna had been thinking: if bricks can kiss, can they be used as objects to think through ideas of caregiving, and be symbolic of togetherness? By this point, Brickfield has produced hundreds of bricks. After each workshop, the participants stack their unfired bricks neatly on pallets. The pallets sit around the site, square grids of pleasing muted colours, some hidden under tarpaulin to protect them from rain. Each brick is a memory of a moment of making, of togetherness, of connecting with the cold clay.

Our shift ends. Two more volunteers emerge from the makeshift encampment, ready to keep the fire burning until dawn. By the time light filters on to this old clay pit, there will be hundreds of hard, hot bricks, each one begging the question of what it might become. From the conditions of scarcity – the limited time the artists were allowed on the pits, the limited waste material they were granted for their brickmaking – they have created a sense of possibility and abundance.

3.7 WHAT HAPPENS TO THE BRICKS?

One brilliant spring day, I head back to Cornwall to find out what happened to the bricks. It's still morning when Rosanna picks me up from the station in her white van, full of dust and rocks. We drive out of town and up to the site, passing two locked gates and multiple warning signs before we reach the familiar plateau that is home to Brickfield.

Today the site is teeming with fashionable architecture students from Falmouth University, getting dirt all over their patchwork jackets and smudges on their spectacles. Many of them have come from far away to study in St Austell because of its well-regarded course.

Their course leader, Tom Ebdon, set up the undergraduate architecture programme at Falmouth in 2014, and a Masters in Architecture programme in 2020. From the beginning, he wanted his students to learn by serving the needs of the local community by using local materials. He figured Cornwall had plenty of architectural dilemmas for his students to work on – not least, high demand for affordable housing. He called his approach, which involved engaging critically with place, radical regionalism.

It was a modern take on critical regionalism, an architecture movement from the eighties. Led by Kenneth Frampton, the critical regionalists argued for architecture on the periphery to respond to the materials and needs of place, in response to the shiny, centralized language of modernism and post-modernism. The modernists designed buildings of concrete and glass in a way that could be replicated anywhere on earth. Regionalism was an attempt to build something that could only exist at its moment, in its place. Tom talked to his students about using the history of Cornwall to make buildings for the future. Materials were at the heart of the idea.

Tom's approach also touches on the developing field of bioregionalism. Bioregionalism is a recognition that the future of humanity is likely to be concentrated at smaller scales. The term refers to geography but also to what some of its early practitioners called a 'terrain of consciousness', or the ideas that have evolved about how to live in that place, or bioregion.[40] Bioregions are defined not by political borders, but by ecological systems, such as river catchments, topography, or areas inhabited by certain plants or animals. Architects working with bioregionalism in mind might look locally for resources and integrate those resources more carefully into their designs, so that humans and nature can both thrive. The practice offers an alternative to global economies in which one culture or people dominates and exploits the land and resources of another. As well as tangible sources of knowledge – rocks, plants, living creatures – bioregionalism values the intangible: the stories, myths, rituals and ceremonies used to pass knowledge about our places and their abundant resources between generations.[41]

We don't value these sources of generational knowledge so much in the West. Zenna's folklore and Rosanna's firing ceremonies remind us of the wisdom that runs through our heritage. Tom has found a place for this wisdom in formal education, by engaging his students with place-based learning. The architecture course is one way of teaching an ethics of stewardship, rooted in the materials and the culture of a place. In the next chapter we travel to the South Wales Valleys. Here, we encounter people setting up apprenticeships and college courses to nurture the skills for a transition to a more sustainable way of living that does not repeat the horrors of the past.

Nina Jones, one of Tom's students, tucks her blonde hair under a bright-blue cap. Her navy sweatshirt is already covered in white powder. She is attempting to make lime mortar using oyster shells. Tom has banned his students from using concrete, which is standard in most modern constructions. As well as being the most widely used substance on earth, concrete is also its most wasteful, sucking up a tenth of the world's industrial water use and producing up to 8 per cent of the world's carbon dioxide.[42]

So, Nina is experimenting with alternatives. Before concrete became widespread in the nineteenth century, lime-based materials had been used since as far back as the Ancient

Egyptians, who used them to build the Pyramids. Lime was normally produced by burning limestone, a rich source of concrete's main ingredient, calcium carbonate. Nina wondered about using oyster shells, an alternative source of high-purity calcium carbonate, since they were in abundance as a waste product from fishing on the Cornish coast. So she got some shells from Porthilly Shellfish and other local fisheries, fired the shells in a kiln and crushed them into dust. Not only was she recycling waste, the oyster shells contain so much calcium that they absorb all the carbon emitted in the process of firing, making her mortar a carbon-neutral building material.

Nina stirs the crumbled shells into water and sand to rehydrate them. When the mixture looks gloopy enough, she spreads it on one of Brickfield's red bricks and sandwiches another on top. Derren, a no-nonsense builder from a local firm, watches from a distance. All morning, he has been teaching these trendy young students how to lay bricks. As well as appropriate materials, Tom wants his students to understand the skills necessary to build structures that respond to the world around them. He is inspired by Rural Studio, an architecture programme at Auburn University in Alabama where, rather than sitting in classrooms, students use locally grown wood to build homes for real people. By using local materials, the course sustains a local timber industry, and by building real houses, it addresses a real need in the area for new homes. Tom hopes this approach is a kind of bottom-up remedy to his experience of planning in Cornwall, where authorities often granted applications to what he saw as non-specific, out-of-place architecture. His students would be the ones to build Cornwall's future infrastructure.

For this project, the architecture students have been working with a dementia walking group from Falmouth. The students are designing and building shelters and benches that will act as stopping points for the walkers, guiding them through the landscape despite the challenges of their illness. To Tom's right, two groups lay bricks for the structures they designed in conversation with the dementia group. One is a dome-shaped shelter from bad weather. The other is a curved seat inside a wall to block the wind. This latter group is working with an Augmented Reality headset, which allows one student to see an outline of the structure before it is built. He looks through the headset and directs the others where to put each brick.

While the students build in the bright sun of the afternoon, another group arrives on site. These are young women from the Clays – Bugle, St Dennis and St Blazey – and they have come as part of a social action project from the organization Empower Her, which supports young women with poor mental health. They gather tentatively around a table covered with clats, or mounds of clay, ready to make more bricks. When they dreamed up Brickfield, Rosanna and her co-founder Katie Bunnell wanted it to be used by different people at the same time – for residents to meet local university students and perhaps be inspired to follow that path. But it's not always been so easy to get local people to come up to Brickfield. People from the Clays have mixed feelings about this site, since so many lost their livelihoods with the mines closed. The untouchable coal tips and spoils are a constant reminder of the past.

Rosanna helps the young women find a place around the

fold-out tables, under the awning, and distributes lumps of clay. Tentatively at first, they touch the cold, clammy matter. But soon they are slamming the clay into moulds and shaking the bricks free, competing to make the sharpest corners. As the session ends, their parents arrive and hover on the fringes of the site, watching from afar as though afraid to cross the boundary and disturb the magic. One of the women calls over: 'We're making bricks, Dad!'

As the day draws to a close, the young women head home and the architecture students pack up. Rosanna lights a little barbecue to make hot dogs. Some of the students have brought cans of beer and drink thirstily. The salty smell of sausages and fire fills the air. The Brickfield team admire the students' structures. The circular shelter isn't quite finished. It's missing a roof and looks like a boiled egg with the top sliced off. 'It is what you expected?' Tom asks Rosanna. She smiles silently as she turns the sausages on the grill. 'No,' Tom continues. 'You probably expected them to make five hundred bricks and finish both their structures!'

Rosanna laughs. 'Maybe. But we're still happy!'

'Well I'm knackered,' Tom says, lying on the floor and propping a can of beer on his chest.

Derren Wilson, the local brickie, goes to leave. 'I've loved it, Tom, thank you,' he says. 'If you ever need anything . . .'

Tom turns to him, but Derren is looking out at the structures, standing proud in the dust of the gravel pit, made of community-thrown bricks of reclaimed clay and the labour of the next generation of local architects. 'To think,' Derren says, 'there was nothing here – and now they have built this.' Both of them are right: Rosanna, who knows they could go further, and Derren, who knows they have come far. Imperfect, unfinished, Brickfield is for that moment a bridge between past and present Cornwall, and onwards to a future where humans exist in harmony with the minerals and the materials of the living earth.

4

FOREST

South Wales Valleys

'People who already live a communitarian experience would say: "You live the commons, you cannot talk about them, and even less theorize them." That I imagine is because of the difficulty to give words to such a powerful and rare experience as that of being part of something larger than our individual lives, of dwelling on "this earth of mankind" not as a stranger or a trespasser, which is the way capitalism wishes us to relate to the spaces we occupy, but as home. But words are necessary, especially for those of us who live in areas where social relations have been almost completely disarticulated.'

—Silvia Federici, *Re-enchanting the World: Feminism and the Politics of the Commons*

4.1 THE FLOOD

It was a Friday, 15 February 2020, when the flood came. It had been a wet winter, so wet it seemed that before the month was out, the brown trout of the River Taff might be washed clean out into Cardiff Bay before the fishing season had even begun. But this is Wales. People are used to a spot of rain. No one realized how bad it would get.

For two days, it hammered on the windows of the houses at the top of the South Wales Valleys, where people tucked in their children ahead of a sleepless night.[1] It poured into the rivers at the bottom. By the time the rain departed again, many people would be standing in water up to their knees. These valleys were wrought by heat and rain. Hundreds of millions of years ago, Wales was a speck near the equator drenched in the hot mist of the rainforest.[2] Here grew the tallest trees in the history of the earth. Giant dragonflies, spiders and scorpions lived among the teetering trees. Reptiles roamed the forest floor, stomping fallen branches and floating leaves into the muck of ancient swamps to be buried, over and over again, in layers of sediment and sand.[3]

First the layers compacted into peat beneath the surface of the earth. Over hundreds of thousands of years, the peat hardened into coal as the layers were forced down and the plates spun north to cooler climes. Then this sooty earth crystallized and became chalky black anthracite, left behind in thick seams just below the surface, where it stayed until humans arrived.

It took thousands of years for humans to work out how to extract minerals from the earth. In Swaziland they cracked it, forty thousand years ago, digging up red ochre from the iron deposits of the Lion's Cave, not to make fuel, or weapons, but for paint.

Then, a mere ten thousand years ago, mining began in earnest. The extraction of flint and metals transformed human settlements into civilizations. During the Bronze Age, up to around 1200 BC, cities emerged and trade networks stretched across the globe. Across the turquoise seas of the Mediterranean, the Minoans carried their precious metals. They loaded ships with copper, lead, silver and gold and headed for the horizon, to make a fortune trading with Egypt, Syria and Mesopotamia.

In China, miners in their thousands drew metals like copper, lead and iron from the earth with picks and shovels. They dug tunnels and shafts into the earth in Henan, Shaanxi and Shanxi, extracting ever deeper deposits. In Shanxi, the miners discovered black rocks that burned with more power than wood. Today, Shanxi, with its population of 36 million, still produces 10 per cent of the world's coal.[4]

Over the other side of the world, hundreds of years apart, those same forces – the miner with his pickaxe, the industrialist with his machines – transformed the valleys of South Wales, turning mountains into heaps of coal spoil, throwing waste from the pits to one side to create jagged coal tips, reshaping the land like mortal gods.

The Rhondda Valley forks at Porth, splitting into Rhondda Fawr and Rhondda Fach, into the large river and the small. Prospectors packed their bags and hiked up the valley to look for coal, digging with no promise of payment until they found their black gold. They delivered their wares back down the valley first by packhorse, then by laying down railway lines.

By the end of the nineteenth century, mining had exploded, levelling the peaks, sinking mines into the sides and filling the bottoms of the valleys with identical terraced homes for miners who came home proud from each day's backbreaking labour black with soot.[5]

Pentre, the village that flooded, had been nothing but scattered farmland owned by absentee landlords until the discovery of coal. But in the middle of the nineteenth century, expeditions arrived from the Dinas Rhondda in the south. Soon businessmen opened mines at two levels of the hillside, one called the Pentre, one called the Church, before sinking them deep into the earth. The mines in the Pentre became some of the most profitable in all the Rhondda.

It took millennia for the coal to form. But humans mined what they could within a hundred or so years. The trail of industry formed long dark ribbons rippling down the valleys towards the ships of Cardiff Bay. When the mines closed, they left scarred mountains with unnatural peaks. Valleys that would have once been open grassland were now forested with monocrops of larch. The rivers ran black with coal and sewage. The land that had once belonged to the reptiles and the dragonflies was left to ruin by landowners and those who leased the mines. By the time of the 2020 storms, there were thousands of tips in Wales and hundreds considered so unstable they might be a threat to life. Pentre was surrounded by them, mountains of coal spoil dug from the earth to get at the black gold, left teetering on the tops of the valleys, overlooking the villages below.

The coal tips were notoriously dangerous. Many locals still held vivid memories of the Aberfan disaster in 1966, when 110 cubic metres of spoil, dumped on a spring at the old Merthyr Vale Colliery, slid down the mountainside and covered over Pantglas Junior School, killing 109 children and five teachers. Many of the survivors suffered nervousness, isolation, enuresis and early death.[6]

In the aftermath, the chair of the National Coal Board declared that the presence of the spring was unknown, even though the villagers and the survivors knew it had caused at least two other, earlier landslides.[7] The authorities tightened their grip on the land, anxiously monitoring the tips for signs of movement, enacting an exacting schedule of tree felling and ground maintenance in the name of public good.

Meanwhile, the man-made forests became overgrown and impenetrable. Under the coal board, villagers were warned off entering these forests. Before the Pentre floods, local authorities stepped in with felling licences, drawing the ire of dog walkers and hikers when they sent in their machines.

Three public bodies merged to manage the wild plantations and the teetering tips under the name Natural Resources Wales. Its executives declared they needed to stabilize the peaks and thin out the larch thickets in the name of safety. When a deadly disease hit the larch trees, they sent in workers with machinery and saws.

In the months before the 2020 flood, Natural Resources Wales had been issued with an order to clear the larch above Pentre.[8]

Larch disease had been carried by spores to Pentre from the Afan Valley to the west. Larches were planted by the Forestry Commission because they grew happily and quickly on the steep slopes of the valley, where young trees provided strong and durable wood. Even after the mines closed, programmes of tree-planting continued. But because the authorities planted only larch, the forests became a monoculture, making them susceptible to disease. When disease came, devastation was quick.

Early in 2002, the fungus *Phytophthora ramorum* was first found in the UK, on an imported viburnum plant in an ornamental nursery in Sussex.[9] [10] Just a few months later, forest workers found resin bleeding from the branches of larches in Afan. The trees were shedding leaves, their foliage gingering to a burned orange colour as the fungus travelled from the spores of one tree into the live tissue of another.

Once the pathogen got beneath the bark of the next tree, it made its way to the trunk, forcing resin out of lesions in the surface and causing the bark to die and sink in patches known as cankers. Bald rings of missing bark, known as girdles, appeared around the trunks of the dying.

Overnight, Natural Resources Wales was given a blanket clear order to remove all infected species. The kill order applied to six million trees.[11] Workers swept into the forest in helmets and hi-vis with chainsaws and pulleys. Everything had to be handled carefully: even the tyres of vehicles had to be washed before workers left a site to try to avoid the spread to another valley. Far above them, the fungus travelled for miles on spores in the wind.[12]

Getting to the larch was not an easy task. The forest was

overgrown, untouched since some of the trees had been planted fifty years earlier, and the sides of the valley were too steep for machinery. The workers installed a system of winches and wire cables to airlift felled trees to the nearest road for stacking, a process called skylining.

Larch is naturally light, and the trees in these plantations were old, brittle and diseased. During the felling and the winching, dead material and branches snapped and dropped on to the forest floor. Many felled trees were left to be dispatched by vehicles later.[13] Deadwood was often left to decay in place, as part of conservation efforts to keep the nutrients cycling through the ecosystem.

Brash and debris accumulated on the steep slopes of the valley. Over the wet winters, the downpours shifted the ground. The snapped and sawn twigs inched into the gullies and the culverts. These were the waterways where the rain found its route from the hilltops down to the river. Only now, they were blocked.

The high street in Pentre had never flooded. But that night in February, the rain could not find its natural course. It collected in the broken brash like a tide against a dam. It pooled into plateaus and pushed against the deadwood. Eventually, with a crack barely audible against the downpour, the banks broke and the water gushed towards the houses below.

Cars sank into roads that became rivers. Gardens turned into lakes. Water entered the houses and rose up to head height in the lowest lying areas. A woman was found clinging to a bare branch. Another had to be dragged out of her home with her dogs on an inflatable boat.

Pentre high street flooded twice in five days. Fifty metres

above the river, nestled up the valley, Pentre was not a village where people expected floods. In the search for the cause, people found the culvert and took pictures of diseased trees tangled in the mud, surrounded by water.[14]

An inquiry was promised. No wrongdoing was found. But the people of the Valleys knew the land with its knotted forests, old mines and ancient springs. They feared the felling done by public bodies in their name. The summers were getting warmer, the winters, wetter. The diseases thrived on the damp, stressed trees. A different way was needed to manage the Valleys. Not by profiteering businessmen, nor paternalistic government, but by the locals themselves.

4.2 FIELD TRIP

The Acharossan Forest sits on a steep hillside in West Scotland's Kyles of Bute. This narrow sea channel is rich with sandy beaches, lush forests and mountainous peaks where feral goats and wild birds make their home. I visited in autumn 2018, two years before the flood in Wales, and on a day so bright the sun dazzled as it reflected the peaks back to themselves in the still waters of the Kyle. I was among a motley crew gathered in a clearing of the forest, hundreds of miles from their own valleys in South Wales.

The Acharossan may be a long way away from the forests of the Rhondda. But all Ian Thomas could think, standing in that field of tree stumps one damp autumn morning, is how alike they seemed. How the frontier is always just moments from your doorstep. Ian is a slip of a man, with thick glasses and the energy of a terrier. He had spent the night at a hotel in nearby

Tighnabruaich, a village sitting on the shore of the coastal channel, with his friends and neighbours from the Rhondda, who had travelled this far north in search of a new model. They wanted to prove to the Welsh authorities that they could look after their valleys themselves, and they had invited me along for the ride. But they needed to find proof that others had done the same first.

In the morning, after a hearty breakfast in the mustard-yellow stucco and wooden beams of the hotel bar, the group piled into a minibus and drove five short minutes up the mountainside to the Kilfinan Community Forest. A sign, so small it might easily be missed, welcomed them on to the land with the words: 'A forest is for life.'

Just a few decades earlier, the dense woods on these mountainsides were barred to local people like the woods surrounding the villages of the Rhondda Valley. The family who had owned the Acharossan Forest since the 1940s had sold it to the Forestry Commission when they decided to move to Canada.[15] Under public ownership, the plantations of spruce went wild, growing ever closer together. It became impenetrable, unpassable for villagers in nearby Tighnabruaich. Meanwhile, over time, people started to leave the village, travelling to the nearest towns in search of jobs.[16]

Those who remained realized that something was necessary to bring the village back to life. They began to imagine a different relationship to the forest, where they could enter for walks. A forest that was returned to broadleaf species like oak, where the plantations of spruce could be felled to create jobs for local people and timber homes on the site.

After five years of planning and fundraising, some residents formed the Kilfinan Community Forest Company. Eventually they were able to buy the Lower Acharossan Forest on behalf of the residents of the Kilfinan parish in 2010.

As soon as the deal went through, the steering group started to submit proposals. First, they needed funding to build a road up to the site, securing access for the first time in decades. Then, slowly, they began to realize their dreams. Polytunnels to grow food. Water and electricity. Salaries for the forest company's first employees. In 2015, they bought the Upper Acharossan Forest from the Forestry Commission, and now own and manage 561 hectares, or 1,300 acres of woodland.[17]

We emerge from the minibus to see the beginnings of a timber house. Just behind, the community have built a huge polytunnel heated by waste wood and lit by electricity generated by the forest company's hydro scheme. To one side, an open barn is surrounded by logs stacked as high as a house: this is the woodland sawmill.

A woman in a green hoodie wearing both a woolly hat and a pair of sunglasses leads the group to a mountainside covered in stumps. This is Marylou Anderson, who moved here with her family from Skye. She explains that she was drawn by the opportunity to come and live on the land without having to buy it. Instead, she was given a secure tenancy that she could pass on to her children.

Ian scratches his head. 'How are you passing it on to your family if you don't own it?' he asks.

'It's called a croft,' Marylou says. She explains that crofting emerged in the late 1700s, after people had been repeatedly displaced from the Highlands by landowners seeking to enclose the fields and develop them for agriculture. After a potato famine in the 1840s, the situation worsened, leading to protests and demands for security of tenure. Eventually, the protesters succeeded in getting tenants' rights recognized under the Crofters Act of 1886.

Under the terms of the Act, crofters were offered protection from being unfairly removed from the land, along with what was considered fair rent and the right to compensation at the end of a tenancy.

In 1976, tenants were given the right to buy their crofts.[18] That right was cemented in 2003, legislation granting crofting communities the right to buy their crofts on a collective basis – even when the landowner objected.[19]

This was community power to cleave back land from unwilling lairds and landowners. And it was on a scale and directness the Welsh visitors could only dream of. By the time of our visit, more than 750,000 hectares of the Highlands and Islands of Scotland were crofted by around 33,000 people, with rights to live and work on the land through the decades.[20]

Ian could scarcely believe his ears. For generations, his family had existed at the whims of the landowners and the authorities. His grandparents had been prospectors, those miners who travelled up the valley to dig unpaid, in the hope of finding coal. The family had searched the Rhondda for their black gold, so hungry between jobs they resorted to poaching for food.

When the coal mines closed down, Ian's dad got a job as a builder in Bletchley. At the age of four, Ian and his family moved into a council house in Milton Keynes. The town was so new when he arrived in the late seventies, it was empty. Ian remembers being surrounded by car parks with no cars, and municipal spaces from supermarkets to football pitches, built according to the aspirations of a generation of town planners, just waiting to be filled up with people.

His cousins would visit his council house and marvel at the inside bathrooms, believing the family had made it big. But his heart was in the Rhondda. When his parents talked of home, he knew that's where they meant. Ian's mum moved back to South Wales at the turn of the millennium. Not long afterwards, his beautiful girlfriend Andromeda fell pregnant and the two of them decided to move back there too, to be near family. Then two more children arrived and soon they were making a life in the Valleys.

Ian worked in local warehouses, desperate to find a job that would allow him to be outside. Then he discovered a community group called Welcome to Our Woods in Treherbert, a village to the north of Pentre, and applied to join them as a community worker. The steering group that set up Welcome to Our Woods had started in the nineties. Barred from entering the woods, local teenagers rebelled by driving used cars from the village into the thicket and setting them alight. Until one day, when Ceri Nicholas, a youth worker with a local charity, had an idea: he would teach the teenagers how to light fires safely.[21]

Not everyone thought it was a good idea. Teaching teenagers to start fires! It sounded counter-intuitive. But Welcome to Our Woods drastically reduced the amount of arson. In the forest above the council houses, groups of young people helped to build a proper fire pit. They chopped wood and learned how to hold sparks beneath kindling, nurturing a glow into flames around which they could cook food and pass the time. Soon the fire pit became a meeting point – a safe place – in that forbidden forest.

Suddenly those in power wanted to be closer to the project. When Natural Resources Wales was created out of the former Countryside Council and the Environment Agency in 2013, the new authority chose to host its launch event at the community building that became the new headquarters for Welcome to Our Woods, a new organization local people established to nurture relationships with the forests.[22] At the launch, the chief executive of Natural Resources Wales surveyed the land, covered in disused plantations, and complained that it was 'uneconomic.'[23] 'Think of a better way to use it and we'll work with you on it,' he said.

Ian, who joined Ceri at Welcome to Our Woods that same year, never forgot those words.[24] Together, they started to nurture other ideas for the forest. Hiking trails and dens for children. Signposts and swimming groups. Rather than exporting timber, they dreamed about what would happen if it stayed in the area, to be used in construction of sustainable, affordable housing. But first they needed access to the land and the right to fell the trees for the use of the people in the villages. A croft sounded like just the thing.

'Can we get one of these tenancies?!' Ian asks Marylou on the mountainside in Kilfinan.

Step forward Chris Blake, the visionary researcher who has organized the trip. Chris came to the Black Mountains of Wales after burning out from his publishing career in London. He is the kind of dogged optimist who doesn't let half a millennium of the Enclosure Acts, those laws that, over centuries, removed the rights of commoners to use land in England and Wales, get him down. 'First, we need to get the Welsh Assembly to agree,' he says.

This is exactly why he organized the trip. He spent the best part of a decade working with communities on hydro energy schemes in Wales, which is where he met Ian. Chris had set up a company that was commissioned by the council to look at installing hydro schemes on publicly owned land in the borough of Rhondda Cynon Taf. At that moment, the government was offering a feed-in tariff so lucrative that had they built a dam in Treherbert immediately, it would have guaranteed an income for the community of £30,000 a year for twenty years. But the land manager stalled. It took four years of wrangling to get an agreement. In that time, the feed-in tariff dwindled to almost nothing.

Chris's company built the hydro scheme. But the experience sparked Chris to change direction. Years earlier, he had been on holiday to Knoydart in Scotland on what happened to be the tenth anniversary of the community buyout of the remote estate on which they lived. There, he saw first-hand what community ownership of land, coupled with hydro schemes, jobs and accommodation, could achieve. Hydro schemes alone were nothing, he realized, unless communities could get the economic rights to the land around them. So he set up a new project to see if some kind of alternative ownership model might work in the South Wales Valleys. And then he won some grant money to explore community ownership of hundreds of hectares of land with three groups in the area. As part of the project, he planned this inspirational visit to community-owned lands in Scotland, in Kilfinan and on the Isle of Mull.

Crofting law gives families the right to live in security and profit from the land, creating the incentive to steward it in such a way that their children and grandchildren will also benefit. But it comes with responsibilities. The Kilfinan Community Forest Company must, as part of its contract, replant canopy. 'Crofting law is about fair share and future share,' Marylou says. She pays rent for her land and agrees, under the terms of her lease, to have canopy cover of 80 per cent. That takes some of the reforesting burden off the company.

Then there is the land itself, which had been left, untended, for so many decades that the only solution was to cut all the trees down. 'We mustn't glorify it; it's a hill full of stumps,' Marylou says, matter-of-factly.

We look around us. The hillside is indeed covered in ugly stumps and brown earth. It's hard to imagine this land as abundant. Marylou says she had exactly the same thought. 'When we first came here I thought, "Hmm, have we taken on too much?" but I've spent the last two years really getting to know it.' She asks us to take a closer look at the stumps. They look dead but there are signs of life: fungi and bracken. Marylou is a permaculture designer, someone who creates systems of managing land that aim to be self-sufficient, resilient and balanced between the needs of people and the environment. She has been carefully replanting native species to create what she calls 'food corridors' in the forest. Her family have already planted 250 trees, including five fruit trees. They used the stumps to protect the seedlings and chose to plant only native species, like alder and fruit bushes.

The bracken can be turned into compost to grow potatoes, beans and nasturtiums, edible flowers that are packed with vitamins and minerals. Every year they are learning: this year the slugs got the beans, but there was a healthy crop of potatoes. Marylou and her partner have supported the local school with their visits to the community forest. They also hold permaculture courses on site, drawing visitors and locals up from Kilfinan.

Soon, the timber house will be a show home for affordable timber accommodation, as part of a plan to build five more. There are plans for a forest centre, available to rent by local groups, to add to the activities on the site. Already, woodworkers meet here twice a week, making nesting boxes for owls and squirrels and fixing them to the old trees. The group is working on wooden signs for the new paths around the mountainside, cleared by volunteers.

An allotment group has been growing on the site, bringing local people to the forest to grow their own fruit and flowers. Schoolchildren come up to explore the lower forest, squealing as they run between the trees and over new bridges, and hiding from one another in shaded dens. There is work in the Acharossan Forest. Not full-time jobs, yet, but work for painters and decorators, landscapers, joiners, plasterers, plumbers, tree surgeons, secretaries and bookkeepers. A self-sustaining economy emerging between the land and its stewards.

Over lunch, the visitors from Wales are buzzing about the possibilities for the Rhondda Valley. The sun is shining over the sparkling waters of Bute as we sit on picnic benches on the side of the hillside, between the forests and water, surrounded by spectacular mountain views.

Welcome to Our Woods already has its small turbine scheme and a spot on the high street in Treherbert, in a former library the community wants to turn into a classroom for everything from carpentry to yoga.[25] If they could only steward the forests, they could bring money and skills into the village, just like the community at Kilfinan. Instead they are constantly fighting the authorities, draining all their energy. They feel that those in charge have been doing their own thing for so long, they don't see the value in collaborating with the people of the Valleys. Someone asks Chris if the community could buy land in the Valleys just like the communities have in Scotland, and rent it out to crofter tenants.

'Virtually impossible,' Chris sighs. Chris might be an optimist, but he knows what they are up against. There's no crofting act in England and Wales, and short of organizing several decades of bloody protests, no clear way of getting one. The Welsh authorities are nervous. There have been too many landslides. The coal tips are unstable, and as the management body, the buck stops with Natural Resources Wales. The authorities need to know a community business model is sustainable, that process will be properly followed, that they won't get in trouble again, Chris says. So the group will have to use all its creativity and commitment to convince the authorities to give it the right to use the land, even as a tenant. 'That's what this project is about,' Chris says. 'We need to show that the community wants to manage the land – and that it can.'

4.3 FIGHT FOR THE FOREST

In the cool, dappled sunlight of a clearing in the Rhondda Valley, birds sing. A stream rushes by below. On the left, a larch tree stands tall but dead. Its black branches turn like spindles in the breeze, covered in black and yellow burrs. Behind the dead tree the valley drops sharply, covered in forest.

It is autumn 2021, three years after the field trip to the Acharossan Forest in West Scotland, and one year after the Pentre floods. A handful of people jostle for space on the uneven ground around Richard Phipps, an official from Natural Resources Wales, the body that manages these valleys. But they don't look at Richard, in his hiking boots and a regulation beige shirt. Everyone is looking up at the dead tree.

'It's a fire hazard,' Richard says. He sounds so certain, and so officious in his uniform, that it's hard not to believe him. He explains that the longer a dead tree is left in the ground, the harder it is to get it out as the forest grows around it, and the harder it is to use the timber, which degrades over time.

He has been put in charge of drawing up the official Forest Resource Plan, a document created every twenty-five years. These plans detail how the authority will manage the Welsh government's woodland estate, including how and when tree felling will take place. In order to meet certain standards, Natural Resources Wales has to consult the public, so it normally makes the documents available in online portals. Few look for them, and those who do find colour-coded maps that are meaningless without explanation. So this kind of engagement – coming to the forest for a tour of the trees – is somewhat new. Richard wants to help. But every moment standing on the hillside is a moment he isn't at his desk finishing the plan.

'I've always said,' one of his colleagues chips in, 'there's no such thing as a safe tree.'

We stare at the lifeless tree, a dead dot in a woodland teeming with life. It is hard to imagine that this tree – in fact, all trees – pose a threat. For as long as they can remember, the villagers have heard these kinds of warnings about the forest. Industrialists barred people from entering, protecting their crop of pit props. That narrative was inherited by the public body, Natural Resources Wales. As part of its mandate to maximize profit from the timber, it restricted access, rather than welcoming people to the forests as a public good. For many years, this status quo has been unchallenged.

But something changed after the visit to Scotland. The community started to see that perhaps the narrative could be different. So they asked Natural Resources Wales if they could have a hand in designing the next plan for the forest. Then they set up a series of meetings – ten, to be precise, over the course of a whole year – and invited Richard and his colleagues to join them as they discussed the many aspects involved in managing the forest and how they might play a part.

They want to work towards producing a forest plan cooperatively. That means that, rather than taking orders, they want to build a relationship with the public bodies who claim to represent them, and work together to look after the land.

This trip up the side of the valley is the second meeting of ten. Already, Richard bears the demeanour of a decent man who, though he wants to be kind, does not relish the thought of another eight discussions about how to do a job the authority has been doing, basically independently, since it was formed.

'One of the problems here is access,' Richard continues, trying to educate the group gently about the need to fell the trees. To get to this clearing we have turned left at Treherbert train station and crossed a bubbling stream on a tiny wooden bridge. The path is made of sharp rocks in mud and would be lethal to any vehicle. The bridge is barely wide enough for more than a couple of people, let alone forestry machinery.

It's enough for locals, who take their dogs up through the forests, and a local walking group, which meets every week. But the authorities do not want access to the forest for hiking and biking. Quite the opposite. 'Once we can get in, we can clear away all the trees,' Richard explains, describing the process of 'clear felling', a term used to describe cutting down all the trees in an area in order to extract all the timber in one go and to allow new trees to be planted uniformly.

There is an angry muttering. 'Do you have to do that?' someone cries.

'We don't have to, but if we leave it, it could be a fire hazard. We have to make the paths better.'

'Better for machinery,' a woman says flatly.

'Better for machinery, but better for everyone else as well,' Richard says patiently. He puts his hands in the pockets of a pair of brown shorts. His beard is streaked with grey. Official policy is to thin the trees when they are between the ages of twenty and thirty years. But thinning only works where there's good access. Most of the trees were planted in the seventies, which means many of them are overdue. In places that have been left un-thinned for decades, where the slopes are treacherous, the authorities have a policy of felling everything, the so-called clear fell.

This forest is now so overgrown, it's taken Natural Resources Wales six years to get access to this stretch of path to make a plan to fell the trees. But it's taken local people much longer to get to the point where they can fight back to try and save them.

One thing unites the managers and the residents: everyone

knows the forest is suffering. The Rhondda Valley is in the middle of the larch epidemic. As we stand looking at the latest casualty, these locals want to know: if the authorities are going to start cutting down trees here, who's profiting from the wood?

Some of the timber is bought when the roots are still in the ground, Richard explains. After the trees are felled, they are sent to processing plants around Wales: 'Could be biomass, could be other things,' he says.

There are murmurs of dissatisfaction. Biomass, a way of generating electricity by burning wood, is generally seen as a last resort for timber that could otherwise be used to make things, from tables to houses.

Conifer, including larch, is considered uneconomic in the Valleys, since it is hard to access from the steep sides. Despite this, it is tough and dense, excellent for building and joinery. The community have an idea that if they could steward the land, they would be able to access the larch by quad bike and fell it with chainsaws, allowing them to use the felled timber to build affordable housing, like they saw in Scotland.

One of the women from the trip steps forward and says they want a plan where they manage the woodland alongside Natural Resources Wales, fifty-fifty. 'Not eighty-twenty,' she says. 'We need to have a say in what happens.'

'Hear, hear,' Ian says.

The question about who gets to control the forest in South Wales goes back further than the recent flooding and disease brought on by climate change. It's about the legacy of families who came to these valleys to find work in the mines. Many people at these meetings descend from skilled, hard-working labourers who carved precious coal from seams of rocks, only to be pushed off the land and left in poverty.

A cocktail of economic factors led to the closure of the mines. In the 1930s, as coal was discovered in countries overseas, the Welsh supply was replaced by foreign mines using more modern excavation techniques.[26] Oil became more popular, replacing some of the former uses for coal. Sterling was expensive compared to other currencies, making Welsh coal less attractive. The US started importing heavily from South America. Germany, a major European coal producer, paid some of its reparations from the First World War in coal, skewing the market.

These factors combined to create a slump in demand, forcing mines to close. Unemployment among men in South Wales rose to 43 per cent in 1932, making Wales one of the most depressed countries in the world.

Decades on, that legacy of low employment persists. People are more likely to be in ill health in the Rhondda and to die earlier – the life expectancy for men is more than a year shorter than the Welsh average.[27] The work on offer is often precarious and involves travelling to other towns. When Covid arrived, the villages suffered some of the highest death tolls in the whole of England and Wales.

The community's right to steward the forest is about more than looking after the trees. It's a matter of life and death. Galvanized by their trip to Scotland, the people of Treherbert are going to fight for a say in what happens to the land and, in turn, their future in the Valleys. Over the next year, they will meet with Natural Resources Wales and consider every aspect of their relationship to the Valleys, dreaming up plans from beekeeping to producing renewable electricity using water and wind. It's a blueprint for a different way of stewarding the land. A first for Wales, and a signpost to other post-industrial communities across the world.

4.4 FINDING A WAY

It could have been so easy. In 2020, a year before the meeting with Richard Phipps, Chris Blake came within a whisker of winning community stewardship of the forest near Treherbert, including the economic rights to develop the woodland.

The Welsh minister gave her blessing, Natural Resources Wales agreed and an agreement in principle was drafted. Now they were just waiting for a proper contract. It would have been unbelievable: an agreement for Welcome to Our Woods to manage 84 hectares of forest for twenty years, with the right to harvest trees as long as they didn't profit from them. Ian could almost see the wood processing plant, the brewery, the community buildings and social housing made of local timber.

Then Natural Resources Wales pulled out. They had to be able to prove they were maximizing the available profit for the land. Without a way to calculate other benefits, like social and environmental value, profit was the only viable motive.

It was no coincidence that Natural Resources Wales had recently been involved with a timber scandal that claimed its chief executive, after it failed to offer timber grown on publicly owned land for sale on the open market. In a national audit in 2018, Natural Resources Wales was found to be selling timber below market value in deals that were 'not entered into lawfully', because the timber was not tendered to other potential buyers before it was sold.[28] It followed a similar case just a year earlier, when Natural Resources Wales was found to have offered £72 million worth of timber to a single sawmill operator without tender.

Considering Natural Resources Wales was only formed in 2013, the 2018 audit query marked the third time the accounts had been questioned in five short years. In comments, senior Welsh politicians questioned whether it was suffering from 'corruption or incompetence' and accused it of being 'out of control'.[29]

Chris considered the sequence of events. A long history of mistrust between the Welsh people and the authorities had ended in catastrophic flooding. A string of recent irregularities had emerged about the awarding of timber contracts. Plus, the head of Natural Resources Wales had admitted, standing with the community workers of Welcome to Our Woods at the community centre in Treherbert, that the public body would welcome new ideas. It was time to broker a better deal, if ever there was one.

A simple land transfer – the freehold or leasehold control of the land – had fallen from view. Instead the community took the long road. They would embark on designing a different way of living in the Valleys: one in which the land was held publicly but managed in partnership with the people.

As soon as his three children could walk, Ian Thomas would take them up the sides of the valley. He'd show them the way the light hit on the hillsides – the rough-hewn faces of rock carved by glaciers millions of years ago. From the top of the Rhondda, he could almost see the ghosts of their ancestors picking their way north, knocking on the doors of the mine owners, getting by on grit and luck. 'All this is yours,' he told his children. He saw the future in their little faces – the beauty of the valley, the declining fortunes of the towns and the legacy of heat and rain and disease.

So it was a surprise, the first time he heard someone from Natural Resources Wales refer to 'their' forests. 'This is public land,' he liked to remind them. Natural Resources Wales was set up to manage the forests, but the land belonged to the people of Wales. So why shouldn't the people from the valley towns have a say in the forest plan?

The two sides differed on one major issue: whether or not to cut down all the trees, all at once. Over the eighteen months of talks, this point came up over and over again.

The authorities had always gone with this policy of clear felling. It was cheaper, quicker and more profitable, since the timber could be loaded on to the back of trucks and taken away for processing – or burning as biomass. At the first meeting, fuelled by satsumas and KitKats, the people of Treherbert, some thirty of them, listened to Richard from Natural Resources Wales and his colleagues talk about clear felling as 'the simplest and most economical system in time, effort and return'. 'We're moving away from clear felling,' Richard reassured them, 'but it still has its advantages. Older, unthinned crops still need to be cleared.'

But the community hated clear felling. Clear felling, it seemed, was responsible for some of the worst natural disasters in the area in recent years. A clear fell by Natural Resources Wales preceded the flooding in Pentre, even though the body said in a report that its actions had nothing to do with the flood. And the frequent landslides were thought to have something to do with clear felling since tree roots – even dead ones – bind together the soil. There were stories of the coal authority refusing so-called 'restoration' of historic culverts on the coal tips, or efforts to return the waterways to their pre-industrial course, to protect dead pine that was supposedly binding the soil, preventing the tips from slipping down the sides of the valley.

So at the first meeting, when Richard advocated for clear felling, Ian piped up. 'That's your version of the truth, not ours,' he said. Ian had worked with the woodland in Treherbert for long enough to have seen whole forests disappear, leaving empty hillsides where once people walked, hiked and found solace in the shade of the trees. Once felled, it took thirty years for the trees to grow back. Some of the forests around Treherbert were so old, clear felling had become the only option. But the community wanted to change the policy for the future so that the forests would be continually thinned, taking out the biggest or the weakest every year, to maintain their productivity for hundreds of years. By thinning, not clearing, the ecosystem survived, allowing nature to thrive – and people could still enjoy the trees.

The authorities were tying themselves in knots. Clear fell for profit and efficiency, they said, but be careful of disturbing the tips. Meanwhile local people, paralysed by the fear of another landslide or flood, felt powerless to speak up with alternatives. So Chris suggested the two sides work on co-producing a plan, drawing on the authority's knowledge of forest management and local people's knowledge of the woods on their doorstep.

Something magical happened in these meetings. The group – some thirty people in the end – turned up at one of Treherbert's community spaces: the Railway Canteen, the Pensioners' Club, or the sheet-metal Treherbert Boys' Club, now the Boys' and Girls' Club. A kettle went on. Bread rolls wrapped in foil tumbled out of an old Sainsbury's carrier bag on to a table. People stuck their names on their chest, in felt-tip on envelope labels. Teacups in hand, paper spread wide, the dreaming started.

It began with amorphous ideas: bike trails, disabled access, selling items made of timber. Over the course of the year, concrete plans emerged. People needed confidence to strike out into the forests for hikes and walks – so the community imagined a visitors' centre, signposted routes, guided walks, resting places and wind-up information panels, and bunkhouses or hides for birdwatching where people could spend time with a ranger.

By imagining what they needed to give them the confidence to go into the forest, the community began to imagine what other people might need too. Not just a muddy path. But tapping points to guide blind people walking with sticks, and sensory gardens.

As well as confidence, local people wanted strategies and plans: to know what was going to happen to the forest ahead of time. They began to formulate the designs to thin, not clear, the next generation of forests. It was called continuous cover, a method of forestry more popular in Alpine regions than the UK. It takes many decades to establish a continuous cover of forests, planting trees with a mix of ages, so bigger trees can be removed without destroying the whole habitat. With smaller amounts of timber from regular thinning, a local forestry company could be established to process the wood and use it to build everything from houses to tables, creating jobs in the village.

As the sessions came to an end, eight clear strands emerged, including renewable energy production, growing food in the forest, a timber processing plant, and a place for learning, from nursery forest schools to woodworking skills. It was a visionary piece of work. But Chris wanted to go one further. He still remembered the U-turn by Natural Resources Wales at the beginning of the project, when they promised to give the land to the community on a long lease and then backtracked because they couldn't prove the scheme offered value to the taxpayer. He wondered, what if Treherbert could test a way to measure the value derived from the land beyond pure profit? A mechanism that took into account job creation and educational value and even the environmental worth of the trees. As well as the co-production process and a land management agreement with the authorities, Chris proposed a pilot to calculate the social value of the land, so if the community gained timber worth £5,000 and created jobs worth £5,000, that was just as valuable as if the timber was sold on for profit. After the workshops, the co-production group shared their ideas with the wider village, some six thousand people. None of it could happen without their say.

At the end of March 2022, eighteen months after that first meeting when the community and the authority clashed over clear felling, Richard Phipps stood up in front of the people of Treherbert once again, to share the Forest Resource Plan. The community assembled nervously to hear how much from the co-production process had translated into the official document.

'The Forest Resource Plan which I am putting together is part of the stewardship of our land,' he said. He explained that the plan was a loose idea of how management will work over the next twenty-five years. 'But what I want to make sure is that what we're putting in here will allow the community vision to be delivered through our management.'

Sitting on a fold-out table covered in paperwork in his brown tweed jacket, Richard explained the plan in thirteen steps. There were points about improving access and mitigating flood risk. Points about changing the way the forests were managed so that once the diseased larch had been clear felled, it was replaced with a mix of broadleaf and other native species, managed for continuous cover.

And the felling would be done differently: instead of cutting down forests covering whole sides of the valleys, Natural Resources Wales would work in blocks over the course of a decade, so the community always had some forest to use. Near the end of the points, Richard said the plan was to work more closely with communities in the future. 'I want to reduce conflict,' he said, 'to make sure the community doesn't feel ignored and Natural Resources Wales doesn't feel attacked, by working together.'

It sounded so good. Native species. Thinning not clear felling. Working in partnership. But the community had heard it all before. They gave Richard a proper grilling.

'I go up in Cwm Saerbren every day, and it's a complete mess,' one man said. 'You're just not doing what you need to be doing up there.'

A woman agreed. People had too many bad experiences with Natural Resources Wales. This sounded like it was all talk. 'There has to be realistic timescales,' she said. 'We need to see progress.'

A man recommended setting some small goals: the opportunity for the public body to prove it was truly invested in
managing the forest with the community for the long term.
'You need to have two or three things that you're going to do
in the next two years and if you demonstrate you're able to do
those and do them successfully, then you get the community
more on board,' one participant said.

Afterwards, Richard felt more committed than ever to the
co-production process.[30] He could see that, even though the
forest management plan reflected the ideas of the community, the people in Treherbert needed more than a plan. They
needed to see that partnership in action. The next few years
would be crucial.

4.5 SURVIVAL SKILLS

In 2010, a dozen or so years before the people of Treherbert
met to discuss the future of their forest under the dappled
light of the trees, the British writer Ben Rawlence arrived at a
sprawling refugee camp on the Eastern Kenyan border to find
a city made of mud and thorns. Golden-brown soil stretched as
far as the eye could see, interrupted only by thorn bushes that
had been stripped bare by people desperate for wood to make
fires and shelter. Hundreds of thousands of people were living
in squat, half-canvas shacks around narrow corridors, passing
through doors made out of blocks of wood and straightened
out USAID tins.

Dadaab had been established in 1991 to contain thousands
of people fleeing civil war in Somalia. Over the next four years,
Ben returned to this strange city for long periods of time to

follow the lives of nine people in limbo, lives he recounts in his book *City of Thorns: Nine Lives in the World's Largest Refugee Camp.*

Ben was an experienced human rights worker. But nothing could prepare him for Dadaab. The camp sprawled as wide as the city of Bristol. But it had no power, no roads, no sanitation. Its inhabitants could not work – and they could not leave.

The refugees lived in tents, donated by the UN, until the tents disintegrated in the 45°C heat or dissolved in the floods that swamped the camp every rainy season. Each person was granted a finely balanced, finely costed daily ration amounting to around 2,000 calories. Some of them had been eating that diet for twenty years.

In his book, Ben documented, in heartbreaking detail, the ordinary people forced to make a life in those camps. But his lasting impression was way broader. This was the future, he realized. Entire cities of displaced people, dependent on aid to survive. Sweltering heat. Flash floods. Not just in Africa, but in Europe – even in the UK. Nobody realized what was coming, or how soon.

Back home in Wales, Ben began researching for another book called *The Treeline,* about the trees in the Arctic. He discovered the line where the tundra turned into vegetation was zooming north at hundreds of feet a year as the planet warmed, turning the white Arctic green. With these two poles of firsthand knowledge – the melting ice in the Arctic and the refugee crisis in Africa – Ben had a unique vantage point on where the planet was heading. And it did not look good. He realized that all the talk of climate change was wrong. The climate had already changed. Instead, he saw that humans had just a few decades to learn how to adapt.[31]

Around that same time, the Welsh government made a stunning decision. It became the first nation in the world to pass a law requiring the government to think about future generations as much as current ones. As long as democracies had existed, they had been governed by elected officials, interested only in maintaining the support of the voting public until the next election. It created a terrible short-termism: whole systems of governments with no motivation to think beyond a few years ahead. But Wales bucked the trend. In 2015, this small nation passed the Wellbeing of Future Generations Act, putting in place seven wellbeing goals to safeguard the future of the country in the interests of coming generations. It also appointed a 'future generations commissioner' to act as a guardian of these future interests.

The Act was bold. But there was a problem. The requirement to consider future generations created some strange phenomena. In the Rhondda, a road leading out of a housing estate in Llanharan informed drivers they could accelerate to the national speed limit. Metres later the road ended, giving way to brash that had grown over an abandoned opencast coal mine.[32] Llanharan was supposed to be connected up to a bypass, relieving traffic through the town. But the plan was canned in February 2023, one of thirty-one cancelled roads. Believing new roads fuelled new cars and greater emissions, the government had, practically overnight, stopped building them.

Some people were irate. Plans for new houses surrounding the proposed roads were going ahead, but without adequate transport routes for the new residents. The future generations commissioner was sanguine. Sophie Howe, who held the post for the first seven years, foresaw that there would be a delay between cancelling the roads and local people feeling the benefits of better investment in public transport.[33] She had the same problem with government investments in renewable energy. Wind turbines and solar farms would reduce energy costs for residents and create some jobs – but building them made people angry at what they considered to be a blight on the landscape.

The delays were made worse by the fact that there was so little capacity. The government passed the Act, but there weren't enough workers to build the roads and the turbines and the solar farms. It was like the saying: they had pulled on the levers of power, only to discover they were not connected to anything.[34] No skilled technicians to build solar farms. No construction companies specializing in retrofit. Wales had the right ideas and a law to implement them. But it badly needed to create the conditions for change.

Ben saw an opportunity. He was nearing fifty. He had forged a successful career in human rights, then as a speech writer and a journalist. He had two books to his name. But he knew he had to do something more about the massive catastrophe humans were heading towards. He could go into politics and try to change things from the top. But he had seen, like with the Future Generations Act, that top-down politics could only go so far. Instead he decided to start at the bottom, with the culture, or the language and the customs, of ordinary people. And he believed that culture started in the classroom.

He founded a college. He called it Black Mountains, after an experimental college of the same name that formed in 1931 in North Carolina, USA, in a small town called Black Mountain. The college had been created by Jewish refugees from the German Bauhaus movement. It embraced a humanistic ethos, experimenting with the arts and growing food, bringing together life and learning. It had also been radically inclusive, admitting Black students before the Civil Rights Act.

Inspired by these ideas, Ben wanted Black Mountains College in Wales to bridge the gaps he saw between real life and public education, between humans and nature. He assembled a small team, and they began to design courses to teach survival skills. He wanted the ethos of the college to be accessible not just for students, but for people in the surrounding places. He believed such an institution could be not just a place to learn about the current world, but a place to create the next one.

Wales had a law allowing people to act in the interest of future generations, even when that seemed to be at the expense of the people of the present. And Ben had an idea for a new kind of public education that would equip people with the skills to adapt and survive in a changing climate. All Black Mountains College needed was a place where people were starting to think differently about how to steward the surrounding valleys. A place like Treherbert.

4.6 IMAGINE MY VALLEY

One Friday in July 2024, just as the sun is trying to push its way through the clouds hanging over the Rhondda, Andromeda Thomas opens up the gates to an old petrol station on the main street in Treherbert. Her husband, Ian Thomas, is up at the woods, preparing for a group of preschoolers to arrive for a workshop. Her own children are out at work or school. The old petrol station shut down decades ago, leaving a desert of cracked concrete and weeds. Welcome to Our Woods had the idea to use the site, which is in a prime position on the main street through the village, for growing food and other plants.

It isn't an obvious place for growing anything. As part of securing planning permission, Welcome to Our Woods have agreed not to plant anything directly in the ground. With support from the local Housing Association, Andromeda – Drom to her friends – and the team from Welcome to Our Woods spread gravel over the cracked concrete and installed a poly-tunnel and a site office, with space for a classroom, a kitchen and a toilet.

As Drom pushes open the gate she is greeted by a small army of fruit trees in pots. These are the latest crop for the community orchard, which will be planted on the site of a demolished council estate, known locally as the ranch. In the classroom, she clicks on a kettle to make coffee. First, the aeroponics need attention: the salad growing in a green metal shed using water and UV lights. Then it's the turn of the plants in the polytunnel.

Under the awning to the classroom, a single fish swims in a white IKEA bin that has been adapted for aquaponics, a kind of farming that uses bacteria and ammonia from fish waste to grow micro-greens above. The bins have been adapted using inexpensive kits that are simple enough for children to assemble. Drom uses this one as a demo model for school visits. The fish is called Gwyn, after the youngest member of the Welcome to Our Woods team, Gwynfor.

Drom still remembers Ian coming home from work one day to say that Gwynfor, just turned sixteen, had asked Welcome to Our Woods if he could be their apprentice. Gwynfor Jones was pretty typical for a teenager in that he didn't love school. His older brother had been studious, and ended up working as a carer. Gwynfor felt there was no point in working hard at school only to get a job he wouldn't enjoy. When the exams came round, he would stare anxiously at the questions for two hours and then find himself with no time to put down an answer.

When he was twelve, Gwynfor saw a poster for an open day on fire safety at Welcome to Our Woods. His mum, Rhian, encouraged him to attend. In the forest, Ian explained how to chop wood with an axe to feed a big fire, and how to balance a big black kettle on the fire to make tea. When it was Gwynfor's turn to have a go, he felt something click.[35] This was what he wanted, he realized. Something real that he could do outside, with his hands as much as his mind.

But he was just twelve, too young to camp overnight. He waited anxiously for his thirteenth birthday, so he could do more at the day camps each weekend. Within a few years, he was volunteering with younger children, teaching them survival skills, including how to collect the right materials and to safely light a fire, passing on his infectious energy for the forests.

During the pandemic, school moved online, and Gwynfor escaped his GCSE exams when it was decided all candidates would receive their predicted grades. When the world opened up again, he decided to embark on a career in nature.[36] He signed up to an apprenticeship in environmental conservation with Bridgend College, and asked Welcome to Our Woods to host him during his studies. It was a leap of faith for Welcome to Our Woods. Though they'd never done anything like it before, Ian felt, instinctively, that formal education was a way to develop the kinds of skills they were already teaching in the woods. The combination went so well that at the end of his course, Gwynfor was given a prize for being National Training Federation Wales's Foundation Apprentice of the Year.[37] At Welcome to Our Woods, he was soon an essential part of the team, since he spoke Welsh and could run mountain bike expeditions and volunteer groups in two languages.

Through Gwynfor, Ian saw how Welcome to Our Woods could do more than demystify the Valleys – it could support young people with few opportunities into careers around forestry and the environment. At home, he encouraged Drom to apply to do a course in regenerative horticulture with Black Mountains College, in the first year that it was delivered in Treherbert.

After a year of classes, Drom began hosting weekly community days at the old petrol station. People came for coffee and asked questions about what to grow and how – questions Drom felt confident to answer, thanks to the course. She taught them how to propagate plants. She learned how the soil of the orchard on the demolished housing estate was like a microbiome that could regenerate over time, as long as they made good choices, staying away from artificial pesticides and using home-made compost.

As cool as the Black Mountains College courses were, Ian knew most valley kids would never make the journey across the mountains to Talgarth. Some, like Gwynfor, might make it as far as college in Bridgend. But the dream was to offer the training in the heart of the town. So he met Ben, and together they began to think about setting up a proper campus in Treherbert.

That July day, while Drom is at the petrol station, Ian is up at the woods. A procession of toddlers makes its way towards him through Treherbert, holding hands in orange safety vests. Ian welcomes them at the bottom of the old brewery site, where a generator hums noisily: the first clue to the old brewery's new life. The little children make their way up the path and through a metal gate that leads to a timber roundhouse, the height of two men and wide enough to contain a parachute. Then they scatter, skipping over the white shells that make a permeable gravel, poking at the piles of wood, peering into planters. The next hour is a happy chaos of snacks, singing and crafting with cordage, or twisted natural twine.

Next door, a temporary site office has become home to the organization that built the timber roundhouse. This is Down to Earth, which trains people out of work or with long-term disabilities to make timber shelters. Their work ranges from this beautiful, open meeting place, to whole developments of sustainable timber housing, residential accommodation and university buildings in Swansea. The idea is that these buildings are used as shelters under which they can teach the next set of trainees.

The roundhouse is symbolic. It's the first structure to be built from Rhondda larch for many years, proof that Natural Resources Wales can do more with the wood in these forests than chip it and burn it as fuel. Ian has grand plans for the little wood they have acquired from felling. Steps from the roundhouse, safely stowed in a metal shed, is a small green tractor.

Ian dreams of the day the green tractor will be hauling logs at a brand new Welcome to Our Woods timber processing plant. When the children have gone, he walks the site with Seb Haley from Down to Earth, debating where the machinery should go. Ever since that trip to Scotland, Ian has been thinking about how to make affordable homes for people out of timber from the valley. The question is how to get from standing trees to finished houses, while keeping the community involved at every stage.

Ian heads to the old library on the high street that is now the Welcome to Our Woods headquarters. Inside, Chris has joined Ben Rawlence and the other staff from Black Mountains College to interview people to deliver courses in Treherbert. They will teach all sorts: wellbeing in nature, coppicing, green wood trades. They are planning to run their courses in an old grammar school just off the high street, opening up another of Treherbert's vacant buildings. The team talks excitedly about the two candidates. Local people so good, they are going to have to offer them a job share.

In one corner of the library, compost is piled high in plastic sacks from a drugs bust in the pub next door. The old Bute Pub, right in the heart of the village, was sold just a year earlier and covered in scaffolding. Before locals could ask why the works seemed not to be progressing, police broke down the back door to find a forest of cannabis plants in black tubs, state-of-the-art ventilation equipment, UV lights and piles of compost bags.

There have been a spate of such incidents in the Valleys: criminal gangs buying up disused buildings on high streets and carrying out their business in broad daylight. The men joke about the benefits of free compost. But the incident shows how Valley villages can become prey to gangs. How empty buildings make them all vulnerable. How a place like Treherbert might fall to something terrible, without a vision of what else it could become.

A painting hangs above the door-frame of the library, showing the valley transformed.[38] A woman pushes a pram into the forest, following a wooden sign. People sit around a campfire on a clearing with cups of tea on their laps. Someone in a wheelchair crosses a bridge over the river. There are thinner forests, mixed species, a timber processing plant with logs stacked neatly ready to be turned into chips or boards. '*Future of our Forest*', it says at the bottom. '*April/Ebrill 2022*.'

The painting was made at the closing event for the co-production process. Over a campfire and some food, the community reflected on their work towards a future vision for the forest. The artist, listening in, painted their dreams on to the canvas for posterity.

Quietly, Ian and Chris had been working towards raising the money to make the vision a reality, putting in a bid for £2.5 million from the National Lottery's Climate Action Fund. They were hoping to announce that they had received confirmation of the funding at that April 2022 event. When the funding didn't come through in time for the party, they didn't worry too much. The co-production process was reason enough to celebrate. But then the delays started to accumulate. In the end, it would take another year of wrangling with contracts and lawyers to prove the community had the right to the land, before the funders would come through.

It was a difficult year for Ian. The community put their trust in the co-production process. Without money, the vision was out of reach. For some time, the promise of the whole project looked like it would end the way so many other promises to the people of the Valleys had ended: in dust.

Welcome to Our Woods never stopped its good work. The initiatives inched on, drawing on smaller grants and bits of funding where they could. They opened up the farm on the old petrol station site and installed the green metal sheds for hydroponics. The mental health and wellbeing walks in the valley went from strength to strength with the help of Martyn Broughton, a skilled local personal trainer and community organizer. There were beatbox competitions in the old brewery site, festivals and campfires round that original fire pit on the eastern side of the valley.

Without funding to forge ahead with their own vision, Welcome to Our Woods relied on new partnerships to make things happen. Down to Earth came on board, then Black Mountains College. Some of the community's plans seemed like they would be possible without proper funding.

But when the money came through, Ian felt profound relief. There was only so much that could be changed simply by imagining a different valley. A vision takes investment. And an investment like this one needed a new set of criteria to prove that value for money was about more than profit and extraction. Chris doubled down on his work proving social value through the project. Their valley project had nearly fallen apart at least twice. They hoped that by building a new way to measure value, no other community would be faced with the same rollercoaster of hope and fear.

After the meeting with Ben in the library, Ian takes Chris

on a drive to the top of the valley. It's a white-knuckle ride on rough, stony roads that give way to sheer drops. They marvel at the culverts, carved neatly into the side of the road, and the massive cubes of rocks in mesh, put in place to stop landslides and flash floods. Once, not so long ago, men were employed to walk the high roads, removing rocks that could send a car plunging below. All that's left of this tradition is the basic stone shelters where the watchmen used to live.

At the top of the valley, they get out of the car. They are standing on one of the twelve coal tips that surround Treherbert, a man-made mountain that never existed before the mines. The settlements run down the centre of the valley, alongside the River Taff, conjoined like the beads on a necklace: Treherbert, Treorchy, Pentre. From here, it's possible to see the place where the Pentre flood started, just below the square tower of a church. No one could have expected a place like that to flood. It was too high up the valley, too far from the river. But flash flooding and the way the land was managed nonetheless conspired against the people of Pentre that day.

Just below, a flat expanse of grass is all that is left of a colliery, an open-faced coal mine that would have employed some of the men in these villages. The land was long ago returned to grassland. All that's left is the strange plateau.

Mining is not the only industry that has left its mark on the valley. In the village, the flat roofs of former warehouse buildings tell the stories of other employers that have come and gone. A distinctive building with a zigzag roof belongs to a former Burberry factory. Another flat expanse of warehouse belonged to a window and door company called Everest. That one closed down just a few months earlier, leaving one hundred local people without a job – some of whom had worked in the factory for fifty years.

The men talk about it offhandedly, too used to seeing companies leaving. It's as though nothing could shock them any more. Rather than the grief, they feel the possibilities. We could put a timber processing plant in there, Ian says. Plenty of room. In the middle of the two warehouses, the roof of the roundhouse is visible, a grassy roof over a spiral of larch. One day, not so long from now, this will be the entrance to the Cwm Saerbren nature reserve: a permanent place for residents and tourists to celebrate the natural history of this part of the forest. First, the larch must be completely felled, in accordance with the compromise they have made with Natural Resources Wales.

The clear felling has already started on the eastern slopes. The men can just about pick out the fire pit first established by Welcome to Our Woods. It was at this spot, all those years ago, that the chief executive of Natural Resources Wales and the founder of Welcome to Our Woods climbed up into the forbidden forest to look out on the valleys, thick with trees. It was on that day the chief executive had asked for new ideas. Neither of those men could have known that to find a path to the future of the valley, the forest around that fire pit would have to be destroyed. One day, in early 2024, the machines arrived: gigantic trucks and chippers bearing the branding of a nearby biomass plant. Within a day, the forest was gone, driven off to be incinerated. All that was left were piles of brash and tree stumps that quickly covered over with grass and weeds.

Welcome to Our Woods brought people to the forest. But they couldn't save the trees. Instead, what they secured was far greater: a promise that the trees would be cut down on the western elevation in stages. And that what replaced the larch monoculture would never be completely cleared again.

The true economic right to manage the land eludes the people of the Valleys. This is still public land. Only a forest croft of the kind they visited in Scotland gives a community the right to profit from the timber. But the project proves that there are other ways to give communities the control they need to deliver benefits for people and for nature in the long term.

Treherbert will go down in history as the first village to secure an agreement with the government to stand shoulder to shoulder on decisions about how to manage its land. In training a new generation of foresters, the people of Treherbert are showing how civilizations can exist in harmony with a valley – a country, a planet – that can never be unchanged.

5

FACTORY

Birmingham

'Pretty much everyone broadly agrees on what we want: beautiful architecture, generous, affordable, healthy, zero-carbon, circular homes and resilient communities living in green, walkable, prosperous neighbourhoods filled with a thousand small, local businesses. Places where children can grow up happily, where the elderly can grow old in good company, and where everyone has the chance to flourish and realise the best version of themselves. And to create all that, we want a booming, innovative design and construction industry. But yet our land system is perfectly designed to never, ever give us that.'

—Alastair Parvin, 'A New Land Contract' (2020)

5.1 SITE AS CLASSROOM

Two miles west of Birmingham City Centre, a historic kilo-metre of canal curves around the former industrial district to which it gives its name: Icknield Port Loop. I take the bus one summer. The journey is a ten-minute tour of Birmingham's ever-evolving architecture, starting with the minimalist sil-very orbs of the Selfridges building and travelling along the Smallbrook Ringway Centre, a majestic modernist boulevard on stilts, built in the late fifties. From there, the city begins to recede into old redbrick schools and almshouses – a reminder of the civic infrastructure of centuries past – many now repur-posed as bookies' and flats.

Then, suddenly, nothing. I almost miss my stop. The build-ings are gone, replaced by two tiers of metal fencing in front of a concrete expanse overrun with weeds, plastic bottles and old Coke cans. Until the 2020s, this 20-hectare industrial dis-trict was left mostly untouched. A road sign reads: 'Welcome to South West Birmingham, supported by', followed by a big white square, an absence. Scrub as tall as a person grows through cracks in old concrete. Placards warn of trespass and 'demoli-tion in progress'.

The three-hundred-year-old Icknield Port Loop canal runs

under the road, resurfacing outside a derelict factory that looks, to the untrained eye, like any other. A century ago this was a tube works, making metal pipes that carried water and gas through the expanding Victorian infrastructure of the city. On the ground floor, the exterior of the old factory is lined with huge windows and stable doors where canal horses were once kept. In its last incarnation, the tube works became a recycling centre, burning the city's waste, smoke twisting skyward from twin metal chimneys. A symbol, perhaps, of a moment in history when climate change felt reversible. But the incinerators are gone and black paint peels from the panels across the windows. Metal mesh rusts over the doors.

When I visit in 2024, the factory is undergoing another transformation. Pictures have appeared on the sides of the building. Some of the panels have been repaired. Colourful paintwork suggests new residents. The tube works may soon become another stop on that architectural tour: a prototype of a new kind of infrastructure, just as vital as service pipes for water and gas and recycling plants for waste. Under the stewardship of local people, the factory is becoming a centre to facilitate the transition of the neighbourhood, by distributing local, regenerative materials, sharing skills from planting to plastering and providing a place of shelter when weather events strike.

Britain is littered with abandoned factories, each one speaking the dying dialects of industry. From the derelict distilleries of Scotland, to the windmills of East Anglia, to the textile mills of Lancashire and the North West, each region has its own vernacular, etched into the architecture of these crumbling monuments. But the West Midlands is the heartland of Britain's industrial heritage. From the eighteenth century, it became the workshop of the world.[1] The belching dark fumes from thousands of iron and steel works gave the region its nickname the Black Country. Its factories produced materials to support smaller workshops from Coventry to Wolverhampton in the manufacture of a bewildering number of smaller goods, from guns, to locks, to leather products and jewellery. These workshops in turn supplied the British military and the global market with the tools of colonial expansion: the chains that held enslaved Africans on their transit to America, the guns that intimidated people in the colonies, the axes and the spades that were used in infrastructure projects overseas.

I have come to Birmingham to visit Civic Square, a radical community organization made up of a handful of brilliant, creative researchers and local activists. They are united in a belief that the injustices perpetrated against people in the name of imperialism live on in the colonial mindset that continues to plunder one half of the world – its nature and its people – to enrich the other. They point to statistics that show that the Global North is responsible for 92 per cent of excess emissions and the majority of ecological breakdown, and that the richest 1 per cent of people globally is responsible for more emissions than the bottom 50 per cent.[2] [3]

The people behind Civic Square believe that climate change cannot only be addressed with mathematics about emissions. They think we need to move beyond growth as a measure of society's success, or gross domestic product as calculated by the consumption of materials, to survive. They see how a clean energy transition that creates massive demand for critical minerals for batteries, wind turbines and electricity grids will end up repeating the violence of colonialism, extracting minerals from poorer nations to supply those with wealth.[4]

Civic Square is rooted in the Ladywood area of Birmingham, a residential district crossed by several busy roads and the old industrial canal. Immy Kaur, the co-founder at the heart of Civic Square, helped bring TEDx to Birmingham in 2012, and ran it for five years as a place where people with minority ethnic backgrounds, working class and queer people of all faiths could shape the discourse in their city.[5] Even back then, she would find herself walking past patches of land, or derelict shops, and wondering who owned them. What would it take to acquire these lost spaces, she wondered, and to open them up again as places for people to gather?[6]

In 2014, Immy launched a crowdfunding campaign to open a collaborative workspace called an Impact Hub in Digbeth, central Birmingham, where people committed to social justice could work, meet and host events.[7] For five years, this Impact Hub thrived. But no matter how well they did, every year the landlord put up the rent. They could not keep up.

Immy and her collaborators realized, through encounters with the radical architects Alastair Parvin and Indy Johar, this sense of being constantly squeezed beyond their means was by design, as renters in a system where huge amounts of public goods were being channelled into private wealth.[8] In 2019, they were finally priced out, at a moment when the city of Birmingham was being reshaped. Over the winter, the Birmingham Wholesale Market in the city centre had been demolished to make way for a £1.9 billion redevelopment.[9] In Ladywood, the public were asked to give their views on proposals to build houses close to the water of the Edgbaston Reservoir, an oasis of green space heavily used by people from the surrounding estates.[10]

Over the road from the reservoir, the developer Urban Splash released plans for luxury housing on the industrial land at Port Loop. When Immy and her collaborators at Impact Hub first saw the Urban Splash proposal documents in 2018, they thought it sounded better than other urban regeneration schemes sweeping the city. The proposals included green streets, communal facilities, repair workshops and household swap shops.[11] But residents were cautious. They knew the developers were ultimately guided by the pursuit of profit, or the extraction of wealth, even though Urban Splash appeared to be more progressive. No interaction with the Port Loop site could ever be what Civic Square considered 'clean' – every move would increase the value of the private housing.[12]

Immy and her collaborators began to formulate an idea: what if this old factory building could once again bring people together and nurture skills – but this time for reparative rather than extractive industries? They dreamed up plans to put the factory at the heart of a climate transition designed, owned and governed by the people of Ladywood. In 2018, Civic Square made a proposal to Urban Splash: sell us the old tube works and we'll turn it into neighbourhood infrastructure in your new estate – a place for residents to learn skills and dream up new ideas for the challenges to come. They wanted to bring as many people as possible along with them as they learned how to transform this twentieth-century industrial site into a twenty-first-century factory for the future. According to the scientists that advise the UN on the Intergovernmental Panel on Climate Change, initiatives that take learning about the climate out of the classroom are an essential part of nurturing environmental citizenship and activism.[13]

Negotiations for the site began. When Covid hit, Civic Square paused its factory plans to work within Ladywood's neighbourhoods on the challenge of the moment. But in 2022, when normality resumed, they doubled down on their efforts to acquire the factory. Leasing it or occupying it wasn't enough. History had taught them how easily their time and energy could be co-opted by others for private gain. Civic Square wanted community ownership of the factory in perpetuity: not just the purchase of land, but a way of protecting it against profit motives in the future, so it could remain affordable to local people for ever. They chose a name that reflected their vision for the factory as a place of dreaming, sharing, learning and adapting. They called it the Neighbourhood Public Square.

5.2 CONSTRUCTING THE FUTURE

In May 2024, Civic Square opens the gates of the Neighbourhood Public Square for the first time. The building is still a ruin – and Civic Square have not yet succeeded in its purchase – but the courtyard, a kind of depot in the centre of the site, is open.

An A-board welcomes people to come inside for the 'neighbourhood trade school'. Civic Square have been running the trade school every week for several years, inviting people from the neighbourhood to get together to learn useful construction skills and share food. The atmosphere feels more like a festival than a school. Everyone is hard at work screwing together wooden beams to make a gigantic polytunnel in the centre of the site. Over the course of the morning, the workers fix solar panels to the roof and metal gutters down the sides. The water collects in giant cubic butts designed by MJM Bespoke, a fabrication studio based in nearby Digbeth.

The polytunnel has been built to embody the spirit of the Neighbourhood Public Square during the factory's construction. When it is finished, the factory will act as a neighbourhood power station, generating enough solar energy to share with the surrounding streets. The polytunnel demonstrates this vision in miniature within hours of its construction. It starts to rain, and water begins to collect in the water butts. A string of light bulbs sparkle above the workers. Most construction sites are closed, hidden behind hoardings. But the polytunnel, with its clear plastic walls, is the first indication that this is a building site with a difference, where everyone is invited to participate. The prototype is live.

For the retrofit of the building, Civic Square want to use regenerative materials from the local region like clay, gravel, straw, timber and even mycelium, or the spores of mushrooms. They intend to reuse and recycle as much as they can. But salvaged materials, from planks of wood to sheets of metal, take up space. In the bottom of the factory, Civic Square have kept space for a materials lab – a new kind of depot that harks back to Birmingham's legacy as a city of a thousand trades. Instead of steel to make tubes, chains and weapons, this workshop will offer second-hand materials, sustainably constructed components and low-carbon alternatives for builders – from homeowners who want to do it themselves to major regional construction firms.

First on site this May morning: the DIY-ers. The group has won a place on a course hosted by Civic Square and Material Cultures, a not-for-profit design studio that runs a construction skills programme using regenerative materials at Central Saint Martins college in London. Over the summer, they will experiment with biodegradable and regenerative materials in construction. The course offers visits to brickworks and timber yards where the group can learn new – and revive old – construction techniques.

Among them is a young man with a crop of bleached hair and dark sunglasses called Kester Sleeman. Kez bought a doer-upper, a 1930s end-of-terrace in nearby Smethwick, only to find that 'doer-upper' was a bit of an understatement. Alongside tackling the obvious cosmetic challenges – the house hadn't been touched for decades – Kez wanted to learn how to update it to be more heat-resilient, less draughty and more energy-efficient: all the things modern houses should be.

By day he worked for the council on its transport strategy, trying to reduce carbon emissions on the roads with bicycles, buses and charging points for electric vehicles. At home, he moved furniture to find black mould. One week, the walls felt clammy and cold, and the next, spores appeared.

Kez was not one to shrink from a challenge. He had trained as a mechanical engineer and came from parents with a strong DIY ethos. But he was wary of repeating the mistakes of previous owners, who had patched up the house with repairs that turned it into Frankenstein's monster. The old tenants had switched from the original lime plaster to cement, making the walls less and less breathable. They had poured concrete into the cavity beneath the old suspended wooden floor, strangling the air flow, creating the conditions for mould. Kez realized he was facing a massive challenge. He would have to rewire the electrics, change the plumbing, insulate the floors and replaster the whole house.

Every time he saw a job that needed doing, he heard his parents in his head: 'Get on with it then, Kez,' they said. He spent hundreds of hours on YouTube, piecing together the knowledge he needed. But when he looked at the materials on the market, they didn't seem sustainable: concrete, cement, plastic. The same materials the previous tenants had used to ill effect. He felt lost.

That's when he saw the advert for the construction workshops. Four meetings, four different materials derived from biological matter: straw, clay, timber and mycelium. Each offered a chance to consider the origins of materials and how they might create buildings better adapted to heat and cold.

In this first session, the cohort are learning how to make buildings out of timber panels. They don fluorescent jackets ready to start building, under the watchful eye of Dieter Brandstätter, a teacher from the Centre for Alternative Technology, an eco-centre in Wales. The panels will be clad with wood wool, which acts as a natural flame retardant, Dieter explains. The group wrestles with dense straw bales, putting them between timber panels as insulation. Some of them have never used a saw. But the learning is deliberately slow-paced, planned in a way that will allow people to become acquainted with the feeling of working with their hands.

Dieter assures them that the basic skills to build straw walls can be learned in a day, making it possible for anyone to have a go, unlike more specialist methods that require qualifications, training and equipment.

The teachers from Material Cultures split the group up into different tasks. They ask Kez to make giant straw bricks in a small team. He spends the afternoon cutting and tying bales made from Mottram hay and Shropshire straw. Others measure beams, saw timber and hammer nails into the base of the wall they are constructing. Someone sweeps.

Slowly the bales, tied and cut, are assembled in the frame and staked with willow to form a sturdy, insulated wall. The straw needs to be on the inside, they learn, where it stays dry and keeps in human heat. A strong structure emerges with two walls and a hatch to look through. A window into their new world.

Outside the polytunnel, other visitors arrive: families and neighbours excited to finally see inside the grounds of the factory. Under cover, on a wooden table, volunteers from Civic Square in transparent waterproofs cut out grids of coloured card and hand them out. The volunteers send visitors on quests around the neighbourhood, asking them to take pictures of the materials they find. They want to get people thinking about how to build using the resources around them, rather than importing things from overseas – or even from outside the region.

The volunteers spread a huge map of Birmingham on a table under the headline 'Materials Map'. As the day goes on, it fills up with notes as people contribute their knowledge about local resources, from reclaimed timber yards, to tool libraries, to local tradesmen. The map is part of a much wider materials matrix that Civic Square is creating with Material Cultures. The

West Midlands remains abundant with raw materials. There are rich clay seams formed hundreds of millions of years ago, still ripe for extraction, in Dudley, Walsall, Coventry and Solihull, plus gravel and grit from the pits of Staffordshire and an exposed limestone rock face in Dudley.

What's more, the Birmingham Canal Navigation network that runs through Port Loop stretches more than a hundred miles, right through the heart of the city, offering direct but little used access to these mineral resources on their doorstep. These resources, this infrastructure, is barely used since builders and developers are so accustomed to cheap imports of carbon-intensive materials. But it's still there, just waiting to be revived.

5.3 REIMAGINING THE WORLD

Immy Kaur, Civic Square co-founder, stands at the door to the tube works offering people hi-vis vests. She's wearing one herself over a chore jacket with the sleeves rolled up, her hair tucked away under a covering. This is a building site, she reminds people as they come in, with a grin that suggests she is delighted that construction can finally begin. Getting to this point has required many years of research, encounters, fundraising and action with residents in the streets of Ladywood. Finishing the building may take another decade. But the real work is right here, bringing people to this place and inviting them to share in the vision. It's a way of spreading hope and getting people involved in something that could be transformative in the neighbourhood, even as crisis envelops the city.

A few months earlier, in September 2023, Birmingham City Council declared bankruptcy and announced the sale of public assets worth £750 million, including twenty-five of its thirty-six public libraries and eleven of the city's remaining community centres.[14] Under the plans, thousands of children in Birmingham would lose access to safe places to read and learn. Hundreds of carers would be starved of the respite of day centres for people with disabilities.

Immy and her collaborators see how these closures, beyond their immediate, catastrophic impact, will have far-reaching consequences as temperatures increase, hitting 40 degrees every summer by 2030. The death of community spaces will leave the poorest people in the most unsuitable homes, sweating through sleepless nights, struggling to breathe through humid days. The squeeze on local authorities has ravaged people of the gathering places that are essential to survival. All across the country, people submit to the idea that councils have run out of money and that the only answer is more privatization.[15]

Immy, like many of those involved in Civic Square, refuses to believe that privatization is the only option. Immy's grandmother emigrated from India, arriving in Britain with stories of devastation in Punjab under partition, of mothers and babies forced to flee in boats, of train carriages full of slain men arriving at stations, pouring blood. Immy was born in the UK and raised by parents who saw it as their duty not to worry her with this ancestral trauma. Instead, she was surrounded by the abundance of their love and generosity, and brought up with stories that reflected the importance of caring for your neighbour. As she blew the dust off her family history, she began to see her ancestors' capacity for reinvention as a gift.

She saw how a new global gold rush for minerals in the name of clean energy would end in further displacement, splitting families as countries competed over raw materials and pushed indigenous people off their land. And she knew that future was fast approaching. Already, she had heard first-hand from relatives in Punjab about how they sweltered through 40-degree temperatures in apartments without air conditioning. How long until these places were once again made inhospitable, not by the first wave of colonialism but by the impact on the climate of a second?

For Civic Square, the way to reimagine the world is to start in the neighbourhood. Immy is inspired by the founding of the NHS as a neighbourhood medical society in a village in Wales and by the philanthropy of Andrew Carnegie, who built thousands of libraries during the Industrial Revolution. The first has transformed the health of working people for generations, the second put knowledge and education at the heart of local communities. These neighbourhood initiatives changed the course of British society. In the decades before Civic Square was founded in 2022, austerity and local authority collapse had created a gap for a new kind of community organization to emerge at neighbourhood level. But scaling up Civic Square's vision will take forces beyond the neighbourhood, just like it took Acts of Parliament to create the NHS and the deep pockets of industrialists to build municipal libraries in every town.

There too, Civic Square has a vision. In 2024, Civic Square and the radical think tank Dark Matter Labs published an invitation to philanthropists to invest in something called civic infrastructure.[16] They defined civic in opposition to public, or funded by the state. The civic sphere is the one in which people interact with place-based organizations, from credit institutions, to religious organizations, schools and local media. In their definition, infrastructure was not just bridges and cables and roads, but who people are, what they value and what they seek to create. They pointed to the 'compendium for the civic economy' published in 2011 by the think tank Nesta. It included twenty-five examples of civic infrastructures in the UK, from libraries of things, to friendship centres, community hubs, arts venues, playgrounds and public parks, as well as intangible things like local policies and social programmes.[17] All of these ideas and organizations are essential to surviving climate change, Civic Square said – but they need to be properly funded.

The Neighbourhood Public Square was designed to embody many of these things. It has three floors of meeting places and resources, from a book and tools library to a gardening area, bicycle repair centre and a communal kitchen.[18] The ground floor, or depot, will be filled with the fruits of the long search for sustainable local materials: timber, stone and straw for builders, from amateurs like Kez to major construction firms. All the spaces have been designed by Material Cultures and the architecture practice Architecture oo to be adaptable to extreme weather events, so they can serve as shade for people who live in overheating homes in hot summers, and warm rooms for those in damp, cold houses come winter.[19] No one would ever be able to say, looking at the Neighbourhood Public Square, that they didn't know what the factories of the future needed to look like. It would be a beacon to funders and philanthropists of how to fund a just transition: a demonstrator of the next generation of civic infrastructure.

At the end of the day, after the rain has passed, Kez and the other participants of the materials course sprawl on the grass.

They are exhausted from all the physical labour, already talking like old friends from working so closely together on their tasks.

Talk turns to building with straw as a political act – a way to democratize power over built spaces. As well as being easy to build with, straw is adaptable and environmentally sound. It can easily be repaired. Or, if no longer useful, it can be dismantled entirely and left to rot back into the soil. Working with straw is a way to think about the whole life cycle of a building material, unlike many more modern materials whose only future is in landfill.

Kez sees how the narrative of climate emergency plays into the hands of an industry which can promise to insulate your home in an afternoon with completely inert and man-made materials. His house bears the scars of this scarcity mindset with its patchwork of damp and poured concrete. But the pace of working with regenerative materials feels different. He feels free from the pressure of time-limited subsidies, scant suppliers, rising damp, climate emergency. At Civic Square, in the polytunnel, he is invited to go slower. To think more. To work with his neighbour. He finds it way more creative and enjoyable than he expected.

5.4 SKILLS FOR ALL

I travel to Port Loop in July 2024, at the height of summer, to visit a different neighbourhood trade school. Immy meets me at the barge that has served as Civic Square headquarters while they have been working towards accessing the site. It's a humble canal boat stuffed with books and resources, docked on a small jetty next to the tube works. They call it their 'floating front room' – an ark carrying Civic Square and perhaps the whole neighbourhood into the future.

We set out towards the Edgbaston Reservoir, crossing a noisy road. The deafening sound of traffic recedes the moment we enter the greenery of the reservoir. I feel instantly calmed. Without a proper space of their own, Civic Square has been hosting meet-ups and events in partnership with other local organizations. Tonight, the neighbourhood trade school will be hosted at the Midland Sailing Club on the shore of the reservoir and at the Red Shed, an eco-building run by Birmingham Settlement Nature and Wellbeing Centre. The shed sits at the top of the water within a beautiful garden, on land saved for the community under a covenant.

Civic Square see these and the many other community organizations as part of the fabric of Ladywood – the part that needs nurturing as much as buildings need retrofitting and public space needs saving. Alongside their work designing the Neighbourhood Public Square, Civic Square spent a year mapping these organizations through interviews and profiles in their community newspaper, *The Good News of B16*.[20] It was an opportunity to spotlight all the organizations in the area that were moving towards a regenerative future under the surface, despite massive cuts in public funding. They found befriending services for the elderly and for immigrants, mental health services run out of mosques, an Afro-futurist arts festival, urban farming, wildlife trusts and even a Marxist book club.

They asked each practitioner to map their work on a doughnut framework, a circular alternative to linear growth formulated by the economist Kate Raworth, to see how the groups might fit together as part of a bigger story about an emerging, alternative future in Ladywood. People put their work into broad categories, from social equity, to education, to access to nature. But all of them were able to see how they contributed to a much broader, neighbourhood-wide effort to keep Birmingham within the two rings of the doughnut: the inner ring, which set out the basic things people need in order to survive, and an outer ring, in which humans overshoot the planetary boundaries, seeding our own demise. At a moment of diminishing public resources, even as the planet hurtled towards breakdown, the map showed a path forward, towards a regenerative future for Ladywood.

The map also showed what was missing. Many decades of over-reliance on man-made and imported materials had created a skills shortage among builders. Birmingham might still have the raw materials and the abandoned buildings for the civic infrastructure that will be the building blocks of an alternative future. But without the skills – a whole spectrum of skills, within the construction industry and among ordinary people – the real work of building alternative futures will remain a fantasy.

So Civic Square went on a recruitment drive. In partnership with nearby Fircroft College of Adult Education, Civic Square designed a more technical version of Kez's course, aimed at builders and construction firms in the West Midlands. They appealed to builders and skilled labourers in the region to come and learn about regenerative building processes and materials.

On the course, participants visit places already using these practices, like Down to Earth, the natural-construction non-profit working with Welcome to Our Woods in South Wales, and the Ubele Initiative, an African diaspora-led non-profit building structures with clay, wheat, reed and timber in the heart of East London, under the guidance of Material Cultures. They are invited to think about how these materials can be used to retrofit existing buildings, preserving their embodied carbon.

Civic Square hope that, when all these efforts are added together, the components of a truly sustainable construction industry emerges, using matrices of found and regenerative materials and involving networks of community organizations and professions. The industry fits within neighbourhoods of skilled residents and shared tools, creating a system capable of adaptation at scale.

Immy and I walk the perimeter of the reservoir. A young fruit orchard grows on one side. On the other, ducks dip into the rippled surface of the water. People pass us in the opposite direction: couples catching up, parents pushing prams, joggers listening to headphones. It looks like leisure, but green infrastructure like this will soon be essential to survival, Immy says. In the hottest summer days, people already leave their unsuitable housing for the shade of the trees. Even though the reservoir is so vital to people's survival in their neighbourhood, it too is under threat. On its banks, the fortunes of two institutions, with two very different relationships to the land, have informed Civic Square's understanding of the agreements they needed to broker to protect their vision for the Neighbourhood Public Square.

The site of one sits over the other side of the water. The Tower Ballroom was a historic roller-skating rink, built by the Victorians and demolished in 2022. Immy says the building offers a cautionary tale about the limitations of community stewardship in the face of private ownership. Many different, diverse communities danced under its disco ball. Local people campaigned for years to try and save it. But the council decided the land would be better used for housing, and closed it down. A piece of local heritage and vital civic infrastructure, swept away. The story is a warning that communities cannot rely on others to grant them access to public land and buildings. That's why Civic Square have sought ways to own their land at Port Loop.

The other is our destination: the Nature and Wellbeing Centre, a green space at the top of the reservoir which is protected from private sale. An industrial pen-manufacturer called Joseph Gillott once owned the land. Gillott placed on it a covenant, or legal obligation, to make sure local people could use it in perpetuity. A local charity called Birmingham Settlement is now the sole steward of the land, holding it open for community activities including nature clubs, nurseries, a community cafe and the Red Shed, built by local people using clay block and newspaper insulation.[21] At the entrance to the land, a noticeboard is stuffed with flyers for events and workshops: from yoga to gardening, playgroup to theatre. The site stretches before us: a small amphitheatre, two geodesic domes visited by children from the local nursery, and pathways flanked with raised beds.

The Red Shed sits at the far end. Out the front, a motley crew of people have gathered on blue picnic benches for this month's trade school, where they are learning to make cornflour bricks. They mix cornflour, sand and water together in big plastic bowls and turn the thick paste into tiny brick moulds, ready to bake in a microwave.

A young girl with a big scab on her knee runs up to Emily Churchill Zaraa, the Civic Square coordinator running the workshop, to ask if she can try decorating her brick with wild-flowers. Emily helps her push in the stalks and sprinkle on some lavender before they put her creation in the microwave. A ping, and the mulch comes out as hard as a rock. The girl tests it by dropping it on the ground and it lands with a thud, intact. Emily explains that it will stay that way unless it comes into contact with water, in which case it would completely dissolve. The girl picks up her brick and studies it closely, as if considering the possibility that it could start melting away with a drop of rain.

Bricks at this neighbourhood trade school serve the same purpose as they do at Brickfield in Cornwall. They are building blocks, ways into conversations about the materials we use to construct our homes, and how we might begin to use others. Tasneem Akhtar discovered the trade school after attending a Civic Square event on mindfulness and mental health. She's a retired debt adviser who likes to fill up her calendar with activities to get her out of the house. I also meet Madalina Popa, who speaks Romanian with her adorable two-year-old daughter Sophia. Sophia runs between Tasneem and Madalina's two Romanian friends, mothered by them all. Madalina has been coming to the neighbourhood trade school since it started, to learn new things and to meet new people. She can remember almost all of the activities: the week they learned to change a tap washer, the one where they got mud under their fingernails learning how to grow vegetables from seed, and the satisfaction of building planters with a hammer and some nails. Every week she wonders if she'll be able to do it – and every week, she leaves triumphant.

Madalina, Sophia and Tasneem walk back around the reservoir to the Midland Sailing Club. Once a month, as well as a skills workshop and cake afterwards, they share supper beforehand. Tonight it is rice salad with grapes and bananas – funded by Civic Square and free of charge to whoever wants to attend. 'And now,' Madalina announces, grinning, 'it's time for cake!' At the Midland Sailing Club, Madalina learns I haven't had any dinner, and rushes off to find me a box of rice salad. She presses it into my hand with an invitation: 'Come to the next one!' In the back, over hot tea and brownies, everyone gathers to watch a film about Retrofit Reimagined, a festival hosted by Civic Square bringing together people thinking about how to reuse local materials to restore buildings. Two children in the back play chess, watched over by the girl with grazed knees.

At the end, Tasneem offers to walk with me to my accommodation – even though it is out of her way. It's only then I realize I have lost Immy. At some point, she melted away, leaving me held by these strangers who want to see me fed and home. People who, after being pulled in by the orbit of Civic Square, extend their hands to others in a growing network of knowledge and care.

In 2025, ten years after they opened the door to the Impact Hub, Civic Square has a breakthrough. In February, Immy, Emily and many other collaborators, participants, friends and supporters of the organization gather at the tube works in the pouring rain for what they call a 'site warming'. At their 'hub warming' to celebrate the opening of the Impact Hub in 2015, they knew they were taking a huge risk on a lease with a private landowner with barely a penny to their name. A decade on, the stakes are higher, the figures bigger, but they are finally holding some deeds.

Immy steps forwards. For a brief moment the rain pauses, the wind quietens, and she announces that, days before Christmas, Civic Square took ownership of the land, making a clean purchase with funding from the Good Ancestor Movement and the Tudor Trust. Other speakers describe how the factory at Port Loop has become an example of how philanthropists can act in the spirit of abundance rather than scarcity, by moving large sums to support the transformation of neighbourhoods in the face of climate emergency. 'This is what wealth should be doing more of, everywhere,' says Stephanie Brobbey, the founder of the Good Ancestor Movement, an advisory firm for wealth redistribution. 'Ladywood, may you enjoy your abundance and know you're inspiring people far and wide.'[22]

Philanthropists have helped them acquire the land. Ownership isn't the goal, Immy says, but it is the rule in the current system. Next, Civic Square will work towards putting a covenant on the land, like Gillott and the old industrialists, to preserve it for future generations. Simultaneously, they will start retrofitting the factory in earnest, using all they have learned about materials and skills. There is no time, in a climate emergency, to work on one thing at a time, or to tinker at the edges, they say. Philanthropy, finance, governance, construction: everything has to be reimagined and rooted in the neighbourhood at a moment when local authorities are crumbling and central government is stalling. Owning the land is a huge milestone. But it is only the beginning.

6

RAILWAY ARCHES

London's East End

'Start with this principle: don't face your fears alone. Make friends, meet your neighbours, set up support networks, help those who are struggling. Since the dawn of humankind, those with robust social networks have been more resilient than those without.'

—George Monbiot[1]

6.1 AN ORDINARY MECHANIC

I had walked past the little road opposite Haggerston Station in London countless times. But I'd never been down Stean Street until the May day I met Len Maloney. Len ran a Volkswagen garage on the street, in a railway arch under the London Overground line. Stean Street has a single claim to fame: in 1933, it was the birthplace of London's most famous gangsters, the Kray twins. Today, locals use it as a shortcut, slipping behind the Kingsland Viaduct to avoid the chaos of constantly rotating new bars, late night chicken shops, Vietnamese restaurants and phone shops on Kingsland Road.[2] Len has a plan. If he is successful, Stean Street may one day have a new claim to fame as the place that the traders of London started a campaign to save themselves from annihilation.

In over a decade of reporting, I have spoken with countless skilled tradespeople displaced from inner cities because of gentrification. Brewers, jewellers, seamstresses – and especially those in manufacturing. These are the family-run furniture makers, joiners and mechanics who have for generations occupied a place in the pockets of cities. Some of the traders have stuck in my mind, like the taxi mechanic forced into an arch so small the cars would barely fit, squeezed for rent so ruthlessly by his public landlord that he took his own life. For many years afterwards his arch stood empty, just round the corner from Len's, earning the landlord no rent at all. The senselessness made me sick.

This book is mostly about how derelict land and buildings have been revitalized by communities. In this chapter, the story starts a little earlier, before the dereliction starts. Here's how a valued community business is forced out, leaving a shuttered railway arch. Few have fought for their place in their community as courageously as Len. From the depths of his tragedy, Len finds himself at the forefront of the campaign to establish permanent land and security for local businesses like his – the kind that glues communities together in moments of crisis.

Len's garage is packed with cars when I first visit in 2017. He emerges from the entrance to Arch 332, beneath a blue sign bearing the name 'JC Motors: Volkswagen Audi specialists'. He wipes his hands on his blue overalls and smiles a smile that has greeted hundreds of customers, apprentices and employees over the decades. We go inside.

Len's arch is long and narrow and lit by long fluorescent strip lights attached to the walls and the ceilings. Three cars are parked along one side on the concrete floor. Labelled tyres are stacked neatly at the back. Workbenches are lined with tools, gas canisters and car parts. Some of Len's workers raise a car on a ramp and shine torches at its underside. The calm atmosphere is punctuated only by the sound of trains rattling over the rails overhead.

Len and I head into a glass partition office full of box files, Post-its and notebooks. On the glass wall, I notice a sign for a petition to save small businesses, started by something called the East End Trades Guild. Len tells me of a time when the trains didn't run over the viaduct and rain dripped between the tracks into his workshop. But these days his landlord says the arches have become very valuable. His business has already been displaced from its original railway arch. Now he's facing a struggle to stay in this one.

The Kingsland Viaduct was built in 1861, long before Transport for London existed. The viaduct was part of a frenzy of infrastructure built by private investors, fuelled by speculation from the moneyed middle classes and sanctioned by Acts of Parliament. Railways came to London from the North of England in the 1830s, unfurling their tendrils across the city, from London Bridge to Greenwich, connecting Euston with Manchester and Paddington with Swindon and Bristol. London expanded. The speculators fuelled a financial crisis, dubbed railway mania, which ended in runs on banks and major reform of the Bank of England in 1847.[3] Before the crash, the expansion of commercial railways completely changed the character of British life, birthing not just the commuter and the seaside holiday but even time itself, which was standardized in order for people to know when to catch a train.

Beneath the viaducts criss-crossing major cities, light industry found a home. The railways, far from easing urban traffic, filled the streets with building materials, vehicles, goods yards, train tracks, hotels and offices. Railway arches were dirty and noisy, but they offered cheap rents, deep warehouses and ready transport for goods and customers to and from their front door. They were in the heart of some of London's most densely populated boroughs. It's these qualities – then as now – that mark them out as frontiers in the battle for city space.

The North London Railway ran on the Kingsland Viaduct

for almost eighty years. But by the time Len arrived, the passenger trains were gone, withdrawn first during the Second World War and then for good in the eighties,[4] when a new link was constructed between Liverpool Street station and the old North London Railway. Grass grew beneath the sleepers.[5]

It was around this time that Len went on day release from school to apprentice at a local mini garage. It was through this apprenticeship he met Joe Chee, a Chinese-Mauritian mechanic from a BMW garage under the Kingsland Viaduct – right in the spot where the new Haggerston Station, with its futuristic orange lettering, now stands. This was JC Motors' original arch. Joe saw something in the young Len and told him to come by if he ever needed a job. So in 1982, Len went to see Joe, and shortly afterwards the two men began a professional relationship that would define their working lives.[6]

Joe was old-fashioned. He passed on to Len his principles: respect the elderly, help the young. Len learned Joe's quirks. When he said: 'Can you pass me that can of red paint?' it meant that he was dealing with a tricky customer. If it was really bad, he'd step it up: 'Len, can you pass the bucket of red paint?'

The two of them made a good team. As Len grew in confidence, Joe suggested they open a car-parts shop off the Kingsland Road. Joe did the paperwork and ran the garage from its original location and Len sold the parts. It was so successful, they took on three more men.

Joe got cancer in the nineties. Len and the customers could see him growing frail, but they feared asking him how he was doing, knowing how much he hated to talk about it. Before he died, Len and Joe agreed that Len should close the parts shop and continue the garage. So he kept servicing cars for generations of the same Hackney families who had been coming to Joe since the beginning. Joe's principles lived on through Len: respect the elderly, help the young.

Len saw babies in their mothers' prams return as adults to ask advice when the time came for their first car. He knew the customers who just wanted a roadworthy vehicle as quickly as possible, no matter the cost, and those who could only afford for him to do the bare minimum. He was always busy, often excusing himself to take a phone call, or dealing with new customers that would drop in, having walked past his business on their way to work or to the shops. But somehow he still had time for everyone.

A framed photograph in his workshop shows Len with his arms stretched wide around three apprentices, each in their blue boiler suits. Three young men with their sleeves rolled up, heads held high. Len had worked with hundreds of young men like this. They were sent to him by their mothers and teachers or they slipped in when they should be at school. Some needed a wash, some were in trouble. Whenever he could, he found them small jobs to do, or offered them apprenticeships or work experience.

Just like Joe taught him, Len taught these young men how to stand up straight and say good morning. He showed them how to position the legs of the lift so the cars wouldn't get damaged. Which tools to use. What the workshop should look like before they leave for the day. Not all of us can go to university, he'd say, and not all of us should. Len saw them all as people – as part of his community in East London – and valued them as he himself felt valued by his customers and his neighbours.

So it was a surprise when, half a decade before the London

Olympics, urban planners designed a new station right through the middle of Joe's garage. In 2006, Transport for London acquired the dormant North London Line and launched a new body, London Overground, to bring neglected stations like Haggerston into a fully orbital network for the capital.[7]

From that moment, Len's world turned upside down. He was told to leave his arch: the place he'd worked in every day, first with Joe Chee, and now with his own staff. He contacted a lawyer to see if he could be so easily evicted. The lawyer said to contact Transport for London's surveyor to try and find somewhere else to move. But as the deadline approached for him to leave his workshop, Len still hadn't heard about alternatives.

Eventually Transport for London offered him Arch 332, just a little way down. He stepped inside. It was an empty shell: no electrics, no fire exit, with a leak in the extension and a spreading patch of damp on the ceiling. He was granted a short period free from rent in exchange for moving out of the original arch.

Painstakingly, he set about re-establishing his business. He put the JC Motors sign out the front and painted the railings blue. He hired contractors to wire the electrics. Rather than complain, he painted over the dark patch in the arched ceiling with white paint, fearing Transport for London might use it as another excuse to condemn the arch and kick him out.

For a decade, every time it rained, water poured through the leak in the extension. Each time, Len and his workers scooped up the water with shovels and buckets. Len always dreamed of what his garage could be: of expanding into other units and taking on a body shop, like he had once with Joe. But after the shock of that eviction, he felt he could never take the risk. What if his landlord came back for him? Not long before we meet, his worst nightmare comes true.[8]

6.2 THE GUILD

In 2015, Transport for London triples Len's rent from £22,000 a year to more than £70,000. Surveyors and business managers come to see Len with their measuring gauges and their official letters and say that's what other businesses are paying. But when Len looks either side of him he sees only empty arches.

Blindsided by the increase, Len starts a petition on Change.org. A customer tells him about an alliance of local businesses called the East End Trades Guild, started several years earlier by a community organizer called Krissie Nicolson. He doubts he has time for committees and meetings with everything else going on. But he feels desperate, so he signs up online and sends his petition to a generic email address. He gets a reply from Krissie, asking if she can come and see him. In his workshop, surrounded by his life's work, she asks him if he's OK. Then, she invites him to come to a meeting with other local businesses. Len's never done anything like this before, but he needs to know he's not alone – and how he can fight back.

Skilled traders and community businesses like Len's are about more than having a friendly face in the neighbourhood. A shortage of skilled workers is already delaying our capacity to generate renewable energy and to update our homes with more efficient ways of heating and cooling. In 2022, analysts found that the UK is short of around 200,000 skilled workers to plug the 400,000 new energy jobs emerging in nuclear, hydrogen and renewables.[9]

Locally, skilled traders are needed to upgrade homes in all kinds of ways, such as installing heat pumps, solar panels and insulation, connecting residences to thermal bore holes and upgrading existing systems. Mechanics, carpenters, plumbers, electricians, heating installers and people who can operate machine tools will all become even more essential to the national labour force, especially those who decide to update their skills to green technologies and retrofit.[10] As well as these specific trades, people need places to learn how to adapt buildings to use less carbon.

In St Austell, South Wales and Birmingham, artists, community groups and activists have figured out that these skills are missing. They are bringing them back through alternative forms of education: workshops, environmental colleges, trade schools and short courses. But what if those skills were never lost? Many mechanics and machinists still exist on the frontiers of Britain's cities. In these unloved arches and industrial estates, skilled tradesmen like Len train the next generation of young apprentices – just as long as they can survive the global forces squeezing them out.

When the traders meet to discuss how to save their premises, they are engaged not just in the fight for their own livelihoods. They are also fighting for the heart of their neighbourhoods: the places that will sustain people when the next crisis comes.

6.3 HOW TO SAVE AN ARCH

One warm Thursday afternoon in May 2017, Len meets members of the East End Trades Guild outside Il Cudega, a deli in a railway arch by London Fields, in a thriving row of independent businesses including a nursery and a print shop. The tenants, many of whom have never met before, push together the circular metal bistro tables and pass around an agenda prepared by Krissie. They take turns to speak, raising their voices to be heard above the chatter of children and the rumble of overground trains.

The traders have similar complaints: leaking arches, rising rent and a sense of being talked down to or pushed around by their landlords. Some, like Len, are in arches owned by TfL. Around half of the traders have leases with Network Rail.

By the time the traders meet outside the deli in 2017, Network Rail is staring down arrears of almost £50 billion. Rumours the government is planning to privatize part of the network have been circulating since 2011, when a change of accounting rules under European Union legislation meant that Network Rail debt would be counted as national debt.

Since the arches are not part of the infrastructure used to run trains, they can be sold off to a private buyer, bringing in cash and getting debt off the government's books. The Network Rail tenants suspect something is up. They compare their latest round of rent rises: some, like Len's, are as steep as 300 per cent. They fear the rises are part of a plan to inflate the value of their arches in preparation for a sale.

It's impossible to know the truth because the two public bodies keep their methodology for working out the market rate a secret. All the tenants have stories of disproportionate rent rises, difficult negotiations and moments of reprieve. But none of the stories – or the figures – are quite the same.

The first thing the Guild members want to do is improve transparency. They keep getting told that their rent increases are 'in line with other similar businesses in the area' – but they have no way of knowing if that is true.

Len rolls the agenda into a tube and rests his chin on one end. He leans forward to hear Nhi Chu, another car mechanic, who has been collecting information on Network Rail tenants' rent rates. 'We're losing industrial businesses,' she says, gesticulating at the others across the metal table tops. 'The other businesses are managing – they can keep going for a while. But if we don't get this – we're dying.'

Krissie gently taps her pen on the papers in front of her, listening carefully. 'It seems to me there are two things we can do,' she says, during a lull in the conversation. 'We can try and change the policy at Network Rail and Transport for London. Or we can try to bring these properties into community ownership, so that in five or ten years' time this doesn't happen again.'

Both are ambitious. But Krissie's ideas are rooted in reality – she knows the power of community organizing. She is the daughter of a Tottenham legend, Reverend Paul Nicolson, who over the course of many decades sent thousands of letters to newspapers as part of his campaign to end poverty through his two organizations: Zacchaeus 2000 Trust and Taxpayers Against Poverty.

Both have continued campaigning since Reverend Paul's death in 2020.[11] Krissie inherited some of her father's tenacity and sense of justice – but she also saw from his work that gains at the neighbourhood level could have global impact. At the turn of the millennium, Reverend Paul commissioned a piece of work for one of his organizations on minimum income standards. This piece of work would form the basis of the Living Wage – an idea born in East London that has travelled the world, setting a new standard for decent pay.

Krissie has organizing in her blood. She has also refined her craft at Queen Mary University, studying community organizing under the geographer Jane Wills. But it was a most unusual small business that got her interested in the way traders can glue together communities: a fifth generation paper-bag seller in the historic market of Spitalfields, East London.

Paul Gardner sold paper and plastic bags and other sundries to small traders and market stallholders, just like his father and his grandfather before him. But the landlord wanted more in rent than he could afford. After reading about him in a blog called *Spitalfields Life*, Krissie met up with Paul to see if she could put the relationship-building skills she was learning at the university to good use. He introduced her to other businesses facing rent spikes in East London. Krissie discovered that these traders, many of whom had deep roots in the city, felt like they had nowhere to turn.

Once, small businesses might have taken problems with untenable rent rises to their local Chambers of Commerce, an organization that emerged in the Victorian era to speak for their collective interests. But in recent decades, Chambers of Commerce have lost a lot of their collective power as members have aged and the nature of business has become more digital and global. Even if the East End traders wanted to join one of these groups, they would struggle. The East London Chamber merged with the London Chamber in 1999, leaving business owners in Hackney and Tower Hamlets with no local organization.

Krissie's idea was inspired by a model that first emerged in the fourteenth century. In medieval times, every trade, from weavers to goldsmiths to wool workers, had their own guild. Krissie's idea for a guild was different: rather than being united by their trade, the businesses came from all industries and found commonality in the challenge of how to survive in the city. She had revived an ancient form of organizing and reimagined it for the future.

In 2012, Krissie co-founded the East End Trades Guild for the small businesses of London. The guild offered a way for these businesses to join together for a low fee – just enough to pay her salary and some organization costs – and low barriers to entry. She created a way for the traders to come together to speak truth to power at a moment when their rent was skyrocketing. It's the very first of its kind, anywhere in the UK – and maybe the world. And it's become the only hope of small businesses facing an existential threat from financial powerhouses way beyond the control of a single government.

In the race for city space, the industrial tenants are struggling. London lost a quarter of its industrial floor space through conversion to other land uses in the decade before 2021, according to an Industrial Land Commission.[12] In inner London the loss is over 40 per cent. In Hackney, where JC Motors is based, two thirds of industrial floor space has been lost, more than anywhere else in London.

The traders are going head to head with a new competitor. It is called 'last mile': the final stage of delivery from a local distribution centre to a customer's home, and it is being fuelled by the rise of online shopping and food apps. Last mile is the latest trend in the logistics sector and it is being backed by global asset managers working on behalf of the pension funds and sovereign wealth funds that are the deepest pools of money in the world. Previously, these kinds of investors preferred retail properties like shopping malls and out-of-town centres. Now, they see the opportunity to make returns in the least likely of spaces: the unloved arches that have for so long been a safe haven for industrial and neighbourhood businesses.

At the deli, back in 2017, the tenants agree on the first option. They will try to convince their landlords to base their rent not on market values but on a different mechanism they call the London Working Rent. Just like Reverend Paul's Living Wage, the London Working Rent will be set in a transparent way, affordable to tenants who have a valuable place in the community. Crucially, they decide to demand security of tenure, which would give them the confidence to invest in their premises and also in their communities. Len dreams of what he could do without the constant pressure of increasing rent and eviction. Fix his roof, for one, and take on some new apprentices. But the traders know Krissie's other option is in the background: to try to take the properties out of the market by owning them outright, as a collective. Two things are about to happen that will make this option the only one. One of the world's most powerful asset managers is about to become the biggest single landlord of British small businesses. Right as that sale goes through, the traders are plunged into a pandemic that – at least temporarily – changes the rules of the game.

6.4 NEW NEIGHBOURS

In the weeks before Christmas 2017, Network Rail makes its shock announcement. It will sell its entire portfolio of railway arches, comprising more than five thousand properties: anything that is not essential for the running of the railway.[13] In the following months, more than one hundred investors express an interest in the portfolio.[14]

In the end, two US investment firms – Goldman Sachs and Blackstone – go head to head. Blackstone wins. By this time, Blackstone is earning a reputation as the world's most powerful landlord, with an annual investment budget of hundreds of billions of dollars – more than the GDP of Switzerland.[15]

The arches sale goes through in February 2019. It is among Blackstone's biggest British real estate investments, symbolizing the advance of US private equity into the UK economy. Overnight, Blackstone and its London partner on the deal, Telereal Trillium, become the biggest small business landlord in Britain, striking fear into the hearts of almost four thousand mechanics, brewers, bakers, hairdressers and gym owners. They are now at the mercy of the largest commercial landlord in history.[16]

Those in favour of privatization see the sale as 'a bet on the economic prospects of Britain' after the catastrophic consequences of Brexit and the long-term decline of the high street.[17] Others see how it will change the nature of cities. Meg Hillier, the politician in charge of Britain's Public Accounts Committee, calls the deal a 'fire sale' in order to plug a debt, and asks the UK's National Audit Office to look into it.

Many tenants first learn about the sale when their rent increases. Network Rail denies the sale and the rent rises are linked, and says all leases will pass unchanged to the new landlord. Then tenants get notice that their new landlord is called Arch Co: a joint venture formed between Blackstone and Telereal Trillium.

Telereal Trillium, which later changes its name to TT Group, is a good strategic partner for Blackstone. At the time of the sale, it's the UK's largest privately owned property company, with a portfolio worth £8 billion. Adam Dakin, managing director of Telereal, denies Arch Co is planning to drive up revenue solely from raising rents. He points out that nine hundred of the arches are vacant, mostly due to their poor condition, and ripe for redevelopment. But the marriage turns out to be one of convenience. TT lends Blackstone credibility in the UK at the critical moment of its arches bid. Within a few years, Blackstone wants full control. In 2025, Blackstone buys out TT Group, becoming sole owner of the portfolio and landlord to thousands of traders.

Since Network Rail was planning £162 million in investment before it sold the portfolio, Blackstone inherits thousands of arches in need of considerable updating. But there's a golden handshake. Network Rail still owns the tracks above many of the arches, so it is on the hook for routine maintenance. The new landlords theoretically have the power to force tenants into structural inspections, for which the British taxpayer must foot the bill.

After the sale goes through, many tenants find themselves in peril. Arch Co tells a florist in south-west London that their rent is going up from £55,000 to £90,000 a year. The accountant in the company pleads for the rent to be tied to its income – a model that becomes popular in the pandemic – but his pleas are ignored.[18]

A tool hire company finds out its rent is trebling, even while the proprietor fights a previous rent review – leaving it on the hook for hundreds of thousands in back payments if he is unsuccessful. 'It would be the beginning of the end,' he tells a journalist, unhappily.[19]

Leni Jones owns a motorcycle workshop in Bethnal Green with her husband Marcus. She learns about the sale after confronting Network Rail when they tell her to pay four times as much on her lease. When she gets the news of the increase, she looks about the beloved arch. It's been the home of their family business for nearly two decades, a place into which they have poured their money and their dreams. More than anyone, she knows its limitations: a dark and difficult industrial space, with a leaky ceiling and gaps where the rats get in at night. A simple Victorian railway arch, down the end of an alley in a compound, with no passing trade.

They've invested as much as they can to make the space habitable, but its construction, its location, is the same as it was when the Victorians built it nearly two hundred years ago. At night, she lies awake wondering how an arch like that could suddenly be worth so much.

Then the pandemic arrives. High streets everywhere fall silent. Shops are shuttered, workers sent home. But not everyone closes the doors when disaster strikes. All across the country, certain small businesses keep trading. Just as nurses, doctors, care workers and police keep working, so too do bakers, nursery workers, grocers, car mechanics and taxi drivers. Even with the threat of eviction hanging over him, Len never misses a day at the garage.

It's on these quiet days that the traders begin to notice some new tenants. They hear new sounds in the streets. The roar of motorbikes. The hum of loitering mopeds. Suddenly, some of the arches are crowded by two-wheeled vehicles. When the tenants investigate, they find nothing but shuttered units. Or open arches filled with rows of metal shelving, bursting with dried goods and household cleaning products.

These are rapid delivery companies, a new generation of online shopping companies whose advantage is speed, with names like Weezy and Zapp. They aim to shave off delivery time by smashing together two separate businesses – supermarkets and delivery drivers – and leasing 'dark' stores, which are not open to the public, in the heart of neighbourhoods – like railway arches and other vacant retail space.

The space itself is at the heart of the business model: it is only possible to deliver goods to buyers in ten minutes if those beers, toilet rolls and teabags are already sitting in little warehouses around every corner. Zapp says the railway arches make perfect sense for its business: they are in densely populated areas of cities, but not too close to residential buildings. They also tend to be the right size and layout to house the two thousand products Zapp stocks.

Weezy, another competitor, starts leasing from Arch Co in December 2020, snapping up arches across the estate as they become available. Their head of property explains that what the arches lack in space, they make up for in location, often in areas where suitable industrial units are scarce.

The deals are typically fast. Weezy brings a checklist of requirements. Arch Co matches a property. Within weeks, leases are signed, the groceries arrive, the shutters come down and the mopeds start squealing. But the pressure on the workers is immense. Delivery drivers were seen as the heroes of the pandemic: the people who kept people's fridges stocked and their families fed when everyone else was forced to stay inside. In 2020, the government added them to the list of key workers in the UK, alongside doctors, nurses and social workers, which meant they could send their children to school in order to stay out on the road.[20] But delivery drivers do not traditionally have anything like the same level of workers' rights as those professions.

A series of investigations showed that Deliveroo drivers in particular can earn as little as £2 an hour during shifts. That's a mere fraction of the minimum wage and even further from the level Krissie's father, Reverend Paul, established as a living wage. Likewise Amazon, where profits increased by 220 per cent after the pandemic in 2021, has been the subject of numerous investigations.[21] [22] The company has short-changed workers on pay cheques and treated them as disposable, replacing them before they got tired or had to be paid more. It has even failed to protect its workers from injury.[23]

But the costs to the fabric of cities is less well documented. The traders talk about how the street used to be an ecosystem of businesses that served the local community – especially essential businesses like garages and nurseries that served healthcare workers, ambulance drivers and local councillors during the pandemic. During the pandemic, residents complain of noise from motorbikes coming to and from the warehouses day and night. The traders collect horror stories of the worst landlord practices: non-disclosure agreements preventing tenants from talking to one another about rental contracts, business owners who died of Covid, only for their families to be pursued for overdue rent.

Within two years of the pandemic, the bubble of speedy grocery companies, hyper-inflated with equity capital, pops. Zapp withdraws from France and the Netherlands and pulls out of major UK cities including Bristol and Manchester, firing staff. Getir, the biggest company operating in the UK, closes down stores and makes layoffs. The rapid delivery companies are on a lifeline of investment, sustained by boosting customer numbers through short-lived promotions. But app data shows that when the promotions stop, app downloads plunge.[24] That leaves family-run businesses facing rent increases based on tenants who were only temporarily able to afford those rates themselves.

The system is rigged against the traders. It becomes clear that the London Mayor cannot control the corporations. It's been several years since the East End Trades Guild set out to obtain a London Working Rent, a campaign that ended up focusing on leases tied to the social value of businesses, alongside security of tenure for community businesses whose premises are leased from Network Rail and Transport for London. They have had many wins, staving off eviction for several members. At the same time, some local authorities in London have attempted to implement social value leases, which offer more affordable rents to childcare providers or businesses that offer apprenticeships, for example. But the interventions remain only at the goodwill of politicians, who are themselves under pressure from the lack of funding for local authorities; and rely on the cooperation of landlords so big that the plight of tenants comes second to making profit. So the Guild members decide to move to plan B: owning the arches outright.

Ever since the Guild began, Krissie and the traders have used their platform to get those in power to consider alternative ownership models. When Network Rail was sold, they got the Hackney mayor to back an idea to bring the arches into the ownership of local authorities rather than selling them to corporate bidders.

In 2024, in the run up to the London mayoral elections, they go one step further, bringing together all that political will to attempt to gain community ownership of premises for businesses in several threatened arches. In a 'Manifesto for the new economy', Guild members set out a plan to own business premises collectively through a community land trust.[25] The trust would operate as a not-for-profit organization, bringing together a broad base of neighbours, business owners, customers and other people who want to share responsibility for the land and what happens there. The trust holds land for the long term and includes a mechanism where rent is tied to income. Any profit is reinvested back into the properties and into the neighbourhood.

By this time, using community organizing and in-person meetings with politicians, the Guild has already got several borough mayors and the London Mayor to agree to the idea of a community land trust. 'The issue is the timeline,' London Mayor Sadiq Khan told the Guild members, when they asked for his help in 2021 to set it up. 'We need to look at the land as we've got to identify the best site.'

Then, in 2023, Transport for London comes for Len's arrears.[26] Through a property company called TTL Properties, Transport for London demands he pays £70,000, or moves to a cheaper arch when his lease expires a few months later. TTL Properties claims Len is the only garage with arrears and that they can't give him special treatment. The Guild knows, because of the work they have done around rent transparency, that that isn't the case.

It's time, Krissie says. It's taken thirteen years for the Guild to get to this point: taking on landlords, fighting for the survival of these tenants. In 2024, with the community support for Len's case, and an election for London Mayor around the corner, Krissie senses a small window of opportunity. They need to seize the moment to create a community land trust for small businesses. It will be a new model for taking premises out of the market and protecting their place in the neighbourhoods for ever.

Suddenly the best site for a community land trust becomes obvious. It's the one right behind that blue door at Arch 332.

6.5 TRUST

Three premises are chosen for the campaign. Len's arch, a music venue attached to an independent brewery called Signature Brew E8, and a yoga and dance studio called TripSpace.[27] For years, landlords have been playing these sorts of businesses off against one another: the old industrial workshops against the more gentrified bars and gyms. Now they are coming together to figure out a way to survive for longer than the length of a lease.

Len, thanks to the strength of his support among customers and his community, wins a reprieve from Transport for London on his rent and arrears for one more year. It passes quickly, the days ticking past in stained overalls and fixed cars. His loyal customers all want to know how he is holding up. I'm still here, he says. Thanks to you. There are no community businesses without community. If our public bodies disrespect businesses that serve local people, then they disrespect the very people that gave them power.

He sounds brave, but he's leaving nothing to chance. Behind the scenes Len and Krissie are hard at work. They start looking for examples of the kind of community land trust to take the properties out of the market and save Len's arch for good. They find two: a Black-owned neighbourhood in Minnesota, in the United States. And a pioneering Latin market right on Len's doorstep, in neighbouring Haringey.

'Nothing about this has been easy,'[28] says Mikeya Griffin from the Rondo Community Land Trust in the city of St Paul, Minnesota, when Len reaches her. Mikeya's roots run deep in Rondo. Her family moved to St Paul in the 1930s and 1940s where they found a solidarity community in the Black-owned neighbourhood of the city.

People in the Rondo tended to own their homes and a stake in local cooperatively owned businesses, like the grocery store and the credit union. Old and young alike participated in the community, where everyone looked after everyone else in circles of care.

Racial discrimination laid the foundations for the close-knit neighbourhood and its embrace of self-care. But that solidarity could not protect the residents from continued discrimination at the hands of those in power, who considered their thriving neighbourhood to be nothing more than a slum.

In the fifties and sixties, the city of St Paul intentionally approved a new highway that sliced through the Rondo,[29] displacing seven hundred households and three hundred businesses. The trauma of displacement has ricocheted through generations of families. By the eighties, the families sought a mechanism to stop this continual erosion. So in 1993, they registered the Rondo as the first community land trust in Minnesota: forming a trust that could take the land from the for-profit, speculative market into shared equity, community ownership and mutual control.[30] Today there are thirteen such community land trusts in Minnesota, holding more than 1,250 homes.

Alongside housing, the Rondo CLT safeguarded properties for small businesses, recognizing the vulnerability of traders and vital enterprise at the hands of those in power.[31] They developed two new buildings on two blighted lots owned by the city of St Paul.[32] They wanted to create workspaces with permanently affordable leases, and apartments on top. It was an uphill struggle, Mikeya says. Getting the city to buy into the vision took many years.

Since completing those two units, the CLT is looking at space on Selby Avenue, Rondo's high street. Once home to family-run doctors, lawyers, grocers and other vital community businesses, Selby Avenue is now getting more expensive as forces of gentrification threaten to displace the Black community once again.

'We're having to work hard to get land on Selby Avenue,' Mikeya says. Three things have become important, she says: knowing who owns what, having capital up front, and their relationships with businesses. Shared ownership is a totally different relationship to the normal landlord–tenant arrangement, one that people have to buy into. It means sharing the risks, but also the rewards.

Mikeya says that equality of opportunities is at the heart of the need for a commercial community land trust. The CLT model emerged from the struggle of African Americans in the sixties. A community organizer called Charles Sherrod witnessed first-hand the evictions of African American families and the mass imprisonments that resulted from non-violent efforts to oppose segregation.

He decided that the only way to get independence and security was for Black people to own the land themselves. 'All power comes from the land,' he noted.[33] This was the origin of the community land trust: an organization that could hold land on behalf of a community in perpetuity.

Len tells Mikeya about his own experience. He knows his public landlord, Transport for London, is not making loads of profit from the arches. The East End Trades Guild has crunched the numbers on Transport for London and discovered that only 1.8 per cent of its balance sheet comes from the railway arches. It doesn't make any sense that they should be squeezing the tenants so hard – not when the wider benefits of Len's business are so broad.

Len works out that he has helped three hundred young people with work experience, apprenticeships and guidance since the nineties. The majority of these young people are, like him, people from racial and ethnic minority groups who might otherwise have struggled with opportunities.

He collects evidence from his past apprentices, including Hakeem Saunders. Hakeem's dad took him round the corner to Len when he was just twelve, to ask if he had any little jobs for Hakeem to do. He went on to be the youngest qualified apprentice in his first job after leaving JC Motors. 'I know I wouldn't have survived university,' Hakeem tells Krissie on the phone one day. 'Small businesses need to stay around to give people opportunities.'[34] But Transport for London doesn't seem to recognize the vital role that Len and his business have played in the neighbourhood, offering opportunities to young people who might not otherwise have anywhere to go. For the landlords, it's all about profit.

'We know our society is built on some folks being able to amass wealth, take advantage of others' labour where others are not,' Mikeya agrees. 'When we are in a consistent state of crisis, of emergency, we're not healthy, we're not well. But the reparative framework that we utilize gets back to when our communities are stable and thriving. Only then can we experience joy.'

'Stability,' Len says, as if turning over the word. 'It will just give us stability.' He knows what it is like to exist in a permanent state of crisis. He scarcely dares imagine how it might feel to be free.

Yet freedom – even joy – is possible. Just around the corner from Len's Hackney arch, in the neighbouring borough of Haringey, a group of Latin traders have tasted freedom. Since the millennium, traders from across the Latin diaspora and beyond have occupied an old department store on Tottenham's High

Road. The Wards Corner building was once the Selfridges of North London until it was bought by Transport for London to make way for the Victoria Line station at Seven Sisters in the seventies. At the turn of the millennium, traders adapted its insides as a market, adding bars, balconies and mezzanines to serve as offices and spaces for their children to do homework and to nap after school. To enter the market in its heyday was to be transported into a self-contained universe of bakeries, butchers, specialist supermarkets and clothes vendors. Everywhere, Spanish could be heard from the stalls and the televisions. Plastic tables spilled into the aisles, on constant rotation of customers eating plates of rich meat casseroles, pastries and rice.

Latin Village, or Pueblito Paisa, as it is locally known, is the largest concentration of Latin traders in the UK – though Ugandan, Ghanaian, Brazilian and other nationalities could be found among the thirty-eight people in the cramped sixty-one units. Since 2004, these traders have been fighting off bulldozers. That year, Haringey Council signed an agreement with Grainger, the UK's largest listed UK property developer by residential properties, to turn the building into 196 flats and a shopping centre.[35]

The news terrified the traders. Each had their own story of coming to the UK and reinventing themselves on the frontiers of society. There was Vicky Alvarez, who came to the UK in 1996 as a refugee from Colombia, fleeing violence that claimed the life of her father. She felt like she was in a movie when she got her first stall at the market selling silver jewellery and jeans. It was the stuff of dreams: a place to have her own business, among her community, while she raised her daughter. In a nearby unit, a DVD shop covered in silver discs was the life's work of Francisco Yunda, who invested all of his retirement money in the stall when he quit his long career as a chef. Next door, Ben Nyerende had invested £75,000 into a successful letting agents business he started after migrating from Uganda. After the traders received news of the eviction, Ben felt sick every day. He feared the community – and their livelihoods – would be wiped out, forcing them to start again from scratch.

But it never happened. For two decades, with extraordinary persistence and bravery, the traders fought back. In 2017 and again in 2019, they secured recognition from the United Nations that plans to demolish the market were incompatible with the state's obligations to protect minorities – and therefore a threat to the traders' human rights.[36] In 2019, the traders took Haringey Council and Transport for London to the High Court over their plans to demolish the market. Even though the court ruled in favour of the developers, the pressure was too much. In 2021, Grainger took the shock decision to withdraw from the scheme. In 2025, the market – which had last traded during the pandemic – reopened in a temporary space right next door. Negotiations started with Transport for London for an affordable lease on the original market – and a plan for its redevelopment.

Len could scarcely believe the story. Here were traders who had succeeded in getting his landlord to back down. When Len asked Vicky how, she told him how the traders had started a community benefit society to take on the market after Grainger left the scheme. The community benefit society meant the traders could develop the market themselves. It offered them strong democratic control, giving every trader a say, and the opportunity to reinvest all profits in their future. And it provided a mechanism to raise investment for the next stage of their community plan: a restored market, designed according to the needs of the traders, with surplus budget for a market manager and administrative support. Eventually, the traders want to take on the upper floors of the department store too, turning them into business units where other people from minority groups can learn trades and test out ideas.

'Your customers would follow you,' Vicky tells Len, when he worries about being displaced from his arch, 'but it's not about that. You are a safety net for the whole community, just by being there. You have their trust.'

6.6 DEMOCRACY ELECTRIFIED

On 12 November 2024, Transport for London evicts Len a second time. In the two weeks before he has to hand back the keys, his customers and fellow Guild members rally around him. They help him move cars, sell parts and give away bikes, desks and even bricks. Every time, the helpers bring food – huge Pyrex dishes of barbecue chicken and rice, curries and spring rolls, burgers, sausages, cans of fizzy drinks. A spirit of camaraderie takes over. Len feels, more than ever, that the forces evicting him are measuring square footage instead of what really matters: the joy and the trust he has cultivated across four decades of service in his neighbourhood.

He moves to Leyton, to share premises with one of his customers: a van hire firm and a previous victim of eviction at the hands of Blackstone and Arch Co. The van company's old premises in London Fields still sit empty a year later. No one moves into Len's arch after his eviction. Eight months later it sits shuttered and empty, litter gathering behind the blue bars. Two loyal, local businesses, displaced for nothing.

With staggering inevitability, by the following Easter, Transport for London come for another business in the Guild. This time it's the turn of TripSpace, the yoga studio that works with the elderly and those on low incomes. TripSpace have been campaigning with Len for the community land trust. But now their very existence is threatened. They scramble to crowdfund £20,000 towards an unexpected deposit increase, buying a bit more time. But they all know the reprieve is temporary.

Behind the scenes, the Guild members stay focused on the plan to own their arches for the good of the community. They register a community benefit society, just like the Latin traders before them. Len becomes the founding director. They organize a round table with the deputy London mayors to make a case for community ownership, and prepare ideas for potential sites. And they keep showing up to public meetings like Mayor's Question Time, putting their plight on the agenda of the city's powerful.

Zoom out and what you see here is democracy in action. The Guild, under Krissie's guidance, uses all kinds of democratic means to advance their cause. Before the London elections, Guild members run voter registration drives, encouraging people to check where local candidates stand on the issues that matter to small businesses.[37] They know connections to supportive politicians are a vital part of any community campaign.

But they also recognize the limitations of this kind of democracy. Way back in 1762, the French philosopher Jean-Jacques Rousseau understood that British democracy was a kind of farce, exercised only during elections. Rousseau wrote, 'The English people believe themselves to be free; they are gravely mistaken; they are only free during the election of Members of Parliament; as soon as the Members are elected, the people are enslaved.'

The Guild is trying to change this by practising democracy of a different kind. By drawing people around Len – by politicizing the business decision to kick him out of his arch – the East End Trades Guild is electrifying the local systems of democracy by which the future of the city is decided. The Guild is saying: we have this ability to hold our elected officials and our public bodies to account. It is our best hope against the gigantic forces of global capital that will chew through the sinews of our neighbourhoods, spitting out empty remains. Let's each use our voice and collectively figure out how to fight back.

Before every election, the Guild agrees its manifesto: a short document setting out its aims. Then it hosts an accountability assembly – a meeting for its members and supporters – and invites the candidates most likely to win: the future mayors of London and its boroughs. There, the members of the Guild ask the politicians, in front of hundreds of their constituents, to commit to their manifesto. First, to transfer the ownership of land to the Guild's community land trust so that it can own the premises and set rent at an affordable level for ever. Then, to commit to social value leases that recognize the value of businesses that serve the community. Finally, they want regular meetings to hold the elected politicians to account.

Accountability assemblies are one tool used by community organizers like Krissie to grow the collective power of the people. Community organizing is not new. It has roots in the civil rights and trade union movements. But it is being used by the Guild to jump-start tired elected democracies: political systems where real people only have a say every four or five years. Representative democracy has shown itself to be short-termist, victim to corporate lobbying, and susceptible to the cult of personalities, who perform well on camera but flop when it comes to fair governance.

At a moment of ecological emergency, a community organizing approach like the one practised by the Guild offers something different. A chance to come together to work on potential solutions for an issue at hand, whether that be river pollution or water shortages, untenably high rent for small businesses or the lack of skilled apprenticeships for young people.

The historian Roman Krznaric has studied ancient and modern systems of governance, from fourth-century Athens to the Rhaetian Free State of the Napoleonic era, to Igbo governance in Nigeria and the autonomous governments of Rojava in post-war Syria. He says democracy has always had an issue with time, since elected politicians deal with the needs of the present, with no incentive to act in the interests of future generations.[38] He advocates for a different kind of assembly – a citizens' assembly – to embed accountability into democratic systems. Extinction Rebellion, or XR, the non-violent environmental movement that is at the heart of activities to address climate breakdown in the UK, has citizens' assemblies as one of its three key demands.[39] XR believes citizens' assemblies are as important in the fight against climate breakdown as reducing carbon emissions to net zero. A citizens' assembly brings together a cross-section of society to decide, in a truly democratic way, the trade-offs and compromises necessary as we navigate huge changes to the way society works in light of the changing climate.

Krznaric says this method of decision-making has enormous potential. He suggests juries for more than just criminal law. Bodies of citizens to uphold the interests of the public beyond the climate question. Electoral fundamentalism, he writes, needs to become a relic of the past: 'If we really wanted to deal with a civilizational threat such as the electoral emergency, is this the political system we would freely choose and feel confident in?'[40]

The East End Trades Guild, with its assemblies to give everyone a voice and its commitment to holding politicians to account in between elections, offers another alternative and a model for way more than just small businesses. It's a reimagining of democracy at a moment when political extremists are keen to point out the system's weaknesses in order to erode faith in elections. Len and the Guild may only be at the beginning of their long battle for justice under the arches. But like Civic Square in Birmingham, their process – their model – is as important as the milestones along the way.

7

HIGH STREET

Plymouth

'The next big thing will be a lot of small things.'

—Thomas Lommée[1]

7.1 A STREET YOU KNOW LIKE THE BACK OF YOUR HAND

One bright, windy day in September 2023, I stand with Hannah Sloggett on the roof of a derelict Art Deco theatre called the Millennium Building in Plymouth. A strong, salty wind blows in from the ocean, making me think of sailors and stories in this historic naval town. Below us, Union Street stretches from the docks in Devonport to the city in the east. We are in the neighbourhood of Stonehouse, once the heart of Plymouth nightlife, where sailors stumbled from their ships to visit the countless pubs and bars of Union Street as they travelled, sodden and free, back to life on land.

Hannah can draw the street with her eyes closed. The spot where her husband Roland opened his antiques shop, full of modernist treasures. The place where his great-grandfather Jack ran a pawn shop and a jewellers, generations before. The Majestic, which would later become the Millennium Building, where Hannah's father, an apprentice on the docks, plucked up the courage to talk to a pretty girl on the dance floor: the woman who would become her mother. And the bars and the clubs Hannah herself went to when she was barely eighteen in the nineties, in platform shoes and blue eyeshadow. So much of it was gone now: pubs demolished, clubs closed down. The Palace

Theatre, with its handsome brown-tiled facade, shuttered for two decades. The glory days were over, replaced by burned-out stores and shady corners you'd hurry past at night.

Once the Millennium Building was among the wreckage. This beautiful Art Deco cinema had stumbled through the decades in various guises until being left to rot. Then Hannah and her friend Wendy Hart came along. The two had met at Stonehouse Action, a volunteer residents' group. They loved Stonehouse – Hannah with her generational attachments to Union Street and Wendy as a transplant from Liverpool, feeling the same sense of community and togetherness she remembered from her home town. They had both been drawn to jobs that reflected their love of buildings and people. Hannah was a neighbourhood planner for Plymouth City Council and Wendy worked for a local housing association. But over time they began to get frustrated with the limited impact they could have on Union Street in their day jobs.

One day, Wendy and Hannah bit the bullet and registered a community business called Nudge. It became an entity to hold buildings while they renovated them and opened them up to the public. And that's how I came to be standing on the top of the Millennium Building with Hannah, talking about her plans for a terrace overlooking the whole street.

Plymouth is a coastal town: home to the largest naval base in Europe; famed for being the place where the Puritans set sail for America on the *Mayflower* in 1620. These days its proximity to the ocean is causing a headache for the council. As the climate gets wetter and the sea level rises, saltwater and rainwater will start to overwhelm the drains. Plymouth has a single sewer for both surface water from the roads and wastewater from toilets.

When that sewer becomes full, the floodgates are opened and the raw waste flows directly into the sea, with unquantifiable devastation on water quality and biodiversity.[2]

Above ground, the effects are just as bad. Stonehouse, the neighbourhood Union Street runs through, has the highest number of buildings at risk from tidal flooding in the city.[3] Union Street is particularly vulnerable. It appears on the flood maps as a kind of bowl, trapping rainwater.[4] Already, residents are used to seeing the puddles turn into streams. I can see this from the rooftop – the way the water would run down the steep slope of the dual carriageway called the Western Approach and get stuck at the roundabout by the Millennium Building, spilling into the nearby streets.

With enough money, there are solutions. Just below Union Street, the old Bath Street has been turned into the state-of-the-art Millbay Boulevard. The council has installed a 'sustainable urban drainage' system capable of holding 240 tonnes of water – equal in volume to seven standard shipping containers – and an urban park sustained by the water held above.[5] But Union Street has none of this. And it is also grappling with some of the worst health outcomes in the country. People in Stonehouse live on average seven and a half years less than the average person in the UK.[6]

By the time I visit in 2023, a local MP has been pleading for a health centre – a kind of gigantic doctor's surgery – for half a decade. The surgery that the MP was registered at had closed down, along with many others across Plymouth. One of the remaining existing surgeries that was due to get more space for patients in the new supersize health centre was so run down it had been the subject of a *Panorama* investigation.[7] People in

Plymouth simply couldn't find a doctor to treat them. The NHS promised to fund the new centre – then when that fell through, the council offered to loan the NHS the money.[8] The NHS said it wouldn't be able to pay back the loan.

The MP went to Westminster, cap in hand, to beg for money for the 'super health hub' on the site of a car park, in Stonehouse.[9] He described a part of the country with 'extreme levels of poverty and deprivation'. A third of private-rented homes in Stonehouse are classed as non-decent by the Ministry of Housing. Children's grades are a third lower than elsewhere in the city.

'Health problems are exacerbated by poverty,' the MP said. And so too was the pressure on local services. One-fifth of the local hospital's emergency admissions came from these few streets known as Stonehouse. Health, he believed, deserved a place at the heart of the high street. It could be a way to revive and repurpose the city centre. But the begging was in vain. The funding never came. The site sat empty for years. The car park turned to rubble behind a navy-blue hoarding running parallel with the road.[10] I walked past it every time I visited Union Street, wondering what people did instead to get doctors' appointments. How many did without.

People in poor housing and with fewer means are less able to prepare for climate events like flooding, which can itself cause illnesses, whether from waterborne disease or anxiety and trauma. Preventing these kinds of disaster spirals will need more than one giant health centre, or one street with a new floodwater system. It simply costs too much to train the doctors, build the hospitals and dig up half the city to install new drains.

But Hannah and Wendy had a better idea of how to mitigate the worst excesses of climate change and health inequalities in Plymouth. The twin problems turned out to have the same solution: helping people to feel like they could do something themselves. It's a solution that Wendy and Hannah had been practising ever since they started working together on the street.

7.2 UNION CORNER

In 2014, Union Corner became Hannah and Wendy's first derelict premises on Union Street. Back then, it was an old shop that had been empty since the eighties. The side of the building was covered over in black plastic and held up with unsightly metal trusses after its neighbour had burned down. Vegetation crept up peeling green boards, threatening to overwhelm the plot entirely.

The unit next door was home to a strip club. Wendy winced when her daughter asked what went on inside the blackened windows. She saw how one derelict shop affected the whole street, but she never imagined she might be able to do something about it. At that time, she was into putting on events. Every year since 2009, Wendy and Hannah and a group of local volunteers had hosted an annual celebration on Union Street, with music, fancy dress, circus acts, food and games. The first year, they simply sat on a street corner with some bags of shopping and some stuff from the scrap store, inviting people to join them in some crafting and some snacks.[11] Each year it got more ambitious, until the council even gave them permission to close part of Union Street – one of the busiest through routes in the city.

Something happened at those street parties. People stopped trudging along Union Street avoiding eye contact with one another. They started to look up at the buildings and ask questions about why so many were boarded up. So Wendy and Hannah started to put up photography on the windows and walls of the buildings. They adorned some of the facades with flowers made at the street parties out of old rags, and covered one with charity shop jumpers, repurposed by a local student. Small, cheerful interventions to brighten up the outsides. Until eventually, they plucked up the courage to take on one of the buildings themselves.

At first, it was almost too easy. To their surprise, the owner of the old shop was delighted that someone wanted to do something with his empty property after so long. He offered them the keys for free, with an agreement that they would start paying rent after two years. But that's where the easy part ends. They had no money, the shop was a mess, and they didn't really know how they could use it. So the volunteers from Stonehouse Action decided to ask their neighbours. They hosted parties and used the opportunity to talk to local people about what they wanted to see. They started to make a plan for a meeting place and a garden where people could test their business ideas, make things and sit together.

Then there was the building. It was stuffed to the rafters with junk and grime, including the late discovery of enough asbestos to fill several carrier bags. It needed insulation and new doors. Even the electrics needed replacing. And there was the issue of funding it all. Initially, several organizations seemed interested in helping to fund the renovation of the building. But after months of engagement, all their leads went cold.

The volunteers knew it would take months to win a grant. Terrified of raising people's hopes for nothing, like so many other initiatives that had passed through the area, they knew they needed to get the building open quickly. So they landed on crowdfunding. Plymouth City Council, suffering from massive cuts to its central government grant, was experimenting with a new kind of civic crowdfunding, supporting volunteer and community groups to run campaigns. It invested £60,000 from its community infrastructure levy, a tax paid by developers, and invited any project with a Plymouth postcode to apply. Before the council would contribute, projects had to reach 25 per cent of their target through crowdfunding. Within twelve months, Crowdfund Plymouth raised over £430,000 for more than a hundred projects in the city, from TruVision, virtual reality for architecture, to Collings Park Trust, a community garden.[12] Almost two thirds of the 4,550 project backers in the first year said they were motivated by the fact that Plymouth City Council would also back the project.

Hannah and Wendy needed £10,000 to start the renovations at Union Corner, and they set a deadline of twenty-eight days to find it. Then they set out on foot to visit local businesses and to ask them to pledge, with surprising results. One day, Wendy found herself in front of a businessman from a local plating manufacturer, who grilled her for twenty minutes on their plans for the buildings. She thought it was a bit much, seeing as she only asked for £20. But within half an hour, the businessman had pledged £1,000. In return, he was promised the name of his business on the front of the shop: a permanent reminder of the generosity of local traders who had made the project possible.

Crowdfunding turned out to be full of such moments, circling between despair and then sudden joy when money appeared from places where they had least expected it. The process was stressful, but it also felt like they were able to really gauge the public response to what they were trying to do.

The twenty-eight days ended with an auction in a pub, with offerings including a felt-making workshop from a local artist. In the end, it was a simple pub game in which people threw pound coins at a port bottle over the bar that pushed the volunteers over their target. Some 135 people and local businesses contributed.

Crowdfunding made Wendy realize that many other people felt invested in the idea of change. With each donation, even as small as £5, she felt people were giving her not just their cash but their trust and their love. It felt like a big responsibility. One that she did not want to mess up.

7.3 IMAGINATION

Four years after that successful campaign, Hannah leads me through the side of what is now Union Corner. The old boards are gone, replaced with an urban garden. The units that once belonged to the strip club and the porn shop down the alleyway have changed hands. No one can say whether the businesses left because of the work on the corner, but the effects are dramatic to everyone. The alley feels clean and safe.

Inside, Union Corner is buzzing with the soup kitchen.

Aside from a counter at one end, the tables have been arranged into long lines, full of people chatting over hot minestrone and hunks of bread. The walls are covered in simple cork and the ceiling hung with different lampshades. A hotchpotch of salvaged and recycled materials.

Hannah and I queue for our soup and sit down with the regular guests. Among the chatter and the warmth, she explains how she and Wendy work hard to keep the building open for activities for local people, like the soup kitchen, rather than for groups hosted by and for people from further afield. This is the first step in what they call nudging people: making the space available for them to explore their own ideas. Often, people in Stonehouse mentioned to Hannah or Wendy in passing that they had always wanted to host a group, or start something themselves, but they never had the means or the confidence. At that moment, Hannah and Wendy would, in their own words, 'wrap around them', helping them find the will and the resources to finally realize their dream.

Wendy and Hannah have tried all sorts of things to make it easy for people to get involved on Union Street – the kind of 'multiple entry points' I had also heard described by Immy Kaur in Birmingham. They made Union Corner available to hire to local people for just £5 an hour. If that seemed too much, they encouraged people to test out ideas at regular street markets. As they expanded into other buildings on the street, the market grew in importance as a place to try out ideas, from massage to craft to selling soaps or pickles. A market stall had no risk, just the hire for the day. That was the opportunity.

The confidence was a little trickier to instil. There was the promise of a cup of tea. Usually a biscuit. A setting, in other words, where people could feel at home. Wendy described it to me as 'a gentle nudging' for people to pursue their dreams. Above all, they wanted it to be fun.

The work had a surprising outcome. By creating a safe place where people could try something new and hopeful, Wendy and Hannah were helping people to feel better about their lives. As people embarked on some kind of communal activity, whether that was making soup for the soup kitchen or running their own group, they were able to pay that good feeling forward, with a knock-on effect on the neighbourhood.

Wendy spent a whole year with one woman, building up her confidence to start a group for people with anxiety and depression. Eventually, the woman was able to apply for some funding and the group was instantly well attended. Within a year, they had stopped three planned suicides.

Activities like these, which nurture our capacity to make decisions and to imagine a different future, have a positive impact on our health. During the austerity project of the Conservative government between 2010 and 2020, public services were cut and whole communities went into spirals of decline. People were starved of youth clubs, carers, bus routes, libraries. They became isolated and lonely. This had a deepened impact on the health of our children and those of working age when the pandemic hit. In 2024, the number of children being referred to NHS mental health services reached its highest level ever recorded.[13] The number of people out of work because of ill health across the UK rose to a record high of three million by 2024. The mental health crisis has been compounded by constant bad news. Climate breakdown has filled screens and timelines with flooding, heatwaves, wildfires and storm damage where it sits alongside an ever-present cost of living crisis and graphic scenes from war zones. Despair seems like a reasonable response.

But fear, in destroying our curiosity and playfulness, also destroys our ability to imagine something better. Instead we become prey to populist narratives about taking back control from imagined enemies. Donald Trump found support in the former Rust Belt states, where the retreat of industry has led to a rise in 'deaths of despair' from suicide, alcohol and drugs. Brexit votes were at their highest in the UK's poorest regions – not least its coastal neighbourhoods.

Wendy and Hannah's personal, piecemeal approach is about repairing people's ability to imagine their lives and their streets otherwise. It's a project that will become even more important as climate breakdown intensifies. In his book *Drawdown*, Paul Hawken writes that the only way to avoid the worst forecasts and to rebuild the way the world works will be by successfully rallying our imagination.[14] We are going to need our imaginations to adapt to climate change, whether that is inventing new ways to live with flooding, finding new ways to care for the most vulnerable in our communities or experimenting with different ways to grow food.

Eventually, this capacity will become more vital than even the most advanced technological solutions to climate breakdown. The climate will never stop changing. Therefore our adaptability – our capacity to care for one another and to constantly reinvent the ways in which we live – will become the most important measure of our survival.

Because they draw ideas from the people in their neighbourhood rather than imposing their own, Nudge nurture experimentation and adaptability in all these ways. Whenever they take on a new building, they wait to see what uses present themselves. After they discovered Stonehouse had a dispro-portionate population of single parents, they built affordable apartments that were suitable for children to stay in over-night. From one of their front-of-house staff, they learned that young people leaving care were often turfed out of temporary accommodation as soon as they found employment. So they started to work with a local organization to develop accom-modation for children leaving care that would offer stability while they made the transition to work. When local young people told them they wanted to learn skills for the future, they gave space to businesses experimenting with preserving food in jars, sprouting edible mushrooms in dark basements, and growing salad and micro-greens over pools of water indoors. Technological skills for growing edible food in urban environ-ments, for teenagers who might not have their own garden.

As Wendy and Hannah took on ever more complicated and ambitious buildings on Union Street to make space for people's ideas, they began to draft their own guidelines for reimagin-ing neighbourhoods in this way. The elements were there, right from the start. First, they invited people to spend time together at parties and festivals. Later, they commissioned artists to make everything from street photography to massive murals on the sides of buildings. They created a sense of anticipation, making the street feel alive and welcoming.

Then it was about creating opportunities and getting out of the way. Not prescribing or extracting but creating the conditions in which people could figure something out for themselves. Building on what Union Street had, both in people and buildings. Even the most unlikely people and buildings in the worst state of repair.

It was the complete opposite to the way they had worked in their jobs at the council and the housing association. These kinds of organizations might spend thousands on consultants to come up with ideas and plans. Long-term planning had its place, but half the time, like with the giant health centre, the funding would disappear and all the planning would come to nothing. Or, because the authorities acted with such broad brushstrokes, their plans would have unforeseen consequences on the people they were supposed to help. Wendy and Hannah saw a place for more adaptable, iterative planning where results were felt more quickly.

Master planning is written into the boulevards of Plymouth. It was one of the most heavily bombed cities in the UK during the Second World War. In the aftermath of the devastation, planners reimagined the city around Armada Way, the Main Street of Plymouth's city centre. Architects lauded the scheme, while locals talked of a 'concrete jungle'.[15]

The post-war planners had good intentions, but they were able to act with little or no regard for the communities they replaced – especially some of the poorest communities, regarded by those in power to be little more than slum-dwellers.[16] When Wendy and Hannah first started working with their volunteer group Stonehouse Action in 2009, people were still recovering from housing regeneration policies. A master plan for North Prospect in Plymouth saw whole streets torn down and replaced.[17] Master plans usually start with the ideas of those in power, who then impose those ideas on ordinary people. Architects and planners come up with proposals for a parcel of land that prescribe the way it will be used, from offices to car parks to homes.

Nudge did the opposite. First they rescued an old building at risk of further dereliction, then they figured out what would go in it by talking to people about what they needed. They did everything with a sense of fun. Most of all, they never imposed their ideas. They earned people's trust.

But there was a problem. The council and the government agencies and the reporters and all the people with power failed to understand this way of working. Newspaper journalists remarked on Hannah and Wendy's colourful boots and playful jewellery, making them sound like amateurs. Councillors, even as their respect for Nudge's transformative methods grew, still asked for the ideas to be translated into 'our language'.

Wendy and Hannah didn't want to do that. They had come up with their ways of doing things precisely because the old ways weren't working for Union Street. Union Street had been destroyed by cold master plans. Its repair would be fashioned by the opposite: Nudge's mistress plan.

7.4 THE MISTRESS PLAN

As Wendy and Hannah nudged more and more buildings on Union Street, private landlords began to take an interest – starting with Nudge's own landlord at Union Corner. When he saw how the street was changing, he put up the rent in some of his other properties.

It was a wake-up call. Hannah and Wendy realized they needed to own the buildings outright to protect the area from some of the more extractive ways of making money from property. They began to worry about the broader impact of brightening up the street. What if they kick-started gentrification that displaced the very people they were trying to support?

On the flip side, if they did everything with grants and charity, they created a culture of dependency that did not allow people to flourish. They needed to find a balance. Like all the communities I have met over the last ten years, they did not want to – and could not – do all the work themselves. They needed the mix of foundation support, council buy-in, private interest and local people's knowledge and ideas. The modern way of handing power to a private investor had scrambled the balance. Nudge's mistress plan was about getting it back.

So they laid down a set of conditions, rather than outcomes. In a world focused on results, they focused on the process. That process was about collaboration and feelings rather than power and rules. It was about responding to the needs of the present in an incremental – or piecemeal – way. And that made it highly adaptable in the case of instability or crisis, unlike master plans with decades-long time horizons, strict rules and fixed outcomes.

In April, 2024, Hannah and Wendy presented a draft of their mistress plan to the people of Union Corner. They threw open the doors to one of the buildings and filled it with 3D maps and display boards, showing what had been done and asking for ideas for what was to come.

They invited people to put Post-its on a Union Street map showing how the street made them feel: the places where they still felt unsafe or the parts they loved to spend time in. They presented diagrams of crime rates and flooding risk, emboldening residents with evidence. As part of their mistress planning, Wendy and Hannah had crunched the data on every single building on the street: who owned it, what they were doing with it and how much it was worth. The mistress plan might be about feelings, but it was also about data – and using collective wisdom to make sense of it.

Crammed into the front of the building, people crowded round Hannah and Wendy, some on chairs and some sitting on the parquet floor. The window was busy with the joyful remnants of past events: a stuffed woodpecker, a globe made of cocktail umbrellas, a picture frame containing the word 'hope'.

'The beauty of this plan is that anyone can contribute,' Wendy said. 'But with the benefit of hindsight, we have been able to plot some important things.'

First, she said, a mistress plan is about **building a feeling of community**. Lower the boundaries, fit in with other things that are happening, make small interventions like pictures in windows or cleaning up litter. 'Be angry,' Wendy implored, 'about how our community is held back by judgement.' Just starting to do something is valuable, she added, even if it feels small, especially in places where dereliction has taken root.

Two, don't worry about having all the answers at the start – and try to remain adaptable. **Create a street of opportunity**. 'A ten-year plan in place actually holds a lot of change back,' Hannah said. 'This is more about how we work together, how we bring money into an area, how we collaborate to understand change and how we feel about it.'

Three, **invest in vacant buildings and sites**. Even small investments, like the £10,000 they had crowdfunded to transform Union Corner, had a huge knock-on effect about how people felt on the street.

Four, make Union Street **a street you want to spend time on**. Nudge discovered that local homes were among the top 20 per cent most overcrowded in the country, while 90 per cent of residents along Union Street had no gardens or public space. They wanted to make Union Street a vibrant social place, where people felt safe to meet and linger. On a big purple billboard in the back of the Plot, Nudge called on residents and volunteers to identify spaces along the street for art, music, creativity and surprise. Nudge offered to provide infrastructure like lighting and electricity supply, and reduce barriers like insurance and permissions, to help people realize their ideas.

Five, **cherish our heritage**, not just by preserving historic buildings, but by holding collective memories and stories. Union Street was full of stories: of the club nights at the Millennium Building, of the parties at the C103 nightclub, of the old shops and family connections. At the annual Union Street party, Nudge turned a doorway into a 'Museum Of Here' full of found treasures and photos from the buildings they were renovating.

Six, **build our local wealth**. Nudge set out to own the buildings, so that once debts were repaid, the buildings could generate surplus from rent and other activities to circulate in the street and invest in the next project. In every building, they employed local people and gave entrepreneurs business opportunities like space, support and investment.

Seven, Nudge made Union Street **a street for walking**: safe, clean and friendly.

Eight, they planned to **reuse and to use less**. It was a philosophy that started with the promise to improve the existing buildings, and extended to what went in them, prioritizing regenerative businesses that did not rely on extraction to create wealth.

And finally, they promised to **collaborate and take risks together**. 'Doing nothing is not an option,' Hannah wrote on one of the billboards in the back of the Plot. 'The "normal" and "proper" ways of operating have not served our community well.' If everyone gave themselves permission to make a small change, that would create some big shifts.

These are the nine conditions. Loose, ever-changing, just like Nudge and its work. They appealed to feelings: asking people to be angry, to care more, to tune into how changes sit with them. Far from trying to talk like traditional developers to win favour with the council and potential investors, Wendy and Hannah have doubled down on the things that make them different.

In one blog, they tried to define the way that feelings drive them. 'We are angry,' they wrote, about the power structures that had held Union Street in a state of steady decline for so long. 'We trust our instincts,' as residents, parents and volunteers, they said, describing a way of using their experiences and their local knowledge to make decisions, rather than slavishly following cookie-cutter models or the pursuit of profit. 'We recognize whole people,' they said, promising to flex around people's needs and interests, rather than imposing ideas from above. 'There will always be space for whoever comes along.'

Like Onion Collective in Watchet, Nudge's plan builds on the work of scholars like the economists J. K. Gibson-Graham, the shared pen name of Julie Graham and Katherine Gibson, who recognized the economic value of unpaid work with a diagram of an iceberg. J. K. Gibson-Graham used the iceberg[18] to represent the economy. Under the waterline – hidden from view – they imagined all the unpaid work that is necessary for capitalist societies to function, including the care work that goes on in schools, by retired people, between friends, by volunteers, and in the neighbourhood. On a high street like Union Street, the care work that typically goes unrecognized under the waterline of the iceberg is incorporated into the business model – it is made visible and celebrated.

In Plymouth, this work of caring and listening has brought economic benefits. Almost 90 per cent of the money Nudge spent in the financial year ending 2023 went into the local economy – defined as within a mile of Union Street. They've created jobs, supported businesses and let homes. But this kind of development is also an important model as the UK faces increasing political division in communities, at a time when climate change is creating new and unforeseen challenges. Elinor Ostrom, the Nobel-prize-winning economist whose idea of the commons inspired the Hastings Commons, has explored the way that self-governing communities are better than top-down institutions at resolving conflict and social problems.[19]

Climate breakdown will be fraught with all kinds of social problems and conflicts. Hurricane Sandy, which hit New York in 2012, revealed that social isolation could be deadly. In her 2014 book *This Changes Everything*, Naomi Klein found that it was 'the people who did not know their neighbours, or who were frightened of them, who were most at risk'.[20] The mistress plan is more than a friendly alternative to top-down change. As extreme weather events become more common, this kind of neighbourhood model may become a matter of life and death.

7.5 REGENERATIVE NEIGHBOURHOODS

In a world of rising temperatures and frequent flooding, a high street needs to hold more than just chain stores. It might include gathering places, described as 'lifescapes' defined by Lucy Easthope.[21] These include communal spaces where people can shelter in times of disaster and gather together to heal afterwards, like pubs, shops, mosques, scout huts and art galleries.

They might include regenerative businesses, like repair cafes where people get help fixing appliances, second-hand stores where unwanted goods can be circulated and refill shops where customers can get packaging-free products, from soap to cereal. They should include green spaces and trees for shade. And local businesses committed to sourcing locally, reducing the amount of carbon used for shipping and transporting.

It sounds idyllic, but many of us are familiar with these kinds of high streets in gentrified areas, with their mix of expensive delis, bakeries, bars and studios. In the not-so-distant past, most town centres used to be a mix of residential, small-scale commercial and non-commercial spaces, like churches and libraries.

These different types of space allowed for a spectrum of different uses. Some were free to enter. Some supported local businesses and circulated local money. Some were home to residents who cared for the streets after commercial hours. But nearly all those activities depended on low rent. As property prices were forced upwards, the smallholders and the family businesses were priced out. In came chains with bigger pockets and their eye on returns for the benefit of shareholders, sometimes at the expense of the vibrancy of the town.

After the Second World War, as this trend intensified, observers began to talk about 'death by development' along the high street, which went dark outside of trading hours. Those dying high streets weren't just in poorer areas. Between 2015 and 2023, the one hundred towns in England that experienced the greatest increase in properties that had been vacant for more than three years included both Rotherham in South Yorkshire, where vacancy rates were already historically high, and Richmond in North Yorkshire, an affluent, mostly rural area, according to research by Power to Change.[22]

When smaller-scale, locally owned stores are priced out in favour of chain shops and big stores, the kind of jobs available change too. Chain stores tend to offer low-skilled, low-paid jobs, often on zero-hours contracts. They intentionally cut the number of employees with the use of technology like mobile self-checkouts, cleaning robots and robot-powered warehouses.

Chain stores extract profit from the local population and move that money out of the area, in contrast to community-rooted businesses, which have been shown to offer apprenticeships, stronger personal relationships with customers and to circulate profits in the local economy. Just like Len Maloney, the Hackney mechanic, who mentored and trained hundreds of young people from his humble railway arch.

On Union Street, Hannah and Wendy wanted to cultivate a mix of enterprises that reflected the lives and hopes of the people of Stonehouse. After the success of Union Corner, Nudge bought a derelict pub called the Clipper. When I visited on a chilly week in March 2020, I saw the change to the old pub from halfway down the street. It had been adorned in geometric murals – the first sign that Wendy and Hannah were making improvements. It had become their policy to brighten up the exterior of a derelict building as soon as they got the keys. It was about making instant change when so many other buildings sat sad and empty for years. By splashing colour and art on the facades, Nudge were calling time on a culture of abandonment and decay and drawing people's attention to a building that had previously been invisible, as if to ask: what's next?

It was lunchtime and the old pub was full of people stopping by for vegan tacos at No Whey, the food startup Nudge was incubating on the ground floor. No Whey belongs to Fiona Graham and her business partner, who were both still on benefits as they tried to get the business off the ground. Fiona was coming out of a period of ill mental health. She had been a stay-at-home mum, struggling for money but feeling she was unemployable. She found her way to The Prince's Trust, a charity that helps young people get back into work. She was offered some training and ended up on a Master's course for entrepreneurship. The non-hierarchical nature of working with Nudge had been amazing for her mental health, Fiona said. She felt supported, encouraged and capable of achieving what she wanted to do. 'I have a network of friends and people I can talk to,' she said. 'I feel like I have integrated into a community.'

I tucked into my tacos as we talked, crunching through colourful cabbage and carrot slaw and succulent spicy jackfruit. Fiona said it felt great to be with Nudge at what felt like the start of something exciting. 'This is what we want to protect,' she said, feverishly, talking about Nudge as if it belonged to her – which of course it did. 'We want to expand on the heart of what the community already has; we don't want to gentrify the area.'

After lunch, I walked down to the Plot, then called Plot 34. Nudge signed a ten-year lease on this old furniture shop in 2019. They weren't in a position to buy the building outright – but at the very least, they thought owning the lease would stop it being passed from one speculator to the next as it deteriorated inside. They covered the exterior with colourful geometric shapes. Inside, the building had been stripped and painted white. It was absolutely massive – much bigger than anything Nudge had taken on before. Nudge decided to divide it up, and landed on the idea for an 'allotment' of businesses – or an alternative shopping arcade. They wanted to create a place where entrepreneurs like Fiona could grow their ideas and cross-pollinate with others.

Nudge commissioned an artist to work with the community to make flowers out of paper in neon shades – the first produce from their allotment. The flowers were installed above the doorway around huge block green letters spelling the word 'grow'.

The holes in the ceiling were filled with massive craft paper in the shape of carrots and spring onions. It was a joyful, playful take on the reality of taking on empty spaces: pulling down parts of it, filling holes. Putting in toilets and running water. Fitting the electrics. The shop floor ran deep into the building, opening on to another street on the other side. It would be perfect for an arcade, just as long as they could open up the back doors and create a natural flow of people through to the front.

The only problem was making it warm. So, like any good gardener, they assembled a flat-pack greenhouse to house their first tenant: a place to incubate ideas before they sprouted. In

February 2020, the Centre for Health Technology moved into the greenhouse and set about bringing together Plymouth University students and researchers from computing, medicine, design, robotics and architecture for the shared mission of tackling health inequalities in Stonehouse. In a warm corner, an AI cat mewled. Boxes of papers and gadgets piled up on a garish green and purple carpet. A 3D printer whirred. The project bloomed.

The Plot's generative ethos extended beyond its front door. When the pandemic struck, it supplied Wi-Fi for the whole street, a precious commodity for home schooling and working during lockdown. And it experimented with supplying local people with companion robots to help social isolation, apps and other interventions to reach those at risk. Health had always been at the heart of Nudge's Union Street plans, but at the Plot it found its proper home.

When I visit in 2023, the pandemic is a memory. The inside of the Plot is now crammed with new businesses that spill from units built into the space with chipboard and incongruous, but ingenious, garden sheds. There is so much demand for space that Wendy and Hannah have a waiting list. The back of the arcade is home to a mini food court called Jabulani, a spin-off from a local diversity business incubator run by a businesswoman called Liliane Uwimana. It contains several businesses owned by African women, serving Ethiopian, Eritrean and West African food and Rwandan coffee. The aroma of spices and sweet coffee drifts into the street. I see little girls crowding around their mothers, listening as the women share news.

The back street is full of cars: there are five garages in the area. But the entrepreneurs are making a difference there too. I meet Jabo Butera, the managing director of the diversity business incubator that has supported many of these women on their paths from home cooking to starting a business. 'People in England grow flowers,' he told me. 'But we are growing food.' Outside, I notice that the flower beds are full of lettuce, tomatoes, kale and herbs.

In the centre of the building, Hannah is proud to show me new tenants, Queer Out Loud, a queer support network for the South West, who occupy a shed. Inside, fairy lights give a warm glow to tables crammed with zines, jewellery, prints and poetry anthologies by queer creatives. It is run by Mimi Jones, a trans, disabled poet and community builder.

Around the shed, the units are filled with colour and life. There is Precious Plastic Plymouth, a social enterprise that shreds and melts plastic for repurposing; a business called JarSquad that uses preserves and other things found in jars to explore circular food systems; and a textile business called Flax Project, which aims to grow its own flax for linen and revive an ancient fibre industry in the South West.

The businesses and the people are all very different, which can come with unique challenges. But the tenants also come together to support one another in surprising ways. Vicky Putler from the Flax Project tells me how some of the other tenants helped her to set up a business bank account – a process she was struggling to navigate alone.

Throughout the month, other groups come to use the Plot's resources and share knowledge. Home-educated children come to use the vinyl cutter and 3D printer. Other groups come to sew, make zines, play board games and experiment with fermentation. The model has been so successful, Nudge is working on a plan to turn the massive Millennium Building into a similar mix of regenerative businesses. Together, the buildings in their care form a pipeline, giving people with business ideas the opportunity to try them out on a market stall at Union Corner, then the chance to scale up with a flexible unit at the Plot, which can be hired by the hour or by the month. The Millennium Building will be a home to more established businesses, who can afford leases of five years or longer. But the rules don't make it easy to offer this kind of flexibility to tenants. Because of the way business rates are calculated, the sheds at the Plot don't count as separate units, which means Nudge was initially on the hook for all the individual traders' business rates, until they fought back on appeal. The cost could have put them out of business.

Then there are the hurdles Nudge has to jump through before it can open the doors to a vacant building. Since they are not renting the spaces to people who can pay the most or be the most reliable, it means that they hold a large amount of risk. Sometimes Hannah and Wendy feel overwhelmed by how much work goes on behind the scenes, only to come to nothing: the buildings they missed out on, the funding they didn't get. All sorts of things that could have been. They don't talk a lot about these opportunities publicly, for the same reason of not wanting to over-promise in a place where people are used to disappointment and failed schemes.

Then there is the whiplash of switching between modes – of writing funding applications worth millions, only for someone to walk through the door needing food. It is intense and mentally challenging. And it could be made so much easier. But here, too, Hannah and Wendy have hope. There are signs that the world outside Plymouth is coming around to the ideas in their mistress plan.

7.6 WE'RE RIGHT HERE

What would it take for the high streets of the UK to be filled with organizations like Nudge, Hastings Commons or Civic Square? Organizations growing more regenerative, fairer futures for people in some of the lowest income areas of the country, at the same time as preparing for the challenges of a changing climate?

In 2011, Conservative prime minister David Cameron passed the Localism Act, which contained a 'community right to bid'. Under this right, communities can nominate valuable land and buildings, so that if it ever goes up for sale, the sale can be delayed for six months to give local groups a chance to raise finance and develop a business plan to bid to buy the asset.

The Act all but failed.[23] The right was too weak. Local groups were given just six months to raise what sometimes amounted to millions in order to buy the assets. Only a handful of buildings listed as assets of community value ever made their way into community ownership.

What's more, a community group could spend six months raising money and making promises to their neighbours, raising the hopes of all those around them, only to lose out when a private buyer came in with more cash. It became another microcosm of the failure of Big Society, which lumped responsibility for public services on volunteers at the same time as the government dismantled council funding through austerity policies.

In the decade that followed the introduction of the Local-ism Act, community groups like Nudge gave evidence on how the right could be improved.[24] They came up with a list of sug-gestions: extend the time that communities get to try and put together a bid from six to twelve months. Upgrade from right to bid to right to buy, allowing groups first refusal on assets. They wanted their right to include buildings and land that might be considered valuable to the community in the future, not just the past. And they called for assets to be independ-ently valued, rather than leaving their value to be determined by the market.

All these changes came into view as the Conservatives left government in 2024. Before the election, then Shadow Level-ling Up Secretary Lisa Nandy promised the old right to bid on assets of community value would be replaced by an upgraded 'community right to buy'. It included first refusal on assets of community value and high-street properties that had been vacant in the long term, alongside the right for communities to buy them without competition.

A plan like this would not only revitalize high streets, but start to shift the balance of power in favour of local people, with all their potential to adapt, to include, to regenerate. And it was not without precedent. As Ian Thomas and Wel-come to Our Woods discovered on their field trip to Scotland, the Scottish Land Reform Act of 2003 gave Scots the right to buy land for crofting – rights that extended across 750,000 hectares of the Highlands and Islands. These rights gave land and livelihoods to 33,000 people within twenty years of being enacted.

For the plan to work, people in the rest of the UK had to

rise up and claim those rights, and the government needed to implement a system of funding and support. So in 2024, as the election came into view, Hannah joined a campaign with nineteen community business owners from around the country and support from hundreds more, calling on the next government to share power with organizations like Nudge. In campaign documents, the organizers put their support behind a suite of policies. They called for the right to power-sharing arrangements with local authorities, the right to control local investment, and the right to shape public services. They called it the Community Power Act. 'Whoever finds themselves elected . . . power up local communities,' Hannah said online. 'Let's work together.'

Six months later, in December 2024, the Labour government released a devolution white paper. Buried in the pages, the white paper contained the idea of a community right to buy – a step change in policy that gives local people the first right of refusal when vital community assets go up for sale. Community organizers like Hannah know the right needs to come with proper funding and support from the state to stop it becoming an extension of the Conservatives' disastrous Big Society, offloading responsibility for taxpayer-supported assets to volunteer groups. But for the first time, community groups in England have real rights to buy buildings and land ahead of private investors who have so long held the advantage – rights spelled out in the black and white of policy documents. The possibilities unspool.

Fifteen years after that first Union Street party, in September 2024, Wendy and Hannah turn the annual event into a special anniversary celebration. It is so much more than a few carrier bags of snacks and crafts on a street corner. The minute I turn into Union Street, I see a man at the top of a cherry picker, setting up the main stage. The street is adorned with handmade bunting, giant balloons spelling out the word 'smile', photographs, street stalls, food and colour.

The activity kicks off at midday without fanfare, the women from Jabulani carrying huge metal vats of curries out of the Plot on their heads. A steel band fills the air with instant sunshine. Parents and children dance to the strains of Harry Styles's 'Watermelon Sugar'.

Down the other end of the street, outside Hannah's husband's antiques shop, a folk band is setting up on a smaller stage. Kids queue to have a go on a massive climbing wall, disappearing into the sky like Jack climbing the beanstalk, only to descend, grinning, touching their feet to the ground.

Hannah appears in a pink jumpsuit with high-top boots and gold ribbons in her hair. She switches from party mode to confide about some trouble they are having with a private landlord, before disappearing again into the crowd with her little daughter in matching boots and leggings printed with constellations.

Then I see Wendy, wearing a giant, decorated rucksack and handing out programmes for the day's events: the musical acts, the theatre performances, the street art. The last ten years haven't all been rosy, she says. Alongside all the challenges with running a community business, she's raised two teenagers, with all the difficulties of adolescence and the heartbreak and the letting go.

Here are fully rounded humans: not saying it's easy, not pretending they don't have other important things in their lives.

Giving permission for everyone else to have differences and difficulties and still do extraordinary things.

Then Wendy is gone, and I get shunted out of the way by a tap dancing troupe laying down panels underfoot ready for their performance. I skirt around one of the games, a human fruit machine. A kid pulls a massive lever, held by a grinning man, and three people with cardboard boxes on their knees make a rumbling sound, spin their arms around and pull out a combination of apples, oranges and bananas. And then I'm at Union Corner, where someone offers me a cake and a cup of tea for £1.

Inside there's the familiar lampshades, a piano, the simple kitchen. The garden is full of blooming pots, painted furniture and bright murals. The floor has been freshly tiled and the door is flung open into the alleyway – that old home to the strip bar and the porn shop. Now it is filled with tables and chairs belonging to a trendy cafe, where a DJ spins records.

Like many others, most of them from round here, I pass the day stumbling between stalls, spending little more than small change. Dancing, listening, learning, grinning. Union Street has become a street you want to spend time on, even as it grows into a demonstrator for so much more.

8

HOME

Birmingham

'Infrastructure, at its most fundamental level, is not about roads and bridges, cables and concrete. It's about who we are, what we value, and what kind of society we want to create.'

—Eric Klinenberg[1]

8.1 RETROFIT REIMAGINED

In the last few decades, evidence has shown that treating the home as a financial asset and not a human right is making us ill. One in five renters in one survey said that housing issues or worries made them physically sick.[2] Centric Lab, a community interest company, has studied how cheap materials contaminate our indoor air, making our lungs heave, disturbing our sleep and exposing us to mould. The housing crisis squeezes us into smaller and smaller spaces, squashing the time and space we need for resting, for caring, for dreaming. Our capacity to create ways to escape these conditions diminishes with sickness and exhaustion.

There are ways to make our houses healthier – and more adaptable for the world to come. Scientists from Centric Lab have scrutinized the way Britain's national planning policy hinges on financial viability for the developer, rather than affordability, biodiversity, climate change adaptation or any other social or ecological factors.[3] They have reimagined the policy from an ecological justice perspective in which the land is kin, not a lifeless resource to be exploited. In this reimagining, the housing shortage is addressed not with new homes, but by addressing need within the existing built environment. Houses are no longer considered as tradable entities, but as part of an interrelated network of streets and neighbourhoods, of trees and water, of non-human and human life, in which time passes, marked by warming days and cooling nights.

New ideas that reframe our relationship to our homes are badly needed as the government fails on its target to improve the energy efficiency of all homes to what is known as EPC band C by 2035. So far, less than a third of the UK's 29 million homes reach this standard – a standard still far below the highest performing examples. That means most of us are living in substandard housing, and most of us have no idea how to do anything about it. To reach its target, the government will focus purely on technical improvements to the fabric of houses. This process is described as retrofit: a way of adding or changing something to make the house better suited to its environment. But in pockets of Birmingham and Bristol, people have begun to think of retrofit not just as a process of changing pipes, bricks or boilers. Instead, retrofit has become a way of reshaping power in neighbourhoods. It's become a way to put those in the draughtiest, leakiest homes, or even those without a home, squashed into accommodation with relatives or bouncing between unsuitable beds, at the forefront of a transition to something better.

8.2 ZERO CARBON HOUSE

I wake up in a teenager's bedroom in the heart of Birmingham and take a deep breath. I am an eternal sneezer, overly sensitive to pollen and dust since I am old enough to remember. Most mornings I wake up with a blocked nose. But the air in this house feels different: cool and clean.

I inch my toes towards the edge of the bed and slip them from under the covers, reaching for the floor. A Persian rug has been laid over compacted Midlands clay excavated from the ground beneath the house.[4] It is a striking dark red, its smoothness interrupted only by delicate seams, as beautiful as marble. But clay, unlike marble, retains warmth when the temperature dips, and stays cool when the sun is beating down outside. My feet land on the barely carpeted surface, but I do not flinch from cold.

At the window, I raise the blind and notice the way the glass pane is set deep into the wall on either side. The building is wrapped in almost 30cm of insulation. The inside walls at the front of the house are stuffed with soft recycled newspaper to preserve the existing frontage, but at the back, the insulation is external.[5] The walls are so thick, the windows seem suspended. The deep window ledge contains family paraphernalia: photographs of childhood country walks, a dreamcatcher. The shelves are lined with dusty Lego models. Museum posters are stuck to the walls. Big shoes are stuffed into a bookcase.

But my eye is drawn outside, to the path that runs down the middle of a country garden. The lawn is lined with deep flower beds. A grand old ash tree towers over the back of the house, casting shade. It is strung with a single tyre swing on a rope. A white cast-iron table and some chairs sit before a pergola, woven with pink roses. Here the garden retreats into a vegetable plot waist-high with produce. The sloping roof of a greenhouse is set against a far wall – the perfect English pastoral.

But this is not a country garden. I am in Balsall Heath, an inner city neighbourhood of the UK's second most-populous city. Beyond the garden a row of terraces recedes into the distance. I can just make out the line of chimneys and slate roofs.

The house that stands here was once a perfectly ordinary, damp, cold and leaky Victorian residence, no different from the ones beneath those chimneys. But the current owner, the architect John Christophers, chose it for a few important qualities.

It is south facing, which is essential since most of the home's energy comes from the sun. And it has that beautiful ash tree, whose leaves shade the house in summer and whose bare branches allow the sun to warm the back of the house in winter.

It was next to a vacant space on the street, which allowed John to expand the footprint of the original house while keeping most of the two-storey structure intact. John added a third storey on to the extension. It is a beautiful gallery-like space called the long room, with a ceiling sloped at exactly the right angle for the extensive solar panels on the roof.

I'm visiting as a guest of John, camping in his son's bedroom while he travels around Europe before starting university. Normally guests stay in the long room at the top, John says, but this is already occupied: a mother and her two daughters are staying while they sort out accommodation after being evicted by their private landlord.

I slip out of the bedroom and into the wet room next door for a quick shower before heading down to meet John for breakfast. Everywhere, light ricochets around the house, even on a rather grey summer's day. Most of it comes from a huge skylight in the ceiling. John tells me later that skylights produce five times as much light as vertical windows, while emitting less heat.

The light descends through the house. It slips between the open staircase and a system of shutters that line the double height living room. By day, the shutters allow the sun to pour down into the corners. By night, the flow is reversed, and cool air travels upwards through the same shutters from a vent on the floor of the kitchen designed to draw in the coolest air from under the ash tree.

The bathroom is an experience. It's like washing in a spaceship. The window is surrounded by curved mirrored plastic that reflects light and heat. The taps mix water with air, to reduce the flow. Combined with more efficient appliances, these measures reduce the amount of water used by a single person in one day by roughly half.

The shower is hot, but this house has no boiler. Instead the water has been heated in solar tubes with capacity to last for several days. While the shower water comes from the mains, much of the household water comes from a 2,500-litre tank of rainwater in the basement of the house.

Taken together, all these measures mean that this zero carbon house makes 40 per cent more energy than it uses. By 2030, after more than twenty years of producing energy, this will amount to more than was consumed in its construction; it will be completely carbon neutral.

Downstairs, John offers me tea and we share a few pastries. The children living in the long room buzz about getting ready for school; there is hair to be combed, backpacks to fill.

We sit at a dining table made of two-hundred-year-old Canadian honeydew maple, which is wider at one end. Its shape echoes the slanted kitchen window, angled to catch the sunlight ninety minutes earlier than if it had been flat against the wall of the house. These are precious minutes of extra warmth and heat for a house with no radiators, no heating more than a small wood burner in the living room which is rarely put to use.

John is an unusual architect. He lives with his partner Jo Hindley, a former midwife. Though they have spent many years welcoming people into their home for tours, open days, events in the long room and all sorts of meetings round the dining table, their thinking has moved beyond the extraordinary home they created together.

These days, their work is in the neighbourhood. Together they make a list of the people they want to introduce me to: a local tree planter, clerics from the mosque, several local residents. All people who have come together to think about energy efficiency not on the scale of single houses – but to reduce heating bills for their neighbours, too. These people have become a broad coalition of faith and community organizations under the name Retrofit Balsall Heath.

Before we leave the house, John whisks me round on a guided tour, his enthusiasm undiminished even though he must have done this hundreds of times. As he talks, I type furiously into my phone about sweet chestnut cladding, swift boxes drilled into the roof and salvaged Arne Jacobsen door handles. Everything is so beautiful, so considered, and still seems so cutting edge.

That's the kicker: John's house was completed in 2009. It's already kind of old. Nothing John has achieved with this house relies on the latest technology. Some of his methods would rightly be described as low-tech: using the sun's energy, employing the shade of old trees, stuffing walls with recycled newspaper, storing thousands of litres of water, building with local clay and salvaged materials. Combined, these techniques mean that the zero carbon house puts in 140 per cent of what it takes out of the National Grid, only drawing on electricity when it's dark outside.[6]

After he built the house, John could have become one of the world's foremost practising architects of zero carbon houses, working exclusively for the eco-conscious among the super-rich. Before his own, he designed one other award-winning building: a mud house for a barrister called Nicholas Worsley in Worcester.[7] But after a terrible cycling accident, he had an epiphany. He saw how top-down action at UN climate summits changed little. He realized climate breakdown couldn't be solved with a handful of perfectly designed homes. To truly adapt for the coming climate catastrophe, neighbours needed to act together in their own streets and homes. Today, if anyone asks, he is proud to introduce himself not as a director of an architectural firm, but as a co-founder of that neighbourhood network of lots of local organizations, called Retrofit Balsall Heath. In this group, retrofit starts not with one-off architectural wonders, but with the draughtiest, mouldiest, leakiest homes – and the people stuck living in them.

8.3 BALSALL HEATH

It's raining outside, and I have to skip to keep up with John. He dashes across an intersection of Birmingham's Moseley Road, his yellow raincoat flapping as he dodges the buses and vans.

We weave our way up the high street between bikes, bins and A-boards. This is one of Birmingham's main arteries – a historic route into the centre where five-hundred-year-old buildings sit next to Lidl and Kwik Fit. All the old pubs are gone, replaced with international supermarkets, cafes and shisha shops shaded by giant plane trees.

Not long ago, the local transport agency Transport West Midlands wanted to cut down all the trees on the Moseley Road to make way for a bus route.[8] John joined a community campaign led by a local Friends of the Earth group, which gathered hundreds of signatures to protest against the plans. Covid-19 eventually killed off the idea, since the pavement needed to be wide enough to allow for social distancing.

Instead, Transport West Midlands began work on reopening three old train stations that follow the route of the Moseley Road. For a hundred years, the line carried workers and goods from the suburbs into the centre of Birmingham. Then in 1941, it closed.[9] A goods line was later turned into an industrial estate, joining the garages, builders' merchants, tyre shops and metal workers that crowd the sliver of land in between the road and the old line today.

The reopening of the Camp Hill line signalled a change of heart – a reversal of the prevailing philosophy of the last fifty years that the car was king. The campaigners saw the proposal and the decision to save the trees as a big vote in favour of a different way to think about development: a 'yes' to tree-lined streets, better pavements for pedestrians and public transport.[10] And they put their faith in public bodies to achieve it.

But the promises of the authorities became mired in dithering. The reopening of the railway line was beset by problems. Spiralling construction costs and delays to completion came alongside the shock decision by Birmingham Council to declare itself bankrupt in September 2024. Suddenly, though the trees were saved, hundreds of millions of pounds' worth of local services – including many libraries and public spaces – were at risk.

The failure echoed a much bigger failure on the part of the national government. Under the 2015 Paris Agreement, the UK government committed to limit the increase in global warming to 1.5°C above pre-industrial levels by, in part, phasing out gas boilers, up-skilling plumbers to insulate homes and employing local authorities to distribute grants to make homes greener.[11] Half of carbon emissions in the UK come from its buildings.[12] A mammoth task lay ahead.

But this top-down approach has a dreadful track record. Under Boris Johnson, the UK government introduced a Green Homes Grant totalling £1.5 billion for households to retrofit their own homes. It lasted just six months, leaving the government to claw back 95 per cent of the funding allocated, since demand was so low. Similar schemes have suffered from this short-termist approach, since suppliers and fitters cannot invest in training and equipment when they can't be guaranteed work more than a few months into the future.

In 2022, the UK's official adviser on climate change said the lack of progress towards zero carbon homes was nothing short of scandalous, with the failure to set out a clear strategy for insulating existing homes a 'shocking gap in policy'.[13]

John and other local campaigners had long ago decided they had to find an alternative way to address energy poverty in their neighbourhoods. The situation in Balsall Heath was desperate.

By 2024, fuel poverty rates in Birmingham and nearby Stoke-on-Trent were the highest in the country. Almost a quarter (24 per cent) of families in these cities found themselves below the government's poverty line after they had adequately heated their home.[14] [15]

On the flipside, in the summer, houses overheated. Birmingham has the highest number of neighbourhoods of any local authority in the UK that will become dangerous when the temperature rises by 3°C.[16] Birmingham's city centre is already on average 4°C warmer than the surrounding countryside.[17] Without the shade of trees and the cooling effects of green spaces and open water, the city heats up like an oven.

The results are deathly. More than 4,500 people are believed to have died in the heatwave that hit the UK in 2022, according to the Climate Change Committee (CCC), an independent UK body that advises the government on preparing for and adapting to the impacts of climate change, a figure that could rise to 10,000 every year.[18]

Meanwhile, every winter, tens of thousands more people die than in summer, in part thanks to fuel poverty. A fifth of excess winter deaths are attributable to cold homes, researchers say.[19]

Fuel poverty discriminates. England scores worse than comparable Northern European countries on the index of excess winter deaths. Those in the North of England fare worse than the South.[20] The very worst outcomes are found in neighbourhoods where homes are older than a hundred years, where people have lower incomes, and where there is a higher concentration of residents from global majority backgrounds.[21] Neighbourhoods like Balsall Heath.

Something happened in Balsall Heath. Sick of being at the bottom of the rankings, with the highest need, people decided they would do something themselves. We arrive at the entrance to Melrose Avenue. No road runs through the middle. Instead, the front gardens of the houses face one another, separated only by a slim path. But Melrose Avenue is quite different to the other streets in Balsall Heath.

It all started with a festival on that protected patch of land next to the Edgbaston Reservoir, the Birmingham Settlement. For four days over the summer of 2022, people spilled out of a giant tent surrounded by lights and hay bales and brightly coloured cushions for a festival of ideas called Retrofit Reimagined. The idea for the festival came from a mish-mash of local groups, among them Civic Square. These groups wanted to start a conversation that was fundamentally about power. The government was failing to decarbonize Britain's 29 million homes. So, one architect asked those under the shade of the big tent, how are we going to do it? Over and over again, people talked about the power of people to force the changes necessary to cope with the planet becoming dysregulated. They wanted to make retrofit feel relevant to everyone, not just people with the time and money to install better insulation and solar panels.

And at the end of the four days, they emerged with a question that would guide all the work that followed. The question wasn't about *what* they needed, because everyone was agreed that all Britain's 29 million homes needed to become zero carbon.

It was about *how*. What was the process for transforming the lives of everyone living in unhealthy, damp homes? 'What if,' they asked, 'the climate transition and retrofit of our homes, streets and neighbourhoods were designed, owned and governed, not by politicians or private companies, but by the people who live there?'

In the years that followed the festival, the movement for people-powered retrofit grew. Within twelve months, the festival spread to other cities, including Bristol, Glasgow and London. Within two years, groups in Birmingham and Bristol had begun to trial retrofitting whole streets and neighbourhoods.

In the winter after the festival, Civic Square produced a tool-kit for winter retrofit containing tips and instructions for small DIY interventions, and introducing precedents for street-scale organizing from around the world. They delivered it to all the residents of Link Road, a slip of Victorian terraces in Ladywood, Birmingham, just around the corner from the Edgbaston Reservoir. Link Road is not particularly green – there's only one tree on the whole street, and that's in someone's front garden. And it's not particularly busy, with the main traffic going down the major avenues that run either side. But over the years, the neighbours have got to know one another. They've built planters, sung Christmas carols and hosted summer street parties.[22] Civic Square hoped that the winter toolkit would build on that early sense of solidarity. It contained DIY tips for retrofit and inspiration from other streets around the world where neighbours had worked together on energy efficiency.

The next summer, at the Link Road annual street party, Civic Square set up a stall to demonstrate how different natural resources might be used to conserve heat in the home. The neighbours were invited to feel the materials and learn about their properties, and to think about how they might be used in imaginative ways.

All through 2023, Civic Square supported the residents of Link Road to make tiny interventions, from cleaning up a local noticeboard, to starting a neighbourhood trade school where residents swapped things like unused packets of seeds.[23]

They held pop-up clothes swaps and started a soil maker where neighbours could collectively compost their organic waste. They worked together to create a communal potting shed and install bat boxes on the street. They started a newsletter and nominated ambassador households to start to share the skills residents needed to retrofit their homes. There were local workshops and trips to weekend courses at the Centre for Alternative Technology in Wales, where they learned about community solar schemes and home insulation.

Taken one by one, the interventions sound small. But together they were progressing towards the dream of retrofitting their own neighbourhood in a way that could become a demonstrator to other residents, everywhere.[24]

Melrose Avenue has a similar story, John tells me as we stand at the entrance to the little street. One that started after the Retrofit Reimagined festival and has taken on a life of its own.

8.4 MELROSE AVENUE

At first glance, Melrose Avenue seems just as unremarkable as Link Road. But things are changing on the street. After the festival on the Edgbaston Reservoir in 2022, some of the local organizations in Retrofit Balsall Heath went out to knock on the door of every one of the 4,900 homes in Balsall Heath to ask: did the people living there want to have better insulation and solar panels?

Yes, said 1,400 of the residents who opened the door to their homes. Within a year, 649 of them had some kind of retrofit. On Melrose Avenue, almost all the households signed up, making it the first street-wide demonstrator of this bottom-up approach. Journalists called it 'retrofit road'.

First, they needed money. The group went to the council and appealed for it to distribute any local authority funding to community groups. When Birmingham Councils was allocated £6.5 million to spend on retrofitting lower income homes under an energy efficiency scheme called Local Authority Delivery 3 (LAD3), it contacted Retrofit Balsall Heath to help distribute the funding, so it didn't get blocked, or sent back, like so many other failed schemes. And Retrofit Balsall Heath was able to sign up many of the thousands of needy homes in the area, distributing on average £10,000 for each home.

As we stand at the entrance to Melrose Avenue, John shares a vision for these close-knit residential streets in Balsall Heath. He painted it once in pale watercolours. In his painting, all the houses have solar panels and heat pumps. The most remarkable change is not to the houses themselves, but to the spaces in between the houses. He turned all the existing concrete yards, bricked off from one another, into broad green space with a communal table in the middle, around which sat neighbours sharing food.

He painted an enormous bike shed for zero carbon transport, compost bins and communal water butts for recycling waste and natural resources. In greens and browns, he imagined a big vegetable garden, plenty of fruit trees, beehives and bird boxes for pollinators. Finally, in tiny brushstrokes, he imagined two workmen carrying tools coming through the arched entrance. They symbolize the jobs that could be created for tradesmen with a properly funded, national scale initiative around retrofit.

At the real Melrose Avenue, the reality is still mostly concrete yards and closed front doors. But there are signs of change: a pair of eye-catching orange benches to encourage people to linger outside, wooden planters painted bright pink, brand new saplings with the tags still on, poking out of raised concrete slabs, and a pair of pink shared bicycles, tethered together in the central path.

John has to go to work, so he introduces me to Jan Burley, who lives on Melrose Avenue. Jan has short grey hair and carries the quiet wisdom of a woman who has helped raise several generations of children. Lately, she has become chief gardener, helping her neighbours' children and grandchildren tend to the plants and trees – including a handsome almond tree with two plump nuts – that were planted here using community funding. A surprise to Jan, too, who just a few years ago could not have said where almonds come from.

We slip through her front door, making sure the cats don't escape. Jan puts some coffee on and settles me in an armchair. Opposite, a smart meter is set up next to framed pictures of family. Thanks to LAD3, Jan had solar panels fitted on her roof, which helps with fuel bills, but only in summer, she says.

Five of the houses on Melrose Avenue received solar panels. But not all were happy with the way the retrofit was handled. After coffee, Jan introduces me to Mr Khan over the road, who complains that three sets of contractors spent hours measuring up his home for works, without anyone explaining what was going on – leaving him feeling confused and annoyed.

Some of the residents in Balsall Heath received funding for insulation, only for their installers to go out of business when the funding ended, leaving unfinished works. Jan heard from women in neighbouring properties who were uncomfortable inviting strangers to investigate the private corners of their home. When the work was approached in this top-down way, people felt the attitude was that they should be grateful – even when communication was poor and the works were badly coordinated. It left a bad taste.

But when the community was allowed to take control of the funding, the action took on a different character. Encouraged by John and Jan, and with help from a local charity called Fruit and Nut Village, the residents on Melrose Avenue lifted a concrete slab and planted a tree. They painted the communal furniture, from planters to benches, and slowly people began to nurture saplings, herbs and flowers. They hosted clean-ups of local green spaces and bicycle lessons for women and children. When funding for the core work of installing solar panels and insulating homes ground to a halt, these activities continued, driven forward by local mosques and churches and their communities.

That afternoon, before my train, I head to the streets around Cannon Hill Park, to see the raising of some concrete slabs to make way for some fruit trees. The mosque on Willow Crescent sits at a junction in the road, with a wide pavement that has been turned into a kind of urban park with planters filled with flowers. It's deserted when I get there. Within a few minutes, an eye-catching purple van pulls up, covered in signage offering advice about benefits and housing and debt. It belongs to the MECC Trust, an organization founded nearly fifty years ago by Muslim businessmen and -women. While rooted in Islamic values, MECC Trust supports many different communities across Balsall Heath and beyond. It is also one of Birmingham's leading retrofit charities. Under the LAD3 funding scheme, it has delivered upgrades to homes in and around Balsall Heath. Then Mazar Dad, the chairman and chief executive of the MECC Trust, arrives. They got so many people signed up to retrofit in Balsall Heath, he says, because of the organization's deep roots in the neighbourhood. When people answered the door to someone from the MECC Trust, they knew they could believe what they heard. Although the funding has since ended, MECC Trust has proved that community-led schemes like this can work. Through its coordination and community ties, MECC Trust successfully delivered improvements to over seven hundred of the most energy-inefficient Victorian homes, installing better insulation and solar panels to reduce residents' energy bills and helping them to live more comfortably.

The initiative goes beyond improving individual properties, to include street-wide gardening and planting fruit and nut trees, which come with the dual benefit of shade and nourishment. 'It's more than making the mosque look pretty,' he says, 'We want to create urban orchards in all our streets.'

After prayer, a group of men file out of the mosque. They inspect three small saplings that have been delivered by Dan Burwood from Fruit and Nut Village. There is some discussion about where the trees will go. And then suddenly a spade is in the ground, the concrete slab is raised. Dan lowers a sapling into the murky earth. He carefully dusts the root ball with mycelium to help it grow. A mulberry sapling, native to South East Asia, Maz tells me proudly, where many of these men have close family. As the roots are covered over and pressed carefully into the ground, I get chatting to one of them. 'Our fathers built this mosque,' he says. 'And we are carrying out their legacy.'

Here's an inner city neighbourhood where preparing for the future is about more than material adaptations to houses. Here, the home spills beyond front gardens on to pavements and shared spaces. History breathes meaning into the smallest of interventions. One day the children of these men will benefit from the shade of the mulberry tree outside the mosque. And on that day, they too will be grateful for the foresight of their fathers.

Bristol

'When a complex system is far from equilibrium, small islands of coherence in a sea of chaos have the capacity to shift the entire system to a higher order.'

—Ilya Prigogine[25]

8.5 WECANMAKE

There are more than one million council-built homes across England, all constructed between the two world wars.[26] British housing stock is stuffed with old and draughty houses badly in need of an upgrade. When it was built in the 1930s by the council, the Knowle West estate in Bristol was designed in line with the principles of Ebenezer Howard's Garden City Movement, which tried to remedy the overcrowding of the city slums by bringing the town and the country together in suburban neighbourhoods.

Knowle West seemed like the perfect spot: on top of a hill, surrounded by green. The council filled the area with five thousand three-bedroom, semi-detached homes, with gardens so big the workers who built them called it 'the five thousand island forest'. It was a town planner's dream. But over the years, the gap grew between the physical infrastructure and the needs of residents. Constrained by the layout, the homes were hard to adapt. They were so spread out over the area that it was difficult to sustain community services, and over time, several shops, a swimming pool and a cinema closed down. The major local employer, a tobacco factory, shut in the eighties. In 2021, the bus service stopped.[27] [28] Inside, the houses got cold. They have solid walls, little insulation and a high reliance on gas. A third of families were experiencing fuel poverty in Knowle West even before the Russia–Ukraine war started driving up fuel prices in 2022.

Younger people struggle to move out of their parents' homes into more suitable accommodation nearby, and so multiple generations are forced to share. Then there are the child-free older people who'd rather find a one- or two-bedroom flat or house – something easier to heat – who rattle around in cold, old homes unable to downsize.

At the annual general meeting of a local arts organization, the housing issue reached a tipping point. It was 2016, and Melissa Mean had worked at Knowle West Media Centre for four years. Melissa is pale with unruly dark hair and a kind of maverick energy about her. More than once, I saw her in a colourful boiler suit, a uniform that straddled her background in the arts and more recent work constructing homes. She never set out to build homes – it wasn't top of her job description as Head of Arts. But perhaps the trajectory was inevitable. The centre had already worked on projects around energy, transport and other related themes. It had innovation in its DNA. It was constructed in 2007 on the grounds of a former health centre. Young people from the area were invited to help design the new centre as a model of carbon efficiency, even before that was a mainstream thing to do,[29] repurposing materials from the old building and constructing walls out of straw bales.

By 2016, there was a growing mismatch between people's housing needs and the type of housing available. In the spring of 2017, with a little Arts Council funding, the Media Centre commissioned an artist called Charlotte Biszewski to make a wallpaper-making machine that could turn any item into a print using cyanotype photography. Like a travelling salesman, Charlotte knocked on doors and offered to make people a slice of wallpaper from their treasured toys and their wartime medals. While the sunlight created a chemical reaction on the exposed paper, turning the precious objects into a print, Charlotte asked residents about their experience of living in their homes and in the neighbourhood, about their hopes for the future, and about what knowledge ran through their family about making anything from cakes to carpentry. It was a lo-fi way to canvass people's opinions about their homes, using their own personal items as a way into their memories and imaginations.

In partnership with architecture students from the University of the West of England Bristol (UWE), the team at

the Media Centre were able to map out the contours of the
garden city. They found a place dotted with need for alternative types of housing – and unlikely plots for potential new
homes. They spoke to Miriam and David, who had been residents of Knowle West for thirty years.* Their daughter Jess
had just had a baby and moved into the spare room. Jess was
on the waiting list for a council house. She had been offered
a mother and baby unit in Brislington, which felt like the end
of the world – miles from her support network of friends and
family in Knowle West. Meanwhile, David had a long-term
illness that affected his mobility and sometimes had to sleep
on the sofa. The couple knew they needed to move into a
bungalow, but there was nothing like that in the area, and
they couldn't afford to move out. They decided to try and
adapt their home, and applied for planning permission to do
a side extension on the house. When permission was rejected
at the planning stage, they felt completely stuck.[30] Planning
applications are twice as likely to get rejected in Knowle West
compared to Clifton, a more affluent area of Bristol, the team
at the Media Centre discovered.[31] That pattern is repeated
around the country, as planning offices in poorer neighbourhoods are more likely to refuse planning or even refuse to
engage with it in the first place.[32]

Then there was Diane, who had lived in Knowle West for
sixty years. She had thirty great-grandchildren living on the
estate and three living with her when she spoke with the

---

* Miriam and David, their daughter Jess, and Diane spoke to UWE
researchers who did not publish their surnames, and I have chosen to
respect that here.

young researchers. The grandchildren were all in their twenties and thirties and trying to save to rent or buy their own homes – but found it nearly impossible to save enough on low or part-time wages. Diane said she felt her house had a revolving door. Sometimes she couldn't even keep track of who was staying. And she could only imagine it getting worse.

At the most acute end of the scale, there were people who had lost their homes, like John Bennett. John had the strong jaw and full head of dark hair of a man who should be enjoying his middle age. But his face bore the marks of a hard life. Someone once told him that most people in Britain are just one pay cheque away from being homeless. He guessed he wasn't the only one who had fallen on the wrong side of that statistic. One horrible year, not long after losing his job, John realized he could no longer afford the bills and rent on his own home in Knowle West. So he moved into a shed. His mental health rapidly deteriorated. His own living conditions were one thing, but what really hurt is that he used to help out his daughter financially, who worked nights in a care home, and he could no longer afford to do so.

He started drinking and going to bed as early as possible, just to end the days. That winter, he found himself on the street. By the time John bumped into Melissa, he was living in the shed in a yard with no running water and no bathroom. Melissa saw past John's recent experiences and asked him if he'd like to get involved with the housing project. They came up with the idea for a podcast on housing, continuing the discussions the wallpaper machine had started. The podcast was a place to explore alternative models for housing from all over the world, to help residents come up with a new idea for Knowle West. People saw the need for – and the possibility of – change. They just had to find the materials – and the space.

8.6 THE MODEL

Melissa realized that the abundance of open space in Knowle West could be one way of challenging the ingrained feeling among some residents of disadvantage, or scarcity.

The students from UWE found fifteen thousand examples of space at least 3.5 metres wide – big enough for a one- or two-bedroom home – in back gardens and in the gaps between existing houses. Then, they took a closer look at some of the gardens. Most were 20 metres long and totally overgrown as people struggled with maintaining all that green space. What if the council gave up some in-between areas and residents contributed some of their long back gardens to build new homes and improve their own housing situations? Even if everyone kept a more standard six-metre long private garden, 31.3 hectares of garden could potentially be released, enough for thousands of homes, each the size of a static caravan. Not all of that would be suitable to build on, but if houses could make use of just a tenth of the available space, it would mark a huge amount of new land in the hands of residents, and deliver more affordable housing than had been delivered in Bristol for the whole of the previous year.[33] So they decided to ask residents if they'd be interested in trading parts of their garden. The response was staggering. Eighty responded positively in the first round of surveys, and more than half of these took part in feasibility studies to see if the sites might work.[34]

Bill Kelly, a single dad with a son, Liam, was one of the first to sign up. He had a big garden behind his council house. But it was overgrown and underused: too much for one man to manage alongside working and raising a child alone. Bill liked the idea of offering up some of his garden for a micro-site to build a new home. But he knew he could never offer space to someone who didn't get along with his son. Knowle West Media Centre worked with him to find a match, carefully assessing the needs and lifestyles of Bill and Liam, before they suggested John. When Bill heard about John and his situation, he invited him over for a coffee. No promises – just to see what they thought of one another.

The two men sat down together and shared their stories. Bill was at the end of a messy divorce and trying to rebuild his life with his son. He knew what it was like to be homeless. John sympathized. It was at the end of his marriage three years earlier when things had really fallen apart. Something lovely happened with Liam, who instantly warmed to John. Bill saw how helpful it might be to have a friendly neighbour: some-one to hold a spare set of keys and on whom Liam might call if he ever needed help. But more than that: he wanted to help someone.

There's a bright light that goes on in Bill's blue eyes, behind his owlish glasses, when he talks about the moment he was able to offer part of his garden to John. It was just nice, he felt, to be nice to someone. There was a sense of satisfaction, after so long counting the things he didn't have, in being able to give something to another person. In receiving the gift, John felt a kinship with this man and his son, knowing that they had both experienced the same kind of vulnerability. Both men had gone from feeling isolated in their situations, to feeling seen and trusted.[35]

Melissa noticed this, too. Rather than saying they are building houses, she likes to say they are building relationships between people. She saw how the project invited neighbours to help neighbours, creating stronger networks in Knowle West, even among family members who had been forced into stressful living situations, like a young woman called Toni Gray. Toni was still living at home with her mother when she became pregnant. After her daughter Amancia was born, Toni would avoid the living room, feeding the baby in the kitchen or playing with her in her bedroom as she didn't want to take up any more space in the cramped house.

Toni had been a member of the Media Centre since she was ten years old, going to the after-school groups and later volunteering. But it was her mum who told her about the housing project, when she returned from a meeting at the centre one evening. Here, it seemed, was a solution that could help them both. Toni could learn how to build a house at the bottom of their garden. In giving her the land, her mum could offer her a fresh start with her young daughter, and a way of learning skills and making new friends in the neighbourhood at a moment when she was at risk of becoming more isolated – while freeing up her house. The question was what to build.

Knowle West suffers from a lack of jobs, but no shortage of tradesmen. When the Media Centre and UWE mapped local assets, they discovered that 52 per cent of respondents in the survey had experience at a professional or amateur level in plastering, plumbing, electrics, roofing, carpentry, bricklaying, painting and decorating, or design.

The Media Centre also had a digital fabrication workshop, known to residents as 'the Factory', which was used to train local people in digital design and fabrication skills and to make a diverse range of products, from jewellery to furniture. After working with architecture students at UWE to do that early mapping of assets and skills in the neighbourhood, the Media Centre invited a range of architectural firms to come up with different designs for a modular house. They wanted something that could be made of materials from the bioregion and assembled on site, using the skills and tools that already existed locally.

Over the summer of 2018, Knowle West Media Centre worked with White Design to test out one of the designs on a plot outside a community centre.[36] Four walls made of timber and compressed straw, built on a farm three miles away and assembled in the grounds of a local community centre in just twelve weeks. Inside, the space measured 36 square metres, big enough for a bedroom, a bathroom and a generous living space with a kitchen and breakfast bar.

The model worked. Next, it needed to be tested on a real site, for real residents. They needed people to give consent for the use of their council-owned land – alongside planning permission. To acquire the land, Knowle West Media Centre wanted to start a community land trust, to make sure that land remains affordable for the good of local people. The Media Centre incubated a new organization called WeCan-Make, led by Melissa and staffed by architects, designers and community members, to specialize in housing and construction. Then, they had to get the council to transfer the land to the new community land trust. Under the standard terms, the land could be held for 125 years – a length of time considered as good as owning. The trust stopped speculators from buying the land for profit and selling it on. Instead, the homes would remain in the ownership of the community and stay affordable for as long as they stood.

Next, there was the issue of getting planning permission. Planning is all about precedence: and getting the paperwork to build modular homes in the back gardens of a council estate had not been done before. Plenty of people said it wasn't possible. Melissa knew they were up against it: self-build and custom-build account for just 7 per cent of new homes delivered each year in the UK, compared to 80 per cent in Austria and 60 per cent in France.[37]

WeCanMake worked closely with planning officers at Bristol City Council to make sure that the homes met all their quality and policy requirements. Because the model was new, the council went straight to the top, with a letter to the Secretary of State, who gave consent to build, approving a new model of land supply exclusively for community-led homes.

Soon, Toni and John were at work in the Factory, learning how to build the insulated walls, known as cassettes, for their own homes. They salvaged the floorboards from a local school that was about to be demolished and laid them in their own modular houses. John made seven of the 150 cassettes for his own house. It took a construction crew of six local tradesmen less than a week to assemble the main structure of the homes. Within four months, the cladding and interiors were finished and the homes were ready to move into.

The finished houses weren't just a lifeline to the new tenants. They were also much better for the environment. The modular house performed 50 per cent better in terms of carbon emissions than a brick house, with running costs that were 20 per cent cheaper.[38] Once the two homes had been built, the council started to get excited about the potential to meet the housing need in this way. In 2020, WeCanMake became an independent community interest company, the kind of organization that can hold community land trusts. And the council approved WeCanMake to start doing this kind of infill across the whole of South Bristol.

They applied for planning permission for two further microsites in Knowle West in 2022, at the exact moment the planning department at Bristol Council went into meltdown. It had lost more than a third of its planning capacity due to a recruitment freeze and the struggle to hire planners in the public sector, given the much better salaries at private companies. The delays reached a crisis point in the spring of 2024, and the national government put Bristol City Council's planning department into special measures. This allows some developers to bypass the council planning department and ask the government for permission instead. But most applications, like WeCanMake's, end up in a giant backlog, waiting for council services to resume.[39]

Rather than sit and do nothing, WeCanMake started working on slightly bigger pieces of land, such as car parks and garages, to design low-rise apartment blocks and community space in other neighbourhoods in South Bristol. At the same time, they started working on a 'retrofit recipe' to improve the existing hundred-year-old homes in Knowle West.

8.7 THE TIMBER PROBLEM

Humans have been building with timber for ten thousand years. But it's a dying art in Britain. Partly that's to do with supply: the UK is one of the least forested countries in Europe, with around 13 per cent forest cover compared with an average of 38 per cent across the EU. But it's also about lost skills and the rise of wasteful, short-term uses for the little timber the UK does produce.

Since the UK has so little homegrown timber, it relies on imports. Britain is the world's largest importer of timber, after China, and it is falling behind on government targets to plant tens of thousands of new hectares of forests in the UK to meet demand.[40] Most of the UK's imported wood and more than 80 per cent of its homegrown timber is sent to massive incinerators to be burned as a kind of energy called biomass. Timber is a carbon neutral material, as long as it is used in a way that embodies its carbon for at least as long as it took that tree to grow. Timber from a sixty-year-old tree could be considered carbon neutral if it was used for sixty years. To achieve true carbon neutrality, the chips and scraps should be recycled to make other, less durable boards and planks, like oriented strand board or OSB. But if any part of that tree is burned for biomass, all that carbon instantly goes up in smoke.

In 2025, the UK government published a strategy to start planting trees to revitalize the UK's timber industries, stating that timber manufacturing was one way to alleviate the impact of three of the country's biggest challenges – climate change, the housing crisis and economic growth – by reducing emissions, building more homes and creating jobs. The strategy set out ambitious plans to plant more trees by 2050, but also to support a better supply chain for locally grown timber and to train people to work with timber in construction.[41]

At the Factory, WeCanMake revised its modular housing system to reduce embodied carbon and to maximize the use of homegrown timber. It made two key changes: swapping metal nail plates for timber pegs to join the cassettes together, and replacing mineral wool insulation with wood-fibre insulation. Then it reviewed the whole of its construction process, from the design to the final fit-out, to see what could be swapped from high-carbon imported materials to low-carbon home-grown timber. It is often said that UK timber is not good enough for construction, in order to justify its use in low quality packaging or as biomass. But WeCanMake discovered that if UK timber is chosen carefully for specific uses, it can be great in construction. Soon, WeCanMake was using local, fast-growing cypress for cladding and working with timber merchants to thermally modify ash so that it could be used for windows.

Building low-carbon homes on so-called 'infill' sites in people's back gardens and between homes was one way for local people to adapt their neighbourhoods to better meet their needs. But WeCanMake wanted to open up this process of retrofit and adaptation so more people could be involved. So they began to research smaller interventions, starting in the front garden. Melissa came across a group called Better Block in Dallas, Texas.[42] Better Block had developed a suite of furniture for city blocks and street corners and shared it online in an open-source design library. Anyone could download the designs and, with a digital fabrication workshop like the one at WeCanMake, cut the parts out of wood and assemble them with nothing more than a mallet. The Better Block library included ramps and planters, chairs, chess sets and signs. WeCanMake began to work on a collection of objects, called a 'front garden retrofit kit', which they felt would be most suited to Knowle West. The kit included sharing cupboards that could be used as neighbourhood libraries, benches, and hedgehog houses and planters for the more environmentally minded. Then they tested it in two front gardens in Knowle West, a first attempt at a much broader effort to make the existing streets greener, since a third of the front gardens have been paved over and lost to car-parking.

The interventions in Bristol are still in their infancy. But the process has already been transformational. In Knowle West, WeCanMake selected a single street, called Andover Road, as a demonstrator for more intense retrofit, like Melrose Avenue and Link Road in Birmingham. On Andover Road, from 2023, six families collaborated on a retrofit project to understand how people lived and used their homes, with the idea to co-design a neighbourhood 'recipe' for retrofit. The neighbours collected data on humidity, temperature and environmental performance. The data showed that in some of these homes, carbon dioxide levels were more than three times higher than healthy indoor levels because of overcrowding. They found other things that could affect residents' health, like mould in the eaves and draughts around the doors.

WeCanMake supported the residents to come up with a five-point retrofit recipe – an antidote to traditional retrofit, with its top-down, technical solutions. The recipe included a commitment to use biomaterials, rather than oil-based materials, in any modifications, alongside measures to improve indoor air quality and prevent mould. Residents said they wanted shared renewable energy, from heat pumps to solar panels, and modest changes to their homes to deal with overcrowding. Finally, they committed to making space for nature, with street trees, rainwater harvesting, green roofs, and diverse plants and flowers. As part of this process, WeCanMake ran DIY tool workshops where local people could learn how to carry out simple retrofit repairs on their own homes, and they launched a tool library where people were invited to come and borrow what they needed. Jasmine Tippett, who lives on Andover Road, attended some of the workshops to explore different ways to repair the fencing in the community allotment using mismatched walls, cobble, wicker panels and recycled wood.

In 2024, at the Factory, Jasmine told me how people in Knowle West bond over negativity, both from family traumas and collective experiences in the neighbourhood. Most people hadn't moved there by choice, but were sent from the slums of Bristol to live in social housing. Jas has her own story of arrival that began when her paternal grandmother was rehomed in Knowle West after a house fire in which family members from three generations died. Her grandmother went on to have six sons, including her father. They were one of a handful of Black families living in Knowle West in the seventies and eighties. Jas tells me how a history of violence could have been passed down through the generations in an estate like Knowle West, but she has worked hard to keep it in the past and out of the bloodline. Today, she works as a community development organizer for the council out of a health hub, running community groups in the neighbourhood.

Jas said that getting involved with retrofit – having her home assessed and attending workshops to learn how to build – has improved her sense of self-worth. 'I love being outside and creating spaces where people feel safe,' she told me, on a bright and breezy July day. 'Retrofit for me is wellbeing.' The interventions might be small, but cumulatively they create a symbiotic relationship between residents and their built and natural environment, so that one person's home is no longer seen in isolation, as merely an asset, but as part of an intertwined network of trees and water, timber and straw, shared pavements where children play out and back gardens where others dwell.

Jas's house is right at the top of Andover Road, its beige pebbledash almost completely hidden behind a big hedge. Most of her neighbours' front gardens have been paved over. Arched passageways lead to back gardens. England flags flap against windows. Neighbours shout hello from the concrete and tarmac patchwork of their drives. Behind Jas's house, next to the Springfield community allotment, is a wild bit of parkland that offers spectacular views across the whole of Bristol, all the way to the Clifton Suspension Bridge. We might be stranded in a garden city of one thousand island homes, but there are ideas here in abundance – real, messy experiments in what retrofit means in practice – and how we can return our homes to their purpose as places to rest, to care and to dream up the neighbourhoods of the future.

9

BODIES

Hastings and Gateshead

'What do they do,
the singers, tale-writers, dancers, painters, shapers, makers?

They go there with empty hands,
into the gap between.
They come back with things in their hands.'

—Ursula K. Le Guin, *Always Coming Home*[1]

9.1 STARTING WITH PEOPLE

One evening in the summer of 2024, I head to the Hastings Observer Building for a big party to celebrate its centenary. A lot had happened in a hundred years. A publishing empire had risen and fallen. A neighbourhood had gone fallow: lights out, pigeons in. A new era has dawned for the Observer Building. A few weeks earlier, I'd watched excitedly as the scaffolding was slowly removed to reveal the restored facade of the old printworks, with its handsome steel-framed windows and the F. J. Parsons insignia. While the alley behind had been a symbol of common stewardship, here was its beating heart, the home of the Hastings Commons. It was host to a developing roster of different users from businesses renting office space, freelancers who came in daily for co-working, a CrossFit gym, a creative technology hub and, temporarily, a youth club awaiting the redevelopment of longer-term premises in another Hastings Commons building. Upstairs, yet to be built – as was customary in the Hastings Commons tradition of developing things in a phased, organic way – there would be twelve affordable flats. All kinds of events took over public spaces: dances for the over-sixties, raves for the under-sixteens, craft weekends, makers markets, tech forums.

I made my way through the cool atrium, past a cafe and through to the poured-concrete floors of the main hall, lit up by disco lights. In front of a golden curtain, Jess Steele stood up to give a speech, wearing her best party outfit: white PVC boots and a pinstriped mini-dress. 'We are famous for having 107 funders,' she said of the many pots of money the team had secured over the years to make the renovation happen, each one funding a different part of the work, from health initiatives, to apprenticeships, to construction. 'Each of them has believed in what we're trying to do: taking difficult, derelict buildings back into use for community benefit for ever.'

For the next hundred years and maybe another after that, the Observer Building will remain in the hands of the community. Longer than a lifetime. And so the future of this self-renovating neighbourhood rests in the hands of its young people and their children, people who aren't even born yet.[2] People who will have 9,000 square metres to decide what to do with, whether that be affordable flats, business uses or youth programmes.

Jess, meanwhile, was planning her next move. Within a couple of years, she hoped to pass leadership of the Hastings Commons to a broader base of commoners. She planned to open an international hosting centre on the alley, bringing people from around the world to experience the Hastings Commons and to spread a sense of solidarity far beyond the bounds of the neighbourhood. It is solidarity, she told those gathered at the party, that will get us through the challenges we face – not just as a town and country – but as a planet.

In each of these chapters, people have come together to bravely reimagine derelict land and buildings against staggering odds. And yet, in the decade I have been following these remarkable projects, I've learned that it is never just about the buildings. Indeed, in some of these chapters, the buildings – railway arches, shop fronts, churches, department stores – have been lost. But in each case, the process of engaging with history – the bricks and mortar of our built heritage and the plants and minerals of our inherited earth – has in some way changed the participants, opening up people's imaginations to new possibilities, steering them away from a prevailing culture of despair.

It's hard not to feel despair. More than a decade on from austerity, politicians continue to write policies based around economic scarcity with catastrophic impacts on public health and life expectancy. Meanwhile, tech moguls rise in power by capturing more of our time and attention with terrifying images that blur the boundaries of reality. These twin forces shrink our human consciousness. Without good health, we can't imagine things otherwise. Without time and courage, we cannot manifest change. One of the unifying features of the projects in this book is that they start by engaging not just with maligned land or buildings but with people, in particular those whose health, time or courage is under attack. None of us, not even billionaires with panic rooms – can outrun the many global challenges of climate change. Whatever approach we take to rehabilitating human life with the changing cycles of the planet must begin with those who are most vulnerable: the sick, the old, the young.

9.2 HEALTH

That same year I first encountered Jess Steele in the alleyway in Hastings, my reporting took me to the other end of the country, to a community centre in the heart of a housing estate in Gateshead, in the North East. At that time, the North East had a dubious accolade. It was the region with the worst healthy life expectancy, or the number of years the average person can expect to live in good health, in the whole of England.[3] From 2014, a family of community centres in some of the housing estates with the worst health outcomes were providing physical places for people to take control of their own wellbeing, with remarkable effect.

The experiment, managed by a social enterprise called Edberts House, was in response to the rising number of people making appointments at the doctors with non-medical problems such as debt, issues with benefits, or trouble paying their heating bill. These people simply had nowhere else to turn. Other places of support had disappeared. Jobs in mining and shipbuilding had disappeared, leaving behind high levels of unemployment. The departure of industry took with it support networks at working men's clubs and trade unions, increasing people's dependence on the state. Then, after 2011, the government's austerity mandate pulled the rug from under them. Youth clubs shut down, community workers disappeared and local centres closed. The doctor's surgery became the last place people could turn. By the time of the pandemic, as much as 20 per cent of doctors' appointments in the UK were about non-medical issues, at a moment when GP surgeries were chronically oversubscribed.[4]

In the Gateshead experiment, which has become known as social prescribing, GPs referred such patients to people employed as 'community link workers', who were trained to support them with administrative tasks, like arranging debt repayments, applying for phone insurance, or helping them access housing benefits. These link workers could also direct people to local exercise classes, activities to tackle the growing problem of loneliness and isolation, and other local services. Community link workers were based in GP surgeries or, in Gateshead, in remaining or reopened community centres in the heart of housing estates, where people could also access services like Citizens Advice, translators, fitness classes, playgroups and even supper or breakfast clubs for teenagers. Over the course of a year, social prescribing reduced the number of GP appointments made by patients accessing the service by about 25 per cent.[5]

Social prescribing was never about cheap alternatives to real healthcare. It was about shifting the balance of power in the healthcare system. The first social prescribing centre opened in Bromley-by-Bow in London in 1984. Later, it became the first GP centre in the UK to be owned by its patients.[6] It proved that real power can develop in the hands of neighbours who start to think about health in a way that relates not just to medicine and surgery but to feeling connected, eating well, and having secure housing and access to education.

After the millennium, recognition grew among policymakers that health needed to be thought about in a social context, and in 2014 social prescribing was incorporated into a five-year plan for the NHS. The following plan, initially released in 2017, included a mandate to expand access to social prescribing to 2.5 million people across England by 2024. Gateshead has become a flagship region for the practice, described by NHS England as demonstrating national leadership in the field.[7] But policymakers are yet to recognize the importance of physical spaces and places within communities as part of the social context for this practice.

What does it mean, to be healthy? In Britain, we treat health as a personal responsibility, reducing illness and disease to biological flaws or behavioural faults. Health becomes its own industry of medication and surgeries, personal trainers and diet books. In an increasingly privatized healthcare system, good health becomes accessible only to those who can pay. But good health often isn't in our control and depends heavily on our environment. Prisoners have their access to the outdoors limited, reducing their chance of a healthy life. Workers in unsafe conditions are condemned to injury and disease. Some people have no choice but to consume unhealthy food or contaminated water because of privatization and pollution.

The law is beginning to recognize this. In a landmark verdict in 2020, a coroner ruled that the death of a Black British girl called Ella Adoo-Kissi-Debrah living in South London in 2013 was the result of air pollution from the South Circular, a congested road near her home. The levels of nitrogen dioxide near where Ella lived had exceeded World Health Organization and European Union guidelines, the coroner concluded. On the day of her fatal seizure, pollution levels were abnormally high. In the campaigning that followed, Ella's mother Rosamund Adoo-Kissi-Debrah spoke to one doctor who, confronted with a patient who was also suffering from respiratory issues because of air pollution, did not prescribe an inhaler or a course of antibiotics.[8] Instead, the doctor asked if it was possible for the patient to move home. Later Adoo-Kissi-Debrah took her claim to the High Court, fighting for 'the right to clean air' under the Human Rights Act.

The case recognized in law, for the first time, that where we live impacts our health. The experiment in Gateshead was so interesting because it situated health at the heart of the neighbourhood, within community buildings. It suggests that the closure of such buildings – the dereliction of places to gather – is a health issue.

In 2016, workers at Edberts joined then-director of public health Alice Wiseman, to do something about spiralling childhood obesity in the borough. At that time, almost a quarter of children in Gateshead were classed as obese. Wiseman knew the burden of obesity fell hardest on children from lower-income backgrounds, and that the problem was getting worse. She wanted to develop a place-based, community-centred intervention drawing on all the resources in the one area, but managed and organized by people within the community themselves.

Long-term funding from People's Health Trust, as part of their Local Conversations programme, enabled community workers from Edberts to work with people in the Old Fold and Nest estates of Gateshead. Together they developed ideas to use a derelict shop in the heart of the neighbourhood as a new community centre called Pattinson House. The shop had been used as a credit union and burger bar, and was in a disgusting state.[9] By working together to reopen the shop, residents built more supportive relationships with one another. These relationships were the starting point for meaningful and honest conversations about obesity with the authorities. Through the new hub, local people worked together to create budgets and plan activities for the benefit of their neighbours.[10]

The project required a different approach from Wiseman, who gave time to conversations, activities and lunches with people from the estates. But it was also a test for residents. Could they stand up in front of those in charge of public health and express their ideas for change?

In the process, traditional power structures were upended. The director entered the conversation needing to learn about the estate: a subject in which residents were experts. Local people were trained in PowerPoint to give presentations to the authorities about their ideas for tackling obesity. Over a year of conversations, a bond of trust grew. Residents' initial ideas – cooking and dancing sessions, for example – became more ambitious. They asked the youth worker at Pattinson House to establish a link with the athletic club at the Gateshead Stadium, which is always visible on the horizon, just 500 metres away from the community hub. Many local people had until then never visited the stadium – they didn't even know what was inside. With help from a youth worker, residents started going for sports clubs and other sessions. Some young people even went on to represent the athletics club in regional events.

In another project, people talked about how they could improve road safety outside the local school, so that more children could walk there. A resident went on to run a road traffic campaign in collaboration with an elected ward councillor, resulting in a change to the layout of the road. Children came forward to talk about their experiences of obesity, including being the target of school bullies, and the way this made them afraid to go to the parks and other green spaces. After extensive redevelopment, funding from People's Health Trust and a lot of determination, Pattinson House officially opened in 2016. An embedded researcher on the project reflected that often, initiatives in disadvantaged communities tried to wean people off support, towards total independence.[11] But in these estates, the desire from residents was for the opposite: more, not less, contact. Not dependence, but a collective approach that made people feel part of something bigger than themselves: healthy interdependence. The building had become a key part of this collective approach to addressing an issue of public health. The researcher described the community hub as a 'health-enhancing environment'.[12]

9.3 YOUNG PEOPLE

In Hastings, too, I had seen this desire for places to sustain collective action and community – especially among the young. Local authorities in Hastings, like many around the country, had spent a decade trying to slim down expenses as their government grant had been slashed by austerity policies. Collectively, these authorities cut youth provision funding in England from more than £1 billion to £408.5 million between 2011 and 2021. Hastings had been ravaged of places for young people to gather. In 2019 alone, East Sussex County Council shut thirteen youth clubs and fourteen children's centres.

In the aftermath of the pandemic, economists have struggled to make sense of spiralling economic inactivity: the number of people out of work and not seeking work. Of those, the number of people out of work because of illness has been particularly problematic. In the five years after 2019, economic inactivity due to ill health rose steadily across the UK to stand at a record high of nearly three million people.[13] Nine-tenths of that rise came from two groups: the eldest in the labour market, or those approaching retirement, and the very young.

Recognizing the dire state of mental health among the town's young people, in January 2023 the Hastings Commons secured £8.6 million from the government's Youth Investment Fund to develop places for them to gather. The youth worker, a softly spoken young woman called Sidney Ewing, went out to find young people to invite. It was winter, but she found teenagers hanging around outside, literally standing in car parks or bus shelters. Sidney gave them a voucher for hot chocolate and directed them to a new Hastings Commons youth club. Soon, many of them were coming by every week.

They confided in Sidney that they didn't feel ready to go to university, that they didn't feel prepared to get a job. That there were no good jobs in Hastings, anyway. Many of them suffered from anxiety or low mood. She learned how these children felt about being shut in at home during Covid. At the exact moment they should have been learning how to talk to one another, they had been forced to communicate through screens, using social media that was later shown to have a devastating impact on their self-image and mental health.

I visited the youth club one Wednesday night in 2024, to write an assignment for the *Guardian* about Hastings having the highest number of young people in bad health of anywhere in the country. It was board game night, and a handful of young people were gathered around a table. One peered from behind a floppy fringe, telling the other players of a monster with jaws wide enough to swallow a man whole. Behind him, two boys played pool. For the moment, there was not an iPhone in sight. Each night of the week was dedicated to youth from a different age group, and each night was popular, particularly the 16–18s night. The young people, far from shunning social contact, seemed to be seeking it out.

The money from the Youth Investment Fund was designed to help Hastings Commons develop facilities for young people to gather within the neighbourhood. Some went towards the renovation of another nearby derelict building. Eagle House, an old furniture store, was being transformed into a youth and community centre, including a youth club and a public living room with sofas and comfy chairs. Downstairs, Hastings Commons designed a new home for the creative technology hub that had temporarily taken residence on the mezzanine of the Observer Building. The hub would share the space with Hastings Youth Commons and staff from other youth and community charities.

Even before it was open, I met one former apprentice from the Hastings Commons, a young man called Alex Giles, who gave me a sense of what they were trying to achieve. Alex had dropped out of a diploma in games development at a nearby college during the pandemic, since he didn't have a computer at home. For the next two years he was on Universal Credit, struggling to find work, save for a Christmas job packing boxes in a local warehouse. In 2022, the job centre encouraged him to apply for an apprenticeship at the Hastings Commons, which turned into a job: two years later and Alex was running technology sessions for visiting youth, including sessions where teenagers learn to make a game in a day. More than once, he heard young people say they'd like to do his job.

Yet, as Eagle House neared completion, the whole project to create a permanent place for young people in Hastings hung in the balance because of a shortage of long-term, or core, funding. The Youth Investment Fund had plugged hundreds of millions of pounds into developing community spaces, only to leave a funding black hole for organizations to implement any meaningful youth activities. When I caught up with Jess in 2025, she said Hastings Commons had been struggling to raise anything like the normal amount of funding from foundations, since it was now considered 'too big' for funders who preferred to provide smaller amounts to projects, meeting immediate needs. After years of being told to be more ambitious, Hastings Commons was now suffering from its own success.

Repeatedly, I heard about this funding paradox from the most successful community organizations. These organizations raised millions for building projects and became the flag bearers for the emerging movement of people and groups practising alternative futures. But it was getting harder, not easier, to raise the money from endowments and philanthropists to do the work. Victories like improvements to the community right to buy that appeared in the small print of the devolution white paper in 2024 were not backed by serious government or philanthropic financial and administrative support. A few foundations, confronted with the realities of climate breakdown, had announced intentions to spend down – plugging every last penny of capital into meeting the challenge head-on.

But many seemed to have become shyer, not bolder. And yet the challenge of adaptation has never been greater.

9.4 ADAPTATION

Over the last decade, I have seen relationships develop between many of the groups and people who appear in this book. Melissa Mean in Bristol, Onion Collective in Watchet, Immy Kaur in Birmingham, Jess Steele in Hastings, and Wendy Hart and Hannah Sloggett in Plymouth began, over the years, to refer to themselves jokingly as the Mycelium Gang. The expression draws on the world-building work of mycelium, the tiny spores of fungi that live beneath the surface of the earth and interact with almost all known plant families through mycorrhizal networks. In her book *The Mushroom at the End of the World*, the anthropologist Anna Tsing showed that these networks are a key part of forest ecosystems, without which trees would not survive.

In the same way, many of the organizations and people who appear in these pages have invisible but intricate entanglements through funders, supporters, values and ideas. These entanglements act like mycorrhizal networks, transferring sustenance, information and strength. We see them come to the fore in times of crisis, such as during the pandemic. Or we can trace them using the alternative-futures work undertaken by Onion Collective in 2024. We may find ourselves drawing more on these stories as the extremes of environmental change leave us with no other choice but to adapt. Perhaps one day we will see how these projects were the starting point for the rooted and circular systems we need at the foundation of our national efforts to adapt to the changing climate within neighbourhoods.

The recent appreciation of mycelium is linked to a growing understanding of the way the world is powered by networks. This includes new research on the oscillatory patterns of neural networks in the brain, and the 2018 discovery of the interstitium, a mesh-like network under the skin of the human body that wraps around the organs and blood vessels, carrying fluid and information. The discovery of the interstitium puts a question mark over cells as the basic unit of life – an assumption that has been the foundation of biology since the English scientist Robert Hooke first peered through a microscope in 1665.[14] Only now are scientists reconsidering this view, as they discover the ever-changing, interwoven systems in our bodies, in nature, even in the minerals of the earth's crust. Science is beginning to show that the planet does not abide by discrete systems. The reality of our existence is far more interconnected than we first thought.

We have overlooked mutualistic relationships in nature, believing them unnecessary to understand the world. By seeing ourselves as separate from one another, we have come to view human life within a hierarchy of predator and prey, where every kind must fight for its own survival by obliterating another. We see the terrifying extremes made possible by this assumption in the unchecked individualism of our time. The commoditization of public health and the capture of our consciousness by tech companies have the same effect of isolating us from one another.[15] The dogma of scarcity that characterized the austerity project has left the UK sick, and getting sicker. In 2024, figures from the Office for National Statistics showed that life expectancy in the UK had returned to 2010–12 levels for women and below the 2010–12 level for men, and was falling in all four nations for 2020–22 compared with 2017–19.[16] Worsening health comes at a time of rising fear. It is becoming harder to distinguish between the real and the fake online, feeding into a sense of confusion that is catnip to politicians with extremist views. Such figureheads use these conditions to usher through terrifying political projects: the persecution of immigrants, the dismantling of social support for the vulnerable, the rolling-back of basic human rights.

Detachment is leading us to despair. While people typically spend longer hours alone as they get older, recent data shows that young people are socializing less. People in their teens and twenties now hang out about as much as someone ten years older did in the past.[17] In parallel, rates of mental distress are rising among the young, but not among those of middle age or older.[18]

This is not coincidental, public health data shows. The statistician John Burn-Murdoch has shown how the deterioration in young people's life satisfaction between 2010 and 2023 can largely be explained by a reduction in the amount of time they spent with others. Too much time spent alone is associated with lower life satisfaction and even higher rates of death.[19]

In an article about the interstitium in *Orion* magazine, Jennifer Brandel explores the way our understanding of the units of the world – molecule, cell, organ, person, species – is demonstrated even by the way we speak in nouns.[20] We organize society and work as hierarchies of individual jobs, called departments or companies, and we assign people immutable roles, professions or specialisms, rather than describing what they do using verbs. We ask children *what* they want to be instead of *how* they want to be when they grow up. But it feels like this language is failing us. Individualism – the idea that any of us can survive without others – will prove deadly during the climate crises ahead.

Frontierlands shows that the way out of this existential cul-de-sac is to live in a more relational way, rooted in our heritage. We need to decide not what we are, or what we want to be – but what we are going to do. Attached to our screens, holed up in dark rooms, we become prey to fear, captured by the horrifying images fed to us on a doom scroll of war, starving children, depraved dictators and impending climate catastrophe. Engaging in the physical, communal nature of creating something – from timber shelters and clay bricks, to colourful murals, even digital games – is one way to step outside of the terror when it descends. Among other people, in shared and trusted places, we can begin to repair our relationships to one another and our environment.

For as long as any of us can remember, a doctrine of growth at all costs has squeezed out alternative models and ideas. On the fringes, in the edge-places, new systems and practices have emerged. We find ourselves in a moment when change is accelerating and our place in eternity is shifting; when we can be sure that the growth delusion will lead to our destruction. It is time to welcome the new ways in from our frontiers.

Acknowledgements

Most of all, I would like to thank the people in this book who have, over the last decade, welcomed me into their lives, put me up on my trips, patiently answered my questions and taught me new ways to be. Thanks to Jess Steele in Hastings, who fed me Ronan's fish pie on a first visit to Hastings and whose work inspired me to make Hastings my home. Thanks to Steve Peak for his invaluable local knowledge. Thanks to Naomi Griffith, Sally Lowndes, Georgie Grant and Hannah Griffith Prendergrast in Watchet, whose Friday parties and pints on the Esplanade and at Pebbles showed me a different kind of motherhood when I was pregnant with my first son and badly needed to see one. Especially to Jess Prendergrast: you stretch my brain! To Beki Melrose and Jo Bambrough in Morecambe, for the kitchen disco and the keto curries, and for allowing me to learn from my mistakes: thank you. To Jules Abraham and Bob Pickersgill for sharing your stories. To Rosanna Martin, whose Stan arrived just before my own, for having me at your cottage, waking me up to stoke the kiln and feeding my Stan spaghetti on our visits. To Zenna Tagney, who made Cornwall come alive for me. To Chris Blake in Wales, who invited me on that early trip to Scotland and, much later, had me to stay in his magical Black Mountains cabin. To Ian and Drom Thomas, and to Gwynfor Jones in beautiful Treherbert. To Ben Rawlence for the words of encouragement. To Immy Kaur, who always, somehow, found a sliver of time to talk despite being pulled one thousand ways. To Len Maloney, who taught me the meaning of persistence, and Krissie Nicolson, whose integrity never wavers. To Frances Northrop, Myfanwy Taylor and Vicky Alvarez: to the end I have drawn from the energy of Latin Village. You proved it's possible. To Wendy Hart and Hannah Sloggett, who showed me the importance of joy. To John Christophers and Jo Hindley for their hospitality and generosity of spirit. To Melissa Mean and Athlyn Cathcart-Keays, for your huge effort during the edit. And to Sarah Gorman in Gateshead, who showed me what it means to care for the people you love. And the hundreds of other people who have offered me their time and kindness – too many to list. Thank you.

The reporting that became *Frontierlands* was supported by various grants, fellowships and institutions. I would like to thank Friends Provident Foundation, especially Danielle Walker Palmour, for taking a punt on my proposal for *Far Nearer* and supporting me through two years of invaluable early reporting. To Power to Change, especially Vidyha Alakeson and Alexandra Valk, who helped me meet so many great community businesses. And to Local Trust, especially Jessica Wenban-Smith and Matt Leach, who invited me to write an essay that opened doors. To Susanne Scharnowski and Marie Menzel at the Freie Universität Berlin, who read early chapters and helped me shape my ideas. To the Democracy Collaborative, especially Ted Howard, Joe Guinan, Neil McInroy, Matthew Brown and Sarah McKinley (now freelance), whose work around community wealth-building is fascinating. To people I met through New Economics Foundation who are now all over: Chris Williams, Will Brett, Rachel Laurence and many others, thanks for giving me your time.

Finding a narrative that could hold these vast and complex stories has not been an easy process. Thank you to my agent, Richard Pike, whose calmness and stoicism always steadied my nerves. To my editor, Susanna Wadeson, who believed in the project early on and has been enormously patient and forgiving throughout. Thanks to her team at Transworld/Torva – I feel so lucky to be one of your authors. Thanks to Ian Greensill and Alex Newby for their copy-editing and Vicki Robinson for indexing. Thanks to Kate Samano, Elizabeth Dobson and Bella Bosworth for their sharp eyes. Thanks to the academics on whose work I have drawn and who took the time to respond to my emails, especially Kate Raworth, Robert Hazen and Lucy Easthope. And to the writers who offered words of encouragement when I needed to hear them: Hettie O'Brien, Lamorna Ash, Kassia St Clair, Lucy Jones and Jen Calleja. Special thanks to Laura Snapes for offering nothing but improvements and enthusiasm.

I am also grateful to my editors at newspapers and other publications. As time has gone on and budgets have become smaller, the space for these kinds of stories has shrunk. Some editors showed faith, including Tim de Lisle, a friend and mentor who always makes my sentences better; Cait Morrison, my editor at the *Independent*, who let me file every week on community businesses in a column that was meant to be about Silicon Valley-style entrepreneurs; Alison Benjamin, who commissioned my first *Far Nearer* story in the *Guardian*, and John Collingridge, Angela Monaghan and Juliette Garside, who commissioned some of my later pitches; James Hurley at *The Times*; and Isabel Berwick, another friend and mentor, who commissioned me at the *Financial Times*. Thanks to Larry Ryan, who often found space for my stories at Nesta's brilliant, now sadly defunct, digital publication, *The Long+Short*. And to Jonny Gordon-Farleigh at *Stir to Action*, the only UK magazine dedicated to the next economy: keep going!

Finally, thank you to the people who held the babies, made the tea and put up with me through the darker moments. To our babysitters in Berlin, Pilar Acosta and Dhati Sta, and Nancy Blythe in Hastings; to Stan's beloved nursery teachers: thank you. To my mum Penny Raine and step-dad Steve Raine, and to my mother-in-law Pat Wilkinson, thank you for the long visits when you barely saw me. To my dad, Nigel Sheffield, for your support. To my kind and generous sister, Caroline Sheffield, who loves my children as if they were her own. To Stan and Larry, Mummy is coming out of the shed now. And to Ian Wilkinson, always ready with a hug: thank you. To say I couldn't have done this without you is an understatement. I love that we are finding our village. But I am so grateful that before we found it, you were my village.

Further Reading

Books

Alexander, J. and Conrad, A., *Citizen: Why the Key to Fixing Everything is All of Us* (Canbury Press, 2022)

Beckerman, G., *The Quiet Before: On the Unexpected Origins of Radical Ideas* (Crown, 2022)

Bennett, J., *Vibrant Matter: A Political Ecology of Things* (Duke University Press, 2010)

Berry, W., *The Unsettling of America: Culture and Agriculture* (Counterpoint, 1977)

Brown, A. M., *Emergent Strategy: Shaping Change, Changing Worlds* (AK Press, 2017)

Carson, R., *Silent Spring* (Penguin, 1965)

Easthope, L., *The Recovery Myth* (Palgrave Macmillan, 2018)

Federici, S., *Re-enchanting the World: Feminism and the Politics of the Commons* (Between the Lines Books, 2019)

Fisher, M., *Capitalist Realism: Is There No Alternative?* (Zero Books, 2009)

Gibson-Graham, J. K., *A Postcapitalist Politics* (University of Minnesota Press, 2006)

Gilmore, R. W., *Abolition Geography: Essays Towards Liberation* (Verso, 2022)

Haraway, D. J., *Staying with the Trouble: Making Kin in the Chthulucene* (Duke University Press, 2016)

Hawken, P., *Drawdown: The Most Comprehensive Plan* Ever Proposed *to Reverse Global Warming* (Penguin, 2018)

Hayes, N., *The Book of Trespass: Crossing the Lines that Divide Us* (Bloomsbury, 2022)

Hazen, R. and Wong, M. L., *Time's Second Arrow: Evolution, Order, and a New Law of Nature* (W. W. Norton, 2026)

Hopkins, N., *From What Is to What If: Unleashing the Power of Imagination to Create the Future We Want Now* (Chelsea Green Publishing, 2019)

Kimmerer, R. Wall, *Braiding Sweetgrass: Indigenous Wisdom, Scientific Knowledge, and the Teachings of Plants* (Penguin, 2020)

Kimmerer, R. Wall, *The Serviceberry: An Economy of Gifts and Abundance* (Penguin, 2026)

Kohn, M., *Radical Space: Building the House of the People* (Cornell University, 2003)

Krznaric, R., *History for Tomorrow: How the Past Can Inspire Our Future* (W. H. Allen, 2024)

Le Guin, U. K., *Always Coming Home* (Gollancz, 2016)

Machado De Oliveira, V., *Hospicing Modernity: Parting with Harmful Ways of Living* (North Atlantic Books, 2021)

Ostrom, E., *Governing the Commons: The Evolution of Institutions for Collective Action* (Cambridge University Press, 1990)

Ostrom, E., *The Future of the Commons: Beyond Market Failure and Government Regulations* (London Publishing Partnership, 2012)

Peak, S., *The America Ground, Hastings* (The History Press, 2021)

Rawlence, B., *City of Thorns: Nine Lives in the World's Largest Refugee Camp* (Picador USA, 2016)

Raworth, K., *Doughnut Economics: Seven Ways to Think Like a 21st-Century Economist* (Random House Business Books, 2017)

Sharpe, B., *Three Horizons: The Patterning of Hope* (Triarchy Press, 2020)

Solnit, R., *A Paradise Built in Hell: The Extraordinary Communities that Arise in Disaster* (Penguin, 2009)

Solnit, R., *Hope in the Dark: Untold Histories, Wild Possibilities*, 3rd edn (Canongate, 2016)

Tsing, A. L., *The Mushroom at the End of the World: On the Possibility of Life in Capitalist Ruins* (Princeton University Press, 2021)

Essays, theses and articles

Brandel, J., 'Invisible Landscapes', *Orion*, 16 November 2023, https://orionmagazine.org/article/interstitium-scientific-discovery-anatomy/

Cheetham, M. et al., ' "It's not about telling people to eat better, stop smoking or get on the treadmill" ' in Dorothy Newbury-Birch and Keith Allan (eds), *Co-creating and Co-producing Research Evidence: A Guide for Practitioners and Academics in Health, Social Care and Education Settings* (Routledge, 2019); also available at https://ebrary.net/209732/education/_it_s_telling_people_better_smoking_treadmill_. Mandy Cheetham's work around co-producing research is fascinating and has much to teach journalists.

Civic Square, 'Neighbourhood Public Square', 2024, available on Medium, https://medium.com/neighbourhood-public-square. All of the publications in this series are essential, in particular '3°C Neighbourhood', 'Endowing the Future', 'Physical Infrastructure Design', 'Building Skills' and 'The Land Story So Far'.

Dark Matter Labs, 'A Smart Commons: a new model for investing in the commons', Medium, 13 Sept 2019, https://provocations.darkmatterlabs.org/a-smart-commons-528f4e53cec2

Lowndes, S. and Prendergrast, J., 'Reclaiming hope for alternative futures', Onion Collective, 11 Feb 2025, https://medium.com/onioncollective/reclaiming-hope-for-alternative-futures-a093d99db434. The first essay of four on Onion Collective's Joseph

Rowntree Foundation-funded work around alternative futures. I recommend them all.

Parvin, A., 'A New Land Contract', Open Systems Lab, 21 June 2020, https://medium.com/open-systems-lab/a-new-land-contract-684c3ba1f1b3

Steele, J., 'Self-renovating neighbourhoods as an alternative to the false choice of gentrification or decline', PhD thesis (University of Leicester, 2022)

Tsing, A. L., 'The buck, the bull, and the dream of the stag: some unexpected weeds of the Anthropocene', Suomen Antropologi, 42:1 (2017), https://journal.fi/suomenantropologi/article/view/65084/26231

Endnotes

All website URLs active as of 28 July 2025.

INTRODUCTION

1   Arundhati Roy, 'The pandemic is a portal', *Financial Times*, 3 April 2020, https://www.ft.com/content/10d8f5e8-74eb-11ea-95fe-fcd274e920ca

2   There is an events venue in Hastings called The Printworks – but the printworks I refer to is the Observer Building, which was built as a publishing house and printing facility in 1924.

3   'Rose Cottage, an ironically named, tumble-down stables in the Alley, came on the market in July 2019': Jess Steele, 'Self-renovating neighbourhoods as an alternative to the false choice of gentrification or decline', PhD thesis (University of Leicester, 2022), p. 153

4   Numbers taken from a tour of the building by James Leathers, 12 June 2019.

5   Hastings Commons Neighbourhood Ventures or HCNV (formerly White Rock Neighbourhood Ventures or WRNV) is a company owned equally by three entities. These are: Jericho Road Solutions, a Hastings-based company, led by Jess Steele, specializing in helping local leaders everywhere to make better neighbourhoods; Meanwhile Space, a national social enterprise community interest company set up in 2010 to create temporary uses for redundant space to support community cohesion, place-making and enterprise; and Hastings Commons Community Land Trust (formerly Heart of Hastings CLT), which emerged from White Rock Trust, an organization that itself came from the campaign to rescue the Hastings Pier but collapsed in 2015. Most of the buildings in the Commons have been bought by HCNV and the long-term aim has always been that 100 per cent of the company

share ownership will transfer to the CLT once the buildings have been de-risked.

6   Rob Evans, 'Half of England is owned by less than 1% of the population', *Guardian*, 17 April 2019

7   Sarah Butler, 'One in seven shops now vacant across the UK', *Guardian*, 30 July 2021

8   *Number of vacant and second homes, England and Wales: Census 2021*, Office for National Statistics, 27 Oct 2023, https://www.ons.gov.uk/people populationandcommunity/housing/bulletins/numberofvacantand secondhomesenglandandwales/census2021

9   Liam Geraghty, 'One million homes are lying empty in England. Here's how we can fill them', *Big Issue*, 18 Nov 2024

10 Gareth Davies et al., 'Revealed: The thousands of public spaces lost to the council funding crisis', Bureau of Investigative Journalism, 4 March 2019, https://www.thebureauinvestigates.com/stories/2019-03-04/sold-from-under-you/

11 Polly Toynbee and David Walker, 'The lost decade: the hidden story of how austerity broke Britain', *Guardian*, 3 March 2020

12 Evelyne Hübscher, Thomas Sattler and Markus Wagner, 'Does austerity cause polarization?', *British Journal of Political Science*, 14 April 2023, https://www.cambridge.org/core/journals/british-journal-of-political-science/article/does-austerity-cause-polarization/5A92279ABBEE6 23D38E438848B03C060

13 Thiemo Fetzer, 'Austerity and Brexit', *Intereconomics*, 55:1 (2020), pp. 27–33

14 Lucy Easthope, *The Recovery Myth*, Ch. 6 (Palgrave Macmillan, 2018), https://www.perlego.com/book/3493850

15 Ian Sample, 'Covid poses "greatest threat to mental health since second world war"', *Guardian*, 27 Dec 2020

16 John T. Cacioppo and Louise C. Hawkley, 'Perceived social isolation and cognition', *Trends in Cognitive Sciences*, 13:10 (2009), pp. 447–54

17 A 2020 study published in the journal *Group Processes and Intergroup Relations* found that social exclusion is a leading factor behind radicalization. A 2021 study conducted by researchers at RAND Corporation found that loneliness is one of the predominant reasons people adopt extremist views and join extremist groups; Brad Stulberg, 'Extended loneliness can make you more vulnerable to extremist views', *Time*, 3 Nov 2022

18 Rebecca Solnit, *A Paradise Built in Hell* (Penguin, 2009), p. 2

19 Ibid.

20 Rebecca Solnit, *Hope in the Dark* (Canongate, 2016), p. 13

21 Steve Peak, *The America Ground, Hastings* (The History Press, 2021), p. 13

22 There is only one report of flying the Stars and Stripes, in 1832 at a major carnival event – see Peak, *The America Ground*, pp. 74–6

23 The street became part of the commercial centre of the new town during the Victorian era, with architecture in Italianate and neoclassical styles reminiscent of other expanding European cities at the time: Hastings Borough Council, 'Consulation Draft: Hastings Central Conservation Area Appraisal and Management Plan' (2017), p. 28, in Steele, 'Self-renovating neighbourhoods', op. cit., p. 132

24 Steele, 'Self-renovating neighbourhoods', op. cit., p. 133

25 Speech by Jess Steele during a tour of the Hastings Commons for stakeholders, June 2019

26 Leigh Shaw-Taylor, 'Who had access to common land?', *Top of the Campops* blog, Cambridge Group for the History of Population and Social Structure, Department of Geography and Faculty of History, https://www.campop. geog.cam.ac.uk/blog/2025/02/06/common-land/

27 Elinor Ostrom, *Governing the Commons: The Evolution of Institutions for Collective Action* (Cambridge University Press, 1990)

28 Elinor Ostrom, *The Future of the Commons: Beyond Market Failure and Government Regulations* (London Publishing Partnership, 2012), p. 4

29 Erik Nordman, 'Opinion: In the face of a looming climate crisis, the late Elinor Ostrom gives me hope', *Ensia*, 14 Nov 2019, https://ensia.com/voices/ climate-crisis-elinor-ostrom-common-pool-resources/

30 Elinor Ostrom, *Governing the Commons: The Evolution of Institutions for Collective Action*, op. cit., p. 67

31 Steele, 'Self-renovating neighbourhoods', op. cit., p. 87

32 Indy Johar, 'The need for a civic economy', Dark Matter Laboratories, 27 Feb 2016, https://provocations.darkmatterlabs.org/the-need-for-a-civic-economy-75e924b23373

33 'In systems terms, these organisations must also acknowledge that we are, for now, as Alnoor Ladna and Lynn Murphy describe it in their thoughtful book on philanthrocapitalism, still very much swimming in the soup of late-stage capitalism and therefore inextricably intertwined with neoliberal

capitalist structures': Jessica Prendergrast and Sally Lowndes, 'Resourcing hope for alternative futures', Onion Collective (11 Feb 2025), https://medium. com/onioncollective/resourcing-hope-for-alternative-futures-27fc7 6acf97e

34 Jessica Prendergrast and Sally Lowndes, 'Practising hope for alternative futures', Onion Collective (11 Feb 2025), https://medium.com/@jessprend/ practising-hope-for-alternative-futures-6ec9d22201d9

35 Wendell Berry, *The Unsettling of America* (Counterpoint Press, 2015), p. 122

36 Araceli Camargo, 'Can we transition from economy to ecology?', *Reimagining Economic Possibilities*, 27 Oct 2022, https://medium.com/reimag ining-economic-possibilities/what-if-a-new-economy-was-rooted-in-ecology-3489e9e7808b

37 Adam Tooze, 'Welcome to the world of the polycrisis', *Financial Times*, 28 Oct 2022, https://www.ft.com/content/498398e7-11b1-494b-9cd3-6d669dc3de33

1: HARBOUR

1 Austen Tosone, 'Mierle Laderman Ukeles takes over the Queens Museum', *Nylon*, September 2016, https://www.nylon.com/articles/mierle-laderman-ukeles-nylon-september-2016

2 Eduard J. Alvarez-Palau and Oliver Dunn, 'Database of historic ports and coastal sailing routes in England and Wales', *Data in Brief*, 25 (2019), p. 104188, https://www.sciencedirect.com/science/article/pii/S2352340919305426

3 Ibid., fig.1

4 Helena Vieira, 'Dockworkers and the introduction of containers in UK shipping in the late 1960's', LSE, 10 November 2017, https://blogs.lse.ac.uk/businessreview/2017/11/10/dockworkers-and-the-introduction-of-containers-in-uk-shipping-in-the-late-1960s/

5 'Dawlish rail line: Closure "costs economy up to £1.2bn"', BBC News, 5 February 2015, https://www.bbc.co.uk/news/uk-england-devon-31140192

6 Ben Gouldby and Peter Hunter, 'Climate Change and Ports: Impacts and Adaptation Strategies', HR Wallingford, March 2021, https://www.britishports.org.uk/content/uploads/2021/10/BPA_HR_Wallingford_Climate_Change_Adaptation1.pdf

7 Interview with Jessica Prendergrast, September 2024

8   'Changing face of Watchet harbour', *West Somerset Free Press*, 2 Feb 2001

9   Hannah Green, 'Last chance for Urban Splash developers at Watchet's East Wharf', *Somerset County Gazette*, 25 April 2013

10 Ibid.

11 Interview with Jessica Prendergrast, September 2024.

12 Sally Lowndes and Jessica Prendergrast, 'Connecting hope for alternative futures', Onion Collective, 11 February 2025, https://medium.com/@sally_85532/connecting-hope-for-alternative-futures-32ca83dd318a

13 'The makings of a plan!', Onion Collective, 20 June 2014, https://web.archive.org/web/20210508101437/https://www.onioncollective.co.uk/single-post/2014/06/20/the-makings-of-a-plan

14 'About us', Contains Art, https://www.containsart.co.uk/about.html

15 'Insight. Innovation. Leadership. Annual Report and Accounts 2015', DS Smith, 2015, https://www.annualreports.com/HostedData/AnnualReportArchive/d/LSE_SMDS_2015.pdf

16 Brexit contributed to pushing up the cost of materials in Britain by 60 per cent between 2015 and 2022: Lisa O'Carroll, 'Brexit: UK construction costs "have risen much more steeply than EU"', *Guardian*, 24 January 2023

17 Lowndes and Prendergrast, 'Connecting hope for alternative futures'

18 Vidhya Alakeson and Will Brett, 'Local Heroes: How to Sustain Community Spirit Beyond Covid-19', Power to Change, 5 May 2020, https://www.powertochange.org.uk/wp-content/uploads/2020/05/PTC_3698_Covid_Report_FINAL.pdf

19 Food Standards Agency, 'The COVID-19 consumer research', research project, 2020, https:// www.food.gov.uk/research/research-projects/the-Covid-19-consumer-research

20 'Coronavirus: Made in Hackney launches free food delivery service for vulnerable people', *Hackney Citizen*, 26 March 2020

21 Swedish Civil Contingencies Agency, 'If Crisis or War Comes', 2018, https://ctif.org/sites/default/files/news_files/2018-06/om-krisen-eller-kriget-kommer---engelska.pdf

22 Robert Kirsch and Emily Ray, 'Always prepared: why prepping for doomsday is a logical choice for many Americans', *Guardian*, 10 Dec 2024, https://www.theguardian.com/society/2024/dec/10/doomsday-prepping-america

23 Lucy Easthope, *The Recovery Myth*, Ch. 6 (Palgrave Macmillan, 2018), https://www.perlego.com/book/3493850

24 Interview with Eric Klinenberg, University of Chicago, https://press.uchi cago.edu/Misc/Chicago/443213in.html

25 Bill Sharpe, *Three Horizons: The Patterning of Hope* (Triarchy Press, 2020)

26 Sally Lowndes and Jessica Prendergrast, 'Reclaiming hope for alternative futures', Onion Collective, 11 Feb 2025, https://medium.com/onioncollective/reclaiming-hope-for-alternative-futures-a093d99db434

27 Sally Lowndes and Jessica Prendergrast, 'Practising hope for alternative futures', Onion Collective, 11 Feb 2025, https://medium.com/@jessprend/practising-hope-for-alternative-futures-6ec9d22201d9

28 Gal Beckerman, *The Quiet Before: On the Unexpected Origins of Radical Ideas* (Crown, 2022)

2: HOARDINGS

1 'Birds of the Bay', Morecambe Bay Partnership, https://www.morecambe bay.org.uk/be-inspired/landscape-coast-nature/birds-of-the-bay

2 'In and around Morecambe', Morecambe Bay Local Nature Partnership, https://www.morecambebaynature.org.uk/node/63

3 'Green tiger beetle', Wildlife Trusts, https://www.wildlifetrusts.org/wildlife-explorer/invertebrates/beetles/green-tiger-beetle

4 'A year in the life of a great crested newt', Acer Ecology, 26 Feb 2017, https://www.acerecology.co.uk/great-crested-newt-year/

5 'In and around Morecambe', Morecambe Bay Local Nature Partnership

6 Catherine Oliver, 'Seabirds, environmental change, and Morecambe Bay', https://catherinecmoliver.com/2023/01/20/seabirds-environmental-change-and-morecambe-bay/

7 Catherine Oliver, ' "The birds of the Bay": Avian landscapes of Morecambe Bay', *Landscape Research*, 26 Feb 2025, https://www.tandfonline.com/doi/full/10.1080/01426397.2024.2438765?src=#d1e224

8 https://sandgrownstories.com/category/people/

9 'Fishing in the Bay', Arnside Archive, https://arnsidearchive.org.uk/?MARITIME_HERITAGE:Fishing_in_the_Bay

10 Richard Muir, 'On change in the landscape', *Landscape Research*, 28:4 (2003), pp. 383–403

11 Bob Pickersgill, 'When I painted the boarded up shop at 190 Euston Rd', Morecambe and Heysham Past and Present Facebook group, 24 Jan 2021, https://www.facebook.com/groups/morecambeheysham/posts/3638643546253694/

12 Josh Halliday, ' "It looks like you're a lazy idiot": hoarders welcome medical classification', *Guardian*, 18 August 2018

13 Jack F. Samuels et al., 'Prevalence and correlates of hoarding behavior in a community-based sample', *Behaviour Research and Therapy*, 46:7 (2008), pp. 836–44

14 Wiktionary, 'hoard', https://en.wiktionary.org/wiki/hoard

15 Cassie Barton et al., 'The future of coastal communities', House of Commons Library, 5 Sept 2022, https://researchbriefings.files.parliament.uk/documents/CDP-2022-0153/CDP-2022-0153.pdf

16 According to the 2010, 2015 and 2019 English Indices of Deprivation, https://www.gov.uk/government/collections/english-indices-of-deprivation; 'England's most deprived areas named as Jaywick and Blackpool', BBC News, 26 Sept 2019, https://www.bbc.co.uk/news/uk-england-49812519

17 According to the 2021 census: https://www.ons.gov.uk/census

18 A study by academics at Sheffield Hallam University in 2008 showed that twenty-six of the thirty-seven principal seaside towns in England have an overall level of deprivation greater than the English average, and that Morecambe fares worse than most: Christina Beatty, Steve Fothergill and Ian Wilson, 'England's Seaside Towns: a "benchmarking study"', *Communities and Local Government* (2008), p. 9.

19 'Briefing: The link between inequality and the far right', Equality Trust, 14 Aug 2024, https://equalitytrust.org.uk/evidence-base/briefings/briefing-the-link-between-inequality-and-the-far-right/

20 Amelia Hill, 'UK spends more financing inequality in favour of rich than rest of Europe, report finds', *Guardian*, 27 Nov 2023

21 Nadine White, 'Tommy Robinson stokes far-right riots on social media from outside UK', *Independent*, 5 Aug 2025

22 Aamna Mohdin and Chris Osuh, 'UK Islamophobia assaults surged by 73% in 2024, anti-hate crime charity reports', *Guardian*, 19 Feb 2025

23 'Morecambe arts group's funding bid to save its home', *Lancaster Guardian*, 7 Aug 2018

24 Ibid.

25 'Lancaster City Council church decision gives new hope to Morecambe arts venue', *Lancaster Guardian*, 24 Sept 2018

26 'New art exhibition opens in Morecambe's Arndale Centre', *Lancaster Guardian*, 24 Oct 2019

27 'Co-Operation Street', Good Things Collective, https://www.goodthingscollective.co.uk/cooperationst

28 'Morecambe Matters: A community wealth building manifesto for Morecambe', Good Things Collective, https://www.goodthingscollective.co.uk/morecambematters

29 Art of the New Frontier: https://www.facebook.com/groups/123539369756172/

30 Dominic Moffitt, 'Morecambe's "eyesore" Frontierland border to get artists' makeover after calls for change', *LancsLive*, 5 March 2021, https://www.lancs.live/news/lancashire-news/morecambes-eyesore-frontierland-border-gets-19975041

31 Interview with Dave Harland, 15 October 2019

32 Ibid.

33 'The latest update on Eden Project North', presentation by the Eden Project's Si Bellamy OBE at North Lancs Expo 2019, Lancaster & District Chamber of Commerce, 22 Sept 2019, https://youtube/YygfnINqI9o?si=z3RSv27j2xAQu3R_

34 Elizabeth Hopkirk, 'First images of Grimshaw's new Eden Project', *Building*, 26 Nov 2018

35 'Eden Project North – Report of the Assistant Chief Excecutive', Lancaster City Council, 19 Dec 2018, https://committeeadmin.lancaster.gov.uk/documents/s71523/Eden%20Council%20report%2019-12-18.pdf

36 Ibid.

37 'Land agreement brings Eden Project North one step closer to reality', Eden Project, 4 Aug 2021, https://www.edenproject.com/media-relations/land-agreement-brings-eden-project-north-one-step-closer-to-reality-0

38 *West End Community Profile*, Lancaster District CVS (2015), https://

westendmorecambe.co.uk/wp-content/uploads/2020/08/West-End-Million-Community-Profile-v2.4.pdf, p. 54

39 Interview with Carmen Scott, 24 January 2020; Carmen Scott, 'Hands On Housing', Good Things Collective, 12 May 2021, https://www.goodthings collective.co.uk/single-post/hands-on-housing-by-carmen-scott

40 https://www.powertochange.org.uk/wp-content/uploads/2019/09/ PCT_3619_High_Street_Pamphlet_FINAL_LR.pdf

41 A public consultation to set 'high-level objectives' was held from 7 November 2023 to 3 January 2024; 'Regeneration of Frontierland', Lancaster City Council, 15 Oct 2024, https://www.lancaster.gov.uk/sites/regener ation/frontierland

42 Michelle Blade, 'Hotel plan for key Morecambe Frontierland site after Eden Project go-ahead', *Lancaster Guardian*, 22 March 2023

43 Lee Grimsditch and Dominic Moffitt, 'Bizarre story of the lost "Blobbyland" theme park near Greater Manchester shut down just weeks after opening', *Manchester Evening News*, 19 Dec 2023

44 Paul Wilkinson, 'It's D-Day for Crinkley Bottom saga', *Westmorland Gazette*, 30 Jan 2003

45 Helen Carter, 'Morecambe fights decline with Mars bar effect', *Guardian*, 20 March 2004

46 Michelle Blade, 'Popular Morecambe prom artwork could "end up in a skip", fears artist', *Lancaster Guardian*, 3 July 2023

47 Catherine Oliver, ' "The birds of the Bay"', op. cit.

48 ' "Terning" the tide for seabird decline in Lancashire', Natural England, 11 Dec 2024, https://www.gov.uk/government/news/terning-the-tide-for-seabird-decline-in-lancashire

49 Gayle Rouncivell, 'Protestors gather on beach to oppose controversial Morecambe Bay wind farm plans', *Lancaster Guardian*, 6 Jan 2025

50 'Wintering Geese and Swans', Cumbria Biodiversity Data Centre (2016), https://www.cbdc.org.uk/wp-content/uploads/2019/04/Wintering-Geese-and-Swans-SS-QC-OCT-2016_Revised_2019.pdf

51 'Roanhead Farm development risks irreparable harm to nature – update', Arc Trust, 23 Feb 2024, https://www.arc-trust.org/news/roanhead-farm-development-risks-irreparable-harm-to-nature-update

52 'Eden Project Morecambe, UK', https://www.edenproject.com/new-edens/eden-project-morecambe-uk

53 'Subsidy Advice Unit report on the proposed subsidy for Eden Project Morecambe', Subsidy Advice Unit, 24 Jan 2024, https://assets.publishing.service.gov.uk/media/65b0e88ef2718c000dfb1c27/SAU_Eden_3_pdfa.pdf

54 Interview with Tim Smit, 15 October 2019

55 'Data's role for a post-carbon built environment', Dark Matter Laboratories, 30 March 2023, https://provocations.darkmatterlabs.org/datas-role-for-a-post-carbon-built-environment-7a31b4ebc934

56 Ibid.

57 'Historic Morecambe Winter Gardens reborn with cutting-edge audio from KV2', KV2 Audio, 30 Oct 2024, https://www.kv2audio.com/news/historic-morecambe-winter-gardens-reborn-with-cutting-edge-audio-from-kv2.html

58 'Wild weather: flood takes Morecambe by storm', BBC News, 20 Sept 2010, http://news.bbc.co.uk/local/lancashire/hi/people_and_places/nature/newsid_9002000/9002370.stm

59 'Coronavirus: Eden Project to cut more than 200 jobs', BBC News, 15 July 2020, https://www.bbc.co.uk/news/uk-england-cornwall-53420648

60 Hazel Sheffield, 'Beki and Jo at the Good Things Collective', Revisiting Britain, 24 Feb 2021, https://revisitingbritain.substack.com/p/beki-and-jo-at-the-good-things-collective

61 Robert Macdonald, 'Questions over scrutiny of Morecambe Co-op site's £750,000 revamp and "contracts for out-of-towners"', LancsLive, 29 April 2024, https://www.lancs.live/news/lancashire-news/questions-over-scrutiny-morecambe-co-29075997

62 In 2024, Good Things Collective launched a new venue on Northumberland Street, Morecambe, with a weekend of exhibitions and events. The venue had artist studios and co-working spaces, but nothing public-facing in its first incarnation; Anne Southby, 'Morecambe arts group launches brand new venue', Lancaster Guardian, 18 July 2024; 'Horraaayyyyy the Good Things Collective has a new home at 3 Northumberland St, Morecambe!', Good Things Collective on Facebook, 28 June 2024, https://www.facebook.com/watch/?v=1567708943810841

3: MINE

1   Anna Tsing, 'The buck, the bull, and the dream of the stag: some unexpected weeds of the Anthropocene', *Suomen Antropologi*, 42:1 (2017), https://jour nal.fi/suomenantropologi/article/view/65084/26231

2   Jane Bennett, *Vibrant Matter: A Political Ecology of Things* (Duke University Press, 2010), p. viii.

3   Katie Bunnell, 'Brickfield Fieldtrip – Blackpool Pit and Watch Hill', St Austell, https://www.staustell.co.uk/event/brickfield-fieldtrip-blackpool-pit-and-watch-hill/

4   'Mining the UK', *Mining Technology*, 23 Jan 2018, https://www.mining-technology.com/features/mining-the-uk/

5   Thames Menteth, 'Devon tin mine closer to reopening after key permits awarded', *Ground Engineering*, 4 Jan 2023

6   Linda Pressly, 'How mercury poisons gold miners and enters the food chain', BBC News, 18 Sept 2013, https://www.bbc.co.uk/news/magazine-24127661

7   Jennifer Chu, 'Study: Technological progress alone won't stem resource use', MIT News, 19 Jan 2017, https://news.mit.edu/2017/technological-progress-alone-stem-consumption-materials-0119

8   'Future projections for mineral demand highlight vulnerabilities in UK supply chain', British Geological Survey, 13 March 2025, https://www.bgs.ac.uk/news/future-projections-for-mineral-demand-highlight-vulnerabilities-in-uk-supply-chain/

9   Rob Bowell, 'The United Kingdom has thousands of abandoned metal mines', SRK Consulting, December 2006, https://www.srk.com/en/publica tions/the-united-kingdom-has-thousands-of-abandoned-metal-mines

10 Dave Johnston et al., 'Abandoned mines and the water environment', Environment Agency, Aug 2008, https://assets.publishing.service.gov. uk/government/uploads/system/uploads/attachment_data/file/291482/LIT_8879_df7d5c.pdf

11 Ibid, p. v

12 Ibid.

13 Mark Pilcher, 'A whiter smile, a greener environment: cleaning up with China clay', Environment Agency blog, 25 April 2014, https://environment agency.blog.gov.uk/2014/04/25/a-whiter-smile-a-greener-environment-cleaning-up-with-china-clay/

14 Rosanna Martin, 'Brickworks and Material Connections', St Austell, https://www.staustell.co.uk/brickworks-and-material-connections/

15 Silvia Federici, *Caliban and the Witch: Women, the Body and Primitive Accumulation* (Autonomedia, 2004), p. 200

16 'William Cookworthy, found the china clay in Cornwall', Cornwall Calling, https://www.cornwall-calling.co.uk/famous-cornish-people/cookworthy.htm

17 'China clay', Cornwall Guide, 12 Jan 2022, https://www.cornwalls.co.uk/history/industrial/china_clay.htm

18 Terry Macalister, 'Blow for West Country as 800 china clay jobs go', *Guardian*, 5 July 2006

19 Ibid.

20 'China clay industry (job losses)', Hansard, 575 (5 Feb 2014), https://hansard.parliament.uk/Commons/2014-02-05/debates/14020579000003/ChinaClayIndustry(JobLosses)

21 'Imerys in the UK', Imerys, https://www.imerys.com/united-kingdom

22 Colin Gregory, 'The time the new Emperor of Japan visited a clay pit in Cornwall', *CornwallLive*, 19 May 2019, https://www.cornwalllive.com/news/cornwall-news/time-new-emperor-japan-visited-2874155

23 'Each place judged less valuable than the growth of industry', quote from Zenna Tagney's lecture 'Clay, Folklore, and Landscape in Cornwall's Clay Country', summarized by Zenna in an accompanying video, https://www.youtube.com/watch?v=yuyXc7AXRXQ

24 The Russell Society Guide to Good Practice can be downloaded https://russellsoc.org/safety/

25 'Mineral evolution', Carnegie Science, https://hazen.carnegiescience.edu/research/mineral-evolution

26 'Q&A: Robert Hazen on studying "deep carbon"', US National Science Foundation, 27 June 2017, https://new.nsf.gov/news/qa-robert-hazen-studying-deep-carbon

27 Email correspondence with Robert Hazen, 5 July 2025

28 Robert Hazen, 'The missing law of nature, and how we found it', *The Well*, 24 June 2024, https://www.youtube.com/watch?v=lepxTr9zKDc. See also Robert M. Hazen and Michael L. Wong, *Time's Second Arrow: Evolution, Order, and a New Law of Nature* (W. W. Norton, 2026)

29 Ibid.

30 Nicola Davis, ' "Survival of the fittest" may also apply to the nonliving, report finds', *Guardian*, 16 Oct 2023

31 Angela Mashford-Pringle, 'My story of Mother Earth', Center for Humans & Nature, 10 Jan 2022, https://humansandnature.org/my-story-of-mother-earth/

32 'Ecuador first to grant nature constitutional rights', *Capitalism Nature Socialism*, 19:4 (2008), pp.131–33

33 New Zealand Te Awa Tupua (Whanganui River Claims Settlement) Act 2017, Eco Jurisprudence Monitor, https://ecojurisprudence.org/initiatives/te-awa-tupua-act-2017/

34 Dallas Goldtooth et al., 'Indigenous resistance against carbon', Indigenous Environmental Network, Aug 2021, https://www.ienearth.org/wp-content/uploads/2021/09/Indigenous-Resistance-Against-Carbon-2021.pdf

35 Jenni Monet, ' "Green colonialism": Indigenous world leaders warn over west's climate strategy', *Guardian*, 23 April 2023

36 'Norway and the Sami people end a dispute over Europe's largest onshore wind farm', Associated Press, 6 March 2024, https://apnews.com/article/norway-sami-wind-farm-energy-indigenous-54f4cafbee29578dc9de1f206df3f9ff

37 '3° Neighbourhood' in 'Neighbourhood Public Square', Civic Square, March 2024, https://drive.google.com/file/d/11JLLVqvHeh1c4FULWTJqwjlcoqQo31XO/view

38 Colin Robertson, 'A rush for lithium in Africa risks fuelling corruption and failing citizens', Global Witness, 24 Nov 2023, https://globalwitness.org/en/campaigns/transition-minerals/a-rush-for-lithium-in-africa-risks-fuelling-corruption-and-failing-citizens/

39 '3° Neighbourhood' in 'Neighbourhood Public Square', op. cit., p. 15.

40 Peter Berg and Raymond Dasmann, 'Reinhabiting California', *Ecologist*, 7:10 (1977), p. 400

41 Daniel Christian Wahl, 'Bioregionalism – living with a sense of place at the appropriate scale for self-reliance', *Age of Awareness*, 15 Aug 2017, https://medium.com/age-of-awareness/bioregionalism-living-with-a-sense-of-place-at-the-appropriate-scale-for-self-reliance-a8c9027ab85d

42 Jonathan Watts, 'Concrete: the most destructive material on Earth', *Guardian*, 25 Feb 2019

4: FOREST

1 'How Storm Dennis broke Welsh records ... but couldn't break the Welsh spirit', ITV News, 23 Feb 2023, https://www.itv.com/news/wales/2020-02-23/how-storm-dennis-broke-welsh-records-but-couldn-t-break-the-welsh-spirit

2 'Wales's tropical rainforests', Amgueddfa Cymru (Wales Museums), https://museum.wales/articles/1301/Waless-tropical-rainforests

3 'Carboniferous period', *National Geographic*, https://www.nationalgeographic.com/science/article/carboniferous

4 https://www.iisd.org/system/files/publications/end-of-coal-mining-south-wales-lessons-learned.pdf

5 'Miners believed themselves to be the aristocrats of the working class': Richard Burton speaking on *Our American Stories with Lee Habeeb*, https://www.facebook.com/watch/?v=386577191159313

6 Louise Morgan, Jane Scourfield, David Williams, Anne Jasper and Glyn Lewis, 'The Aberfan disaster: 33-year follow-up of survivors', *British Journal of Psychiatry* (2003), 182, 532–6.

7 'Special report: Aberfan 50 years on', *New Civil Engineer*, 10 October 2016, https://www.newcivilengineer.com/latest/special-report-aberfan-50-years-on-10-10-2016

8 'The coupe area is dominated by larch, which was subject to a statutory notice to fell as a result of *P. ramorum* (PR) infection', 'February 2020 Floods in Wales: Natural Resources Wales Land Estate Management Review', Cyfoeth Naturiol Cymru (Natural Resources Wales), October 2020, p. 53, https://naturalresources.wales/media/692380/february-2020-floods-in-wales-nrw-land-estate-management-review-eng.pdf

9 'Phytophthora ramorum', Woodland Trust, https://www.woodlandtrust.org.uk/trees-woods-and-wildlife/tree-pests-and-diseases/key-tree-pests-and-diseases/phytophthora-ramorum

10 'Phytophthora ramorum: strategy for Wales', Llywodraeth Cymru (Welsh Government), 2019, https://www.gov.wales/sites/default/files/publications/2021-01/phytophthora-ramorum-management-strategy.pdf

11 Steven Morris, 'Larch forests of south Wales fall victim to disease', *Guardian*, 17 May 2015

12 'Phytophthora ramorum', Woodland Trust, op. cit.

13 'dispatch of timber from the site continued until quite recently': 'February 2020 Floods in Wales', op. cit., pp. 53–4

14 'Storm Dennis: Pentre flooded again after tree felling', BBC News, 20 February 2020, https://www.bbc.co.uk/news/uk-wales-51561865

15 Conversation with Marylou Anderson, 10 October 2018

16 'Happy Birthday, Kilfinan Community Forest!', Woodland Crofts, 6 April 2020, https://woodlandcrofts.org/?p=772

17 'About us', Kilfinan Community Forest, https://kilfinancommunityforest.org.uk/about-us

18 Under the Crofting Reform (Scotland) Act 1976: https://www.legislation.gov.uk/ukpga/1976/21/enacted?view=plain

19 Land Reform (Scotland) Act 2003: https://www.legislation.gov.uk/asp/2003/2/contents

20 'Crofters have six months to meet future payment conditions', SRUC, 22 Nov 2024, https://www.sruc.ac.uk/all-news/crofters-have-six-months-to-meet-future-payment-conditions

21 Ceri Nicholas worked for Valleys Kids from 2003 to 2018 and was responsible for delivering the National Lottery 'Create Your Space' project in partnership with Welcome to Our Woods.

22 'About us [Natural Resources Wales]', Gov.uk, https://www.gov.uk/government/organisations/natural-resources-wales/about; 'The Process', Future Forest Vision, https://futureforestvision.co.uk/people-and-process-2/

23 Hazel Sheffield, ' "They look after the land because they feel it is theirs": how South Wales is learning from forests in Scotland', Independent, 23 Oct 2018

24 Ian Thomas joined in 2013: Sheffield, ' "They look after the land" ', ibid.

25 'Welcome to our woods', Co-op Foundation, 1 May 2019, https://www.coopfoundation.org.uk/stories/welcome-to-our-woods/

26 'Wales history: war and depression (part 2)', https://www.bbc.co.uk/wales/history/sites/themes/guide/ch20_part2_war_and_depression.shtml

27 Emily Withers and Claire Miller, 'How long people live in every part of Wales as life expectancy falls for first time in 40 years', WalesOnline, 23 Sept 2021, https://www.walesonline.co.uk/news/wales-news/my-life-expectancy-wales-falls-21658193

28 David Deans, 'Timber scandal: what went on in Natural Resources Wales?', BBC News, 7 August 2018, https://www.bbc.co.uk/news/uk-wales-politics-45097451

29 'Natural Resources Wales seems "out of control", says AM', BBC News, 18 July 2018, https://www.bbc.co.uk/news/uk-wales-politics-44879456

30 'What I've learned is we need to be doing more of this, generally, as an organization': Richard Phipps speaking at co-design session no. 8 of Natural Resources Wales's Forest Resource Plan, 16 March 2022, https://vimeo.com/690008389 (15':14")

31 Ben Rawlence, 'Public education in an era of planetary emergency', Coleg y Mynydd Du (Black Mountains College), February 2023, https://blackmountainscollege.uk/an-essay-by-ben-rawlence-public-education-in-an-era-of-planetary-emergency/

32 Robert Wright, 'Welsh town left on road to nowhere after Cardiff scraps new bypasses', Financial Times, 3 July 2023, https://www.ft.com/content/991edcfa-60b8-4dc9-a523-8dbdf8c39d4a

33 S. Howe, D. Nutbeam, 'Interview with inaugural Future Generations Commissioner for Wales Sophie Howe: Embedding a wellbeing approach in government', Public Health Research and Practice, 2023, 33(2):e3322314

34 Jonathan Powell, 'Trying to govern from a standing start', UK in a Changing Europe, 5 March 2024, https://ukandeu.ac.uk/trying-to-govern-from-a-standing-start/

35 'Fun day in the woods', Welcome to Our Woods Upper Rhondda Valley, 24 June 2019, https://www.youtube.com/watch?v=CEkRJgm12JU

36 'Apprenticeships: Gwynfor's story', Llywodraeth Cymru (Welsh Government), 14 Feb 2022, https://www.gov.wales/apprenticeships-genius-decision/gwynfors-story

37 'Rhondda teenager wins apprenticeship award after achieving "the impossible"', National Training Federation Wales, 27 March 2024, https://www.ntfw.org/aac2024-winner-gwynfor-jones/

38 Future of Our Forest, painting completed April 2022, at Treherbert Old Library, https://io.wp.com/futureforestvision.co.uk/wp-content/uploads/2022/04/image1.jpeg

5: FACTORY

1 https://historicengland.org.uk/images-books/publications/key-industrial-sites/key-industrial-designated-sites/

2 Jason Hickel et al., 'National responsibility for ecological breakdown: a

fair-shares assessment of resource use, 1970–2017', *Lancet Planet Health*, 6 (2022), pp. e342–e349, https://www.thelancet.com/pdfs/journals/lanplh/PIIS2542-5196(22)00044-4.pdf

3   Tim Gore, 'Confronting carbon inequality: putting climate justice at the heart of the COVID-19 recovery', Oxfam International, 21 Sept 2020, https://www.oxfam.org/en/research/confronting-carbon-inequality

4   'Blend the trend – pathways to a liveable planet as resource use spikes: Summary for policymakers', United Nations Environment Programme Global Resources Outlook, 2004, https://wedocs.unep.org/bitstream/handle/20.500.11822/44902/GRO24_Summary_for_Policymakers.pdf

5   Imandeep Kaur, 'Change begins with an idea – launching TEDxBrum 2014', TEDxBrum 2014, 20 June 2014, https://medium.com/tedxbrum-2014/change-begins-with-an-idea-launching-tedxbrum-2014-286bfb0643b8

6   'Neighbourhood Public Square: The Land Story So Far', Civic Square, 4 April 2025, https://medium.com/neighbourhood-public-square/neighbourhood-public-square-the-land-story-so-far-75cc9797f09b

7   'Epic Brum – Making Impact Hub Birmingham a Reality', https://www.kickstarter.com/projects/immykaur/epic-brum-making-impact-hub-birmingham-a-reality

8   'This phenomenon wasn't unique to us, it was systemic, as outlined in Alastair Parvin's *Housing without debt* paper (2016): "a fundamental flaw in our economic model, arguably destroying any reasonable hope for sustainable, equitable urban development in the 21st century." The publishing of Dark Matter Labs' *A Smart Commons* in 2019 helped show this as by design, with huge amounts of private wealth being created from public goods': 'Neighbourhood Public Square', op. cit.

9   '5 photos of the Birmingham Wholesale Markets being completely demolished', I Am Birmingham, 6 Dec 2018, https://iambirmingham.co.uk/2018/12/06/5-photos-birmingham-wholesale-markets-completely-demolished/

10 'Controversial Edgbaston reservoir revamp plan to go ahead', BBC News, 15 Nov 2022, https://www.bbc.co.uk/news/uk-england-birmingham-63626101

11 Port Loop Manifesto, https://apps.urbansplash.co.uk/port-loop/main-menu/about-port-loop/port-loop-manifesto

12 'Neighbourhood Public Square', op. cit.

13 https://medium.com/neighbourhood-public-square/physical-infrastructure-design-4daf850a092a

14 Jane Haynes, '25 community libraries in Birmingham at risk in massive council shake-up to save millions', *BirminghamLive*, 22 Jan 2024, https://www.birminghammail.co.uk/news/midlands-news/25-community-libraries-birmingham-risk-28488801

15 'Neighbourhood Public Square', op. cit.

16 Civic Square, 'Endowing the Future', 29 April 2024, https://medium.com/neighbourhood-public-square/endowing-the-future-65041b0f88cd

17 'Compendium for the civic economy', Nesta, https://www.scribd.com/document/155665115/Compendium-for-the-Civic-Economy

18 Images of the Neighbourhood Public Square by Sonia Dubois, available on her website, https://soniadubois.com/civic-square/

19 Ibid.

20 Civic Square, 'Those Moving Us into the Doughnut', https://civicsquare.notion.site/07-Those-Moving-Us-Into-The-Doughnut-dacb908af9784043917faaf0469b2e53

21 'Neighbourhood Public Square', op. cit.

22 Ibid.

6: RAILWAY ARCHES

1 George Monbiot, 'There are many ways Trump could trigger a global collapse. Here's how to survive if that happens', *Guardian*, 18 Feb 2025

2 This is actually a hectic twenty-minute stretch of the ancient road that follows the Roman route from London up to Lincoln and York, the A10.

3 Gareth Campbell, 'Government policy during the British railway mania and the 1847 commercial crisis', Queen's University Belfast, https://pureadmin.qub.ac.uk/ws/files/18161511/RailwayCrisis.pdf p. 2

4 'The assassination of Broad Street', *London Wanderer*, 10 Nov 2020, https://thelondonwanderer.co.uk/2020/11/the-assassination-of-broad-street/

5 'Broad Street – Dalston (Pt. 3)', *Abandoned Stations*, http://www.abandonedstations.org.uk/Broad_Street_line_3.html

6 'Save JC Motors of Haggerston', *Spitalfields Life*, 7 June 2023, https://spitalfieldslife.com/2023/06/07/save-jc-motors-of-haggerston/

7   'Introducing London Overground – a new era for London Rail', Transport for London, 5 Sept 2006, https://tfl.gov.uk/info-for/media/press-releases/2006/september/introducing-london-overground--a-new-era-for-london-rail

8   Interview with Len Maloney: 'I have a vision of what I want my shop to be like,' Len says. 'But I can't follow through with it because of the constant worry about finances.' 2 Nov 2023

9   'The energy transition and jobs: can people transition to new green jobs?', PricewaterhouseCoopers, August 2022, https://www.pwc.co.uk/who-we-are/purpose/the-energy-transition-and-jobs.pdf

10   'LNPK 156 Geothermal Coalition: regional labor market assessment', Bureau of Business and Economic Research, University of Minnesota Duluth, Sept 2024, p. v, https://conservancy.umn.edu/server/api/core/bitstreams/5e524b99-eff2-4307-9ae1-a50e3bd2934d/content

11   But it is Reverend Paul's earlier work that seems most closely aligned with Krissie's. In the 1970s, before he began training for the priesthood, he founded the Confederation of Employee Organisations. This collective provided collective strength for smaller unions threatened by the closed shop legislation, which made employment in certain workplaces dependent on union membership.

12   'Industrial land shortage is now critical says independent Commission', Centre for London, 27 January 2022, https://centreforlondon.org/news/industrial-land-shortage-critical/

13   Network Rail Commercial Estate Sale fact sheet, https://www.networkrail.co.uk/wp-content/uploads/2019/05/Commercial-estate-sale-fact-sheet.pdf

14   'Network Rail's sale of railway arches', National Audit Office, 2 May 2019, https://www.nao.org.uk/wp-content/uploads/2019/05/Network-Rails-sale-of-railway-arches.pdf

15   Hettie O'Brien, 'The Blackstone rebellion: how one country took on the world's biggest commercial landlord', *Guardian*, 29 Sept 2022, https://www.theguardian.com/business/2022/sep/29/blackstone-rebellion-how-one-country-worlds-biggest-commercial-landlord-denmark

16   Shawn Tully, 'How Blackstone became the world's biggest corporate landlord', *Fortune*, 17 Feb 2020

17   Jack Sidders, 'Blackstone makes a long-term bet on Britain's railway arches', *Financial Review*, 12 Sept 2018

18 George Hammond, 'Blackstone pushes rent rises', *Financial Times*, 12 Dec 2020, https://www.ft.com/content/dfba2558-04cf-4440-89b1-d4b064bd8827

19 Ibid.

20 'Children of critical workers and vulnerable children who can access schools or educational settings', Gov.uk, 2 January 2022, https://www.gov.uk/government/publications/coronavirus-covid-19-maintaining-educational-provision/guidance-for-schools-colleges-and-local-authorities-on-maintaining-educational-provision

21 Karen Weise, 'Amazon profit soars 220 per cent as pandemic drives shopping online', *New York Times*, 29 April 2021, https://www.nytimes.com/2021/04/29/technology/amazons-profits-triple.html

22 Jack Kelly, 'A hard-hitting investigative report into Amazon shows that workers' needs were neglected in favor of getting goods delivered quickly', *Forbes*, 25 Oct 2021

23 Michael Sainato, ' "They're more concerned about profit": Osha, DoJ take on Amazon's gruelling working conditions', *Guardian*, 2 March 2023

24 Miriam Partington, 'The state of play in European speedy grocery: who's left?', *Sifted*, 27 April 2023, https://sifted.eu/articles/state-of-play-speedy-grocery

25 'A manifesto for the new economy', East End Trades Guild, https://eastendtradesguild.org.uk/wp-content/uploads/2024/03/A-Manifesto-for-the-New-Economy-1.pdf

26 'Hackney mechanic faces eviction from railway arch after TfL asks for £70,000 in rent arrears', ITV News, 9 June 2023, https://www.itv.com/news/london/2023-06-09/hackney-mechanic-faces-eviction-from-after-tfl-asks-for-70000-rent-arrears

27 'Community owned arches in Hackney!', East End Trades Guild's Crowd-funder page, https://www.crowdfunder.co.uk/p/take-hackney-arches

28 'Stronger Together: Learning from Rondo Community Land Trust', *Acast*, 16 April 2024, https://shows.acast.com/stronger-together/episodes/learning-from-rond-community-land-trust

29 'Remembering Rondo: a history harvest', Center for the Preservation of Civil Rights Sites, University of Pennsylvania, https://cpcrs.upenn.edu/resource/remembering-rondo-history-harvest

30 'About us', Rondo Community Land Trust, https://www.rondoclt.org/about/about-us

31 Richard Reeve, 'Rondo Community Land Trust starts a new venture to support Black entrepreneurship', KSTP.com, 10 Sept 2023, https://kstp.com/kstp-news/top-news/rondo-community-land-trust-starts-a-new-venture-to-support-black-entrepreneurship/

32 'Welcome to commercial ownership', Rondo Community Land Trust, https://www.rondoclt.org/commercial/our-spaces

33 'The Black history of the community land trust model', Rondo Community Land Trust, 29 April 2024, https://www.rondoclt.org/news/the-black-history-of-the-community-land-trust-model

34 'Stronger Together: Hakeem Saunders, former JC Motors Apprentice', *Acast*, 10 Aug 2023, https://shows.acast.com/stronger-together/episodes/hakeem-saunders-former-jc-motors-apprentice

35 Seven Sisters Regeneration at Wards Corner Equality Impact Assessment, June 2012, https://www.minutes.haringey.gov.uk/Published/C00000728/M00006093/AI00030127/150612SevenSistersEQIAfinal.pdf

36 'Plans to redevelop UK's Seven Sisters market pose human rights threat, say UN experts', United Nations, 26 March 2019, https://www.ohchr.org/en/press-releases/2019/03/plans-redevelop-uks-seven-sisters-market-pose-human-rights-threat-say-un

37 'All top three candidates for London mayor say yes to our relationship ask!', East End Trades Guild, https://eastendtradesguild.org.uk/top-three-candidates-for-london-mayor-agree-to-meet-eetg-if-elected/

38 https://www.involve.org.uk/news-opinion/opinion/does-democracy-need-time-rebellion

39 'What is Extinction Rebellion and what does it want?', BBC News, 14 April 2022, https://www.bbc.co.uk/news/uk-48607989

40 Roman Krznaric, *History for Tomorrow* (W. H. Allen, 2024), p. 149

7: HIGH STREET

1 Written by Thomas Lommée in a mural on the facade of a building at the University of Ghent, 2015

2 Toby Codd, 'Sewage alerts across Plymouth after heavy rainfall', *PlymouthLive*, 24 Feb 2025, https://www.plymouthherald.co.uk/news/plymouth-news/sewage-alerts-across-plymouth-after-9969182

3   'Oxford Brookes students bring creative inspiration to the Stone-house community to talk all things climate', Climate Connections, https:// climateconnectionsplymouth.co.uk/projects/climate-resilience-in-stonehouse/

4   'Plymouth City Municipal Action Plan for Sustainable Drainage Systems', Plymouth City Council, February 2020, https://waterresilientcities.co.uk/ wp-content/uploads/2020/02/Plymouth-City-Centre-SuDS-Municipal-Action-Plan.pdf, fig. 7, p. 11

5   'End of the road in sight', Plymouth.gov.uk, 18 Feb 2021, https://www. plymouth.gov.uk/news/end-road-sight

6   'Plymouth councillors push for health hub in city ward', BBC News, 28 Feb 2023, https://www.bbc.co.uk/news/uk-england-devon-64798017

7   Charlotte Turner, 'What Plymouth is doing to tackle the GP crisis', PlymouthLive, 15 May 2019, https://www.plymouthherald.co.uk/news/health/ what-plymouth-doing-tackle-gp-2872665

8   William Telford, 'Plymouth's health hub doomed after NHS turns down £45m council loan', PlymouthLive, 10 March 2023, https://www. plymouthherald.co.uk/news/health/plymouths-health-hub-doomed-after-8239485

9   'Super health hub in Plymouth City Centre', Parallel Parliament, 25 Oct 2022, https://www.parallelparliament.co.uk/debate/2022-10-25/commons/ westminster-hall/super-health-hub-in-plymouth-city-centre

10 In 2023, Plymouth City Council said that NHS England had confirmed £25 million for a community diagnostic centre on Colin Campbell Court, the former car park that had been earmarked for the £40 million health hub. The diagnostic centre has a different purpose and different sources of funding. It was scheduled to open by April 2026. Luke Pollard, the Plymouth MP who went to Parliament to try and get money for the health hub, said he hoped the diagnostic centre might revive interest in the earlier hub plans: 'Milestone for Plymouth Community Diagnostic Centre as concrete frame takes shape at Colin Campbell Court', University Hospitals Plymouth, 23 April 2025, https:// www.plymouthhospitals.nhs.uk/latest-news/milestone-for-plymouth-community-diagnostic-centre-as-concrete-frame-takes-shape-at-colin-campbell-court-8242/

11 Bluestone 360 interview with Hannah Sloggett, 10 April 2024, since archived, https://bluestone360.co.uk/blog/hey-hannah-sloggett/

12 Hazel Sheffield, 'How UK councils are crowdfunding themselves out of a crisis', *Independent*, 12 May 2017

13 Andrew Gregory, '"Jaw-dropping" number of children in England with anxiety shocks even professionals', *Guardian*, 27 Aug 2024, https://www.theguardian.com/society/article/2024/aug/27/jaw-dropping-number-of-children-in-england-with-anxiety-shocks-even-profes sionals

14 Paul Hawken, *Drawdown* (Penguin, 2018)

15 Owen Hatherley, *A New Kind of Bleak: Journeys Through Urban Britain* (Verso, 2012), p. 180

16 'Book review: *Municipal Dreams: The Rise and Fall of Council Housing*', London School of Economics, 21 Oct 2018, https://blogs.lse.ac.uk/politic sandpolicy/book-review-municipal-dreams/

17 'North Prospect History Project', *Plymouth Culture*, 27 May 2015, https://plymouthculture.wordpress.com/2015/05/27/north-prospect-history-project/

18 The diagram is available to view online https://www.communityeconomies.org/resources/diverse-economies-iceberg

19 Jordan Lofthouse, 'Chapter 2: Self-Governance, Polycentricity, and Environmental Policy' from the book *The Environmental Optimism of Elinor Ostrom*, Center for Growth and Opportunity, Utah State University, 12 Aug 2021, https://www.thecgo.org/books/the-environmental-optimism-of-elinor-ostrom/chapter-2-self-governance-polycentricity-and-environmental-policy/

20 Naomi Klein, *This Changes Everything: Capitalism vs the Climate* (Alfred A. Knopf, 2014), p. 92

21 Lucy Easthope, *The Recovery Myth*, Ch. 6 (Palgrave Macmillan, 2018), https://www.perlego.com/book/3493850

22 Jessica Craig et al., 'Community-powered high streets: how community businesses will build town centres fit for the future', Power to Change, May 2023, p. 18, https://www.powertochange.org.uk/wp-content/uploads/2023/05/Power-To-Change-Community-powered-high-streets-how-community-businesses-will-build-town-centres-fit-for-the-future.pdf

23 Jules Pipe, 'Two years on, what has the Localism Act achieved?', *Guardian*, 2 Nov 2013

24 Josh Westerling, 'Getting it right: introducing and implementing a Community Right to Buy', Power to Change, August 2024, https://www. powertochange.org.uk/wp-content/uploads/2024/09/Getting-it-right-on-Community-Right-to-Buy.pdf

8: HOME

1 Eric Klinenberg, 'Infrastructure isn't really about roads. It's about the society we want', *New York Times*, 26 April 2021, https://www.nytimes. com/2021/04/26/opinion/infrastructure-biden.html

2 'Health of one in five renters harmed by their home', Shelter, 13 Oct 2021, https://england.shelter.org.uk/media/press_release/health_of_one_in_ five_renters_harmed_by_their_home

3 Hannah Yu-Pearson, 'What would an NPPF look like from an Ecological Justice framing?', Centric Lab, https://www.thecentriclab.com/latest-news/ what-would-an-nppf-look-like-from-an-ecological-justice-framing

4 The rug is a family heirloom known affectionately as the 'elephant footprint carpet'.

5 'Insulation and airtightness', Zero Carbon House, https://zerocarbonhouse birmingham.org.uk/design/insulation-airtightness/

6 'Avoiding fossil fuels', Zero Carbon House, https://zerocarbonhouse birmingham.org.uk/about/no-fossil-fuels/

7 Deyan Sudjic, 'Mud, mud, glorious mud', *Guardian*, 14 Nov 2004

8 John Newson, 'Widening of Moseley Road – cancelled', Birmingham Friends of the Earth, 3 Dec 2021, https://birminghamfoe.org.uk/news-events/news/ widening-of-moseley-road-cancelled/

9 'Camp Hill railway station', Wikipedia, https://en.wikipedia.org/wiki/Camp_ Hill_railway_station

10 Newson, 'Widening of Moseley Road – cancelled', op. cit.

11 'Net Zero Strategy: Build Back Greener', HM Government, October 2021, https://assets.publishing.service.gov.uk/media/6194dfa4d3bf7f055507 1b1b/net-zero-strategy-beis.pdf

12 'LETI climate emergency design guide: how new buildings can meet UK climate change targets', London Energy Transport Initiative, Jan 2020, https:// www.levittbernstein.co.uk/site/assets/files/3494/leti-climate-emergency-design-guide.pdf

13 Joey Gardiner, 'Government slammed for "shocking" failure on retrofit', *Building*, 29 June 2022

14 'Can fuel poverty be ended? Committee on Fuel Poverty Annual Report 2024', Committee on Fuel Poverty, https://assets.publishing.service.gov.uk/media/66cdfe604e046525fa39cf78/committee-on-fuel-poverty-annual-report-2024.pdf

15 'What is fuel poverty?', National Energy Action, https://www.nea.org.uk/what-is-fuel-poverty/

16 'Who suffers most from heatwaves in the UK?', Friends of the Earth, July 2022, https://policy.friendsoftheearth.uk/print/pdf/node/275

17 'Birmingham – climate change and vulnerable communities', Local Government Association, 31 Jan 2017, https://www.local.gov.uk/case-studies/birmingham-climate-change-and-vulnerable-communities

18 'Heat resilience and sustainable cooling – fifth report of session 2023–24', House of Commons Environmental Audit Committee, 31 Jan 2024, https://committees.parliament.uk/publications/43103/documents/214494/default/

19 Alice Lee et al., 'Fuel poverty, cold homes and health inequalities in the UK', Institute of Health Equity, 2022, https://www.instituteofhealthequity.org/resources-reports/fuel-poverty-cold-homes-and-health-inequalities-in-the-uk/read-the-report.pdf

20 Ibid., p. 8

21 'Can fuel poverty be ended?', op. cit., p. 7

22 'Link Road St party', Civic Square, https://civicsquare.notion.site/Link-Road-St-Party-61711250c3244e52bc0d0534b70ee7a2

23 Details taken from PDF copies of the Civic Square publication, 'Good News of Link Road'

24 'Civic Square teaser – final cut', 25 Oct 2022, https://vimeo.com/763839354/2cab31b1b4

25 Exact source is unknown but is often attributed to Ilya Prigogine and Isabelle Stengers, *Order Out of Chaos: Man's New Dialogue with Nature* (Bantam Books, 1984)

26 'Homegrown homes for people & planet: a mass local approach to building with timber in every neighbourhood', WeCanMake, July 2024, p. 25, https://wecanmake.org/wp-content/uploads/2024/07/HGH-final-report-Online-version.pdf

27 According to the 2021 census, there were 14,299 people living in Filwood ward, https://censusdata.uk/e05010898-filwood#google_vignette. The Knowle West neighbourhood straddles Filwood and Knowle wards but is mostly in Filwood.

28 According to Melissa Mean, there are 44.7 people per hectare in Knowle West and the minimum requirement for a bus service to operate is 100 people per hectare; https://medium.com/reimagining-economic-possibilities/what-if-the-power-and-resources-to-build-our-neighbourhoods-were-in-community-hands-f3d5c5982ef8

29 'KWMC/Backgrounder', https://watershed.co.uk/archive-sites/engage/wp-content/uploads/2010/06/Knowle-West-Media-Centre_background.pdf

30 Melissa Mean et al., 'We Can Make: Civic Innovation in Housing', Knowle West Media, October 2017, now archived but still available at https://web.archive.org/web/20210624195545/https://issuu.com/knowlewestmedia/docs/wecanmake

31 The team at the Media Centre analysed planning data over a six-year period and compared the planning consent or rejection rate with wealthier neighbourhoods, including Clifton and Redland. They found applications in Knowle West were twice as likely to be rejected; Esme Ashcroft, 'New homes could be built in gardens of Knowle West council houses', BristolLive, 20 Oct 2017, https://www.bristolpost.co.uk/news/bristol-news/new-homes-could-built-gardens-657996

32 John Geoghegan, 'Poorer areas see few neighbourhood plan applications', Planning, 25 March 2013, https://www.planningresource.co.uk/article/1175787/poorer-areas-few-neighbourhood-plan-applications

33 Melissa Mean et al., 'We Can Make', op. cit.

34 Eleanor Young, 'Gardens of interwar estates could house thousands more', RIBA Journal, 16 October 2018, https://www.ribaj.com/intelligence/housing-white-design-we-can-make-bristol-prefabrication-innovation

35 For more on this, see Robin Wall Kimmerer and Jenny Odell, 'Gift thinking: the relationships, abundance, and reciprocity of nature's economy', Orion, 19 Nov 2024

36 Ellie Pipe, 'The Knowle West community that built a home made of straw to address housing need', B24/7, 2 Nov 2017, https://www.bristol247.com/news-and-features/news/knowle-west-community-built-home-made-straw-address-housing-need/

37 Wendy Wilson, 'Self-build and custom build housing (England)', briefing paper 06784, 1 March 2017, https://researchbriefings.parliament.uk/ResearchBriefing/Summary/SN06784

38 Lily Maxwell, 'Tackling the housing crisis one micro-plot at a time', Atlas of the Future, 9 Nov 2021, https://atlasofthefuture.org/project/we-can-make/

39 Alex Seabrook, 'Government rejects requests to take planning department out of special measures', B24/7, 19 Feb 2025, https://www.bristol247.com/news-and-features/news/government-rejects-requests-take-planning-department-special-measures/

40 'Seeing the wood for the trees: the contribution of the forestry and timber sectors to biodiversity and net zero goals – fifth report of session 2022–23', House of Commons Environmental Audit Committee, 19 July 2023, https://committees.parliament.uk/publications/40938/documents/199465/default/

41 'Timber in construction roadmap 2025 – policy paper', DEFRA, 3 March 2025, https://www.gov.uk/government/publications/timber-in-construction-roadmap-2025/timber-in-construction-roadmap-2025

42 Wikiblock Library, at https://www.betterblock.org/library

9: BODIES

1 Ursula K. Le Guin, *Always Coming Home*, Gollancz, 2016, p. 74

2 'That's the thing that wells up in me: a sense that there are people coming who will continue this work long after we are gone, and people coming from other parts of the country who will be inspired by what we have done here, and do the same.' Jess Steele speaking at the centenary celebration of the Observer Building, 18 July 2024

3 'North of Tyne Mayor Jamie Driscoll: UK2070 Commission speech, House of Lords, 24 Nov 2022', UK2070, https://uk2070.org.uk/wp-content/uploads/2022/11/NoTMayorJamieDriscollSpeec_UK2070-Commission_House-of-Lords-24th-Nov-2022.pdf

4 Kerryn Husk et al., 'Social prescribing: where is the evidence?', *British Journal of General Practice*, 69:678 (2019), pp. 6–7

5 Sarah Gorman, 'Edberts House: Impact and Achievements', https://www.peopleshealthtrust.org.uk/projects-we-fund/project-stories/edberts-house-impact-and-achievements

6   Benedict Lejac, 'A desk review of social prescribing: from origins to opportunities', Support in Mind Scotland, April 2021, https://www.rsecovidcommission.org.uk/wp-content/uploads/2021/04/A-Desk-Review-of-Social-Prescribing-from-origins-to-opportunities.pdf

7   'About us', Edberts House, https://edbertshouse.org/about

8   'Strategy thinkpiece: policy, patients and pollution: Ella's legacy', Academy of Medical Sciences, 8 Sept 2021, https://acmedsci.ac.uk/more/news/policy-patients-and-pollution-ellas-legacy

9   Email interview with Sarah Gorman, then chief executive of Edberts House, 14 July 2025

10 Mandy Cheetham et al., ' "It's not about telling people to eat better, stop smoking or get on the treadmill" ' in Dorothy Newbury-Birch and Keith Allan (eds), *Co-creating and Co-producing Research Evidence: A Guide for Practitioners and Academics in Health, Social Care and Education Settings* (Routledge, 2019); also available at https://ebrary.net/209732/education/_it_s_telling_people_better_smoking_treadmill_#182727

11 Cheetham et al., ' "It's not about telling people to eat better" ', op. cit. – 'Our reflections on what helped' to 'References' inc., https://ebrary.net/209734/education/reflections_what_helped

12 Ibid.

13 https://commonslibrary.parliament.uk/economic-update-inactivity-due-to-illness-reaches-record/

14 Jennifer Brandel, 'Invisible landscapes: scientists' recent discovery of a "new" part of the human body, the interstitium, is an invitation to think differently about our relationship with the world at large', *Orion*, 16 Nov 2023

15 'National Life tables – life expectancy in the UK: 2020 to 2022', Census 2021, 11 Jan 2024, https://www.ons.gov.uk/peoplepopulationandcommunity/birthsdeathsandmarriages/lifeexpectancies/bulletins/nationallifetablesunitedkingdom/2020to2022

16 John Burn-Murdoch, 'Young people are hanging out less – it may be harming their mental health', *Financial Times*, 18 Jan 2025

17 David Blanchflower and Alex Bryson, 'Changes in despair by age, USA (2012–2022)' in 'The Global Loss of the U-Shaped Curve of Happiness', *After Babel*, 27 May 2024, https://www.afterbabel.com/p/youth-health-declines-82-countries?open=false#%C2%A7changes-in-despair-by-age-usa

18 Enghin Atalay, 'A twenty-first century of solitude: time alone and together in the United States', working paper 22-11, Federal Reserve Bank Philadelphia,https://www.philadelphiafed.org/-/media/FRBP/Assets/working-papers/2022/wp22-11.pdf

19 J. Henriksen et al., 'Loneliness, health and mortality', *Epidemiology and Psychiatric Sciences*, 28:2 (2017), pp. 234–9

20 Jennifer Brandel, 'Invisible landscapes', op. cit.

Index

Hazel Sheffield is a business reporter and investigative journalist. Her work can be found in national and international publications including the *Guardian*, *Follow the Money* and the *Financial Times*. Before going freelance, she covered derivatives for *Euromoney* and worked as the business editor of the *Independent*. She left the *Independent* in the summer of 2016 to start a grant-funded project called farnearer.org documenting self-organizing communities and economic alternatives in the UK. After a decade of reporting, that work has come together as *Frontierlands*, her first book. She lives with her family in Hastings.